Cross-Border Employment and Social Rights in the EU Road Transport Sector

Cross-Border Employment and Social Rights in the EU Road Transport Sector

Edited by
Bartłomiej Bednarowicz
Amber Zwanenburg

eleven
international publishing

Published, sold and distributed by Eleven International Publishing
P.O. Box 85576
2508 CG The Hague
The Netherlands
Tel.: +31 70 33 070 33
Fax: +31 70 33 070 30
e-mail: sales@elevenpub.nl
www.elevenpub.com

Sold and distributed in USA and Canada
Independent Publishers Group
814 N. Franklin Street
Chicago, IL 60610, USA
Order Placement: +1 800 888 4741
Fax: +1 312 337 5985
orders@ipgbook.com
www.ipgbook.com

Eleven International Publishing is an imprint of Boom uitgevers Den Haag.

ISBN 978-94-6236-964-1
ISBN 978-94-6274-383-0 (e-book)
NUR 825

Table of Contents

1 Introduction

*Amber Zwanenburg & Bartłomiej Bednarowicz**

1.1 Focus of This Book

This textbook aims at providing a thorough analysis of the key concepts of European Union law relating to determining applicable employment and social rights, with a particular focus oriented at the cross-border road transport workers. The European Union cross-border road transport is a truly living organism operating at a supranational level. Due to the fact that the very essence of the road transport sector is dictated by its international element, it is not an easy area to navigate through in terms of finding the applicable laws. This is more specifically the case with the employment and social rights of highly mobile truck drivers. In fact, despite the existing rules on cross-border transport, its application is still sometimes shrouded in ambiguity. In order to bridge the gap between the ambiguous and complex legislation, faulty operating provisions that could serve as a basis for circumvention of the laws and increasing legal uncertainty, this textbook not only provides a better understanding of the topic as such, but also, more importantly, stimulates the problem-solving solutions, especially as far as the grey areas of the laws are concerned. Lastly, the coverage of this textbook does not extend to all legal aspects of the international road transport sector such as working time regulations or typology of contracts, as it focuses on determining applicable employment and social rights.

With regard to its structure, this textbook consists of five contributions from international legal experts, each depicting a vital topic for mobile workers with a particular focus on the EU cross-border road transport sector. We will now briefly introduce the authors and the topics respectively.

Luca Ratti, who is an Associate Professor of European and Comparative Labour Law at the University of Luxembourg, sets forth the general legal framework con-

* Amber Zwanenburg is PhD Researcher and Lecturer in Labour Law, Erasmus University in Rotterdam. Bartłomiej Bednarowicz is PhD Researcher and Teaching Assistant, University of Antwerp.

cerning the basic operating mechanisms of the European Union internal market with a focus shifted at the personal and material scope of the three fundamental freedoms of the Treaty on the Functioning of the European Union (TFEU): free movement of workers, freedom to provide services and freedom of establishment (**Chapter 2**). The core principle governing the fundamental freedoms embodied in the Treaties, is the principle of non-discrimination and the prohibition of imposing obstacles to these freedoms. These principles however, depending on the freedom, may have a different ambit, as shown by important case law of the Court of Justice of the European Union (CJEU), which will be analysed further throughout this chapter.

Hereafter, Zef Even, Ruben Houweling and Amber Zwanenburg – respectively: Professor of International and European Labour Law, Professor of Labour Law and PhD Researcher and Lecturer in Labour Law – from the Erasmus University in Rotterdam together with Professor Mijke Houwerzijl from Tilburg University, dwell into the problem of the applicability of the rules on private international law in the employment contracts in the cross-border road transport (**Chapter 3**). In their contribution, they demonstrate that due to the intrinsic characteristics of the cross-border road transport, which is its extraordinary transnational nature, conflict of laws may and eventually, will arise. The questions that need to be addressed upon such consideration are not only revolving around the law of which Member State is applicable to the employment contracts at hand, but also, around the jurisdiction of the courts over the claim that is to be submitted. To bring coherency to the subject matter, which used to be regulated at the national level by the Member States, some special legal regimes have been adopted by the EU that nowadays form a large part of EU law, which are further set forth in this chapter.

The fourth contribution by Professor of Labour Law Mijke Houwerzijl at the Tilburg University (**Chapter 4**) concerns posted workers, who under EU law are not considered to be workers falling under the ambit of the free movement of workers (Article 45 TFEU), but instead, under the scope of the provisions governing the freedom to provide services. Consequently, posted workers cannot enjoy in full the principle of equal treatment unlike migrant workers do, because as argued, they do not enter the labour market of a host Member State since they are supposed to provide their services only temporary in the first place. Nevertheless, in order to strengthen their protection and to mitigate the risks of unfair competition between undertakings established in other Member States, the (revised) Posting of Workers Directive plays a pivotal role and guarantees a minimum set of hard-core rights for the posted workers. In addition, the Posting of Workers Enforcement Directive seeks to safeguard a proper enforcement of these rules. Since the issue of posting is commonly present in the cross-border road transport, as it happens to be the case that truck drivers are the ones being posted to deliver the goods from one Member State to another, these legal instruments must be scrutinised to unravel the sensitive issues concerning genuine posting and the enforcement of the existing rules on posting to fight abuse and fraud in the field of posting.

Further in this volume, Professor of International and European Labour and Social Security Law Herwig Verschueren and PhD Researcher and Teaching Assistant Bartłomiej Bednarowicz from the University of Antwerp, examine the rules depicting social security coordination at the European Union level (**Chapter 5**). Since the cross-border road transport features a truly transnational element, the truck drivers could fall under a number of national legal social security regimes depending on the country of origin, transit countries and the country of the final destination. Therefore, it is crucial to analyse to which social security should the drivers be subject to in order to make it clear where the contributions have to be paid and where the workers could enjoy the corollary social security rights and benefits. Consequently, this part of the textbook dwells not only into the existing legal provisions regulating EU social security coordination but also into case law, which particularly in this field, forms a substantial bulk of the available interpretative rules.
Finally, Professor of Labour Law Monika Tomaszewska and dr. Michał Szypniewski from the University of Gdańsk, dive into the EU social dialogue framework (**Chapter 6**). Their starting premise is that social dialogue attempts to facilitate the cooperation between a vast array of stakeholders who represent different positions, also often in forms of collective bargaining. What social dialogue aims to achieve is the overall improvement of the strategic legal instruments as it takes into account a wider perspective worked out in a course of negotiations and consultations. Thereby, at the European level, social dialogue plays an important role between the associations of employers, trade unions and essentially the EU institutions that are obliged to consult the stakeholders during the legislative process. Therefore, as the authors put forward, social dialogue cannot be omitted, nor disregarded, quite the contrary, it needs to be strengthened to achieve a level playing field for all involved in the cross-border road transport.
Before we proceed to the legal parts of this book, as the editors, we find it crucial to briefly sketch out: why we consider this book as interesting for students and legal practitioners (para. 1.2); then to present the overall project by virtue of which this book was compiled (para. 1.3); and finally to provide the readers with some further information on how we think this book could be used by our target audience (para. 1.4).

1.2 Why This Book?

The EU transport sector – which includes various modes of transportation of goods and people – is a genuine transnational sector. It involves many countries and stakeholders, each having its own different economic, social and legal systems. If, for instance, goods are transported from the Netherlands to Poland and *vice versa*, the transport activity is carried out on the territory of different countries, despite at the first sight being it irrelevant for the purpose of moving these goods to either engage a Dutch or a Polish company. The choice of company and where it is established, however, turns out to have major economic, social and legal consequences not only for countries and companies but also, for employees and other involved actors. This is specifically so, if on a large scale similar choices are made. Imagine for instance such an assumption like favouring Polish transport companies over companies established in the BeNeLux countries. The freedom to make such choices is nevertheless accepted and forms a crucial part of the EU fundamental freedoms, such as free movement of goods and services. At the same time however, if these choices are made solely on the basis of the lower costs of labour, this may result in 'abuse' of the rules, commonly referred to as social dumping. Here, we see a potential clash between the EU freedoms on the one hand and the protection of employment and social standards of Member States on the other.

Perhaps surprisingly, there are still great gaps in the legal knowledge and education because of all the complications in the field of social and legal policy concerning the EU international transportation. The currently available know-how in different Member States happens to be also quite scattered. Unfortunately, the cooperation between universities and other stakeholders is still sometimes scarce and high quality education is not always within reach. These emerging problems perfectly show that the EU urgently needs properly trained legal professionals able to solve the problems at hand and to also develop further best practices. In consideration of these flaws, this textbook will provide a sound educational basis for a better understanding of the legal setting and will steer its readers towards fine-tuning their problem-solving skills. Moreover, this textbook will provide better understanding of the new challenges regarding the workers' mobility within the ambit of the EU transnational transport sector.

In light of the foregoing, the main learning objective of this book is to raise the awareness of the paramount importance and the significant impact of European Union law on the applicable employment and social rights of mobile workers, with a certain focus on truck drivers engaged in cross-border road transport. Due to the inherent interrelation of different provisions of EU law that are applicable to such mobile workers, it is crucial to unravel all the particular connections between different fields of EU law in order to understand the core legal problems arising from the application of the legal norms. Furthermore, this book is intended to accommodate readers with an opportunity to benefit from mutual learning opportunities by making use of all available legal sources ranging from the Treaties, directives and regulations through case law, which in majority of the cases, supports the application and interpretation of EU law.

1.3 How Was This Book Compiled?

This book was compiled in light of an Erasmus+ project called SENSE.[1] The project, which is funded by the European Commission, was launched in late 2016. Five universities (Erasmus University Rotterdam, University of Antwerp, Tilburg University, University of Luxembourg and University of Gdańsk) from four EU Member States (The Netherlands, Belgium, Luxembourg and Poland) were

1 www.project-sense.eu.

actively involved. The project aimed to contribute to the development of the problem-solving mechanisms in the field of EU transnational road transport by providing well-tailored understanding of the entire legal setting, both at national level and at EU and also at the comparative level. In order to achieve this objective, all the five partners developed high quality education programmes in their curricula.
This textbook forms the educational basis for the part of the project that focuses on the existing law at the EU level. The book provides first and foremost an inventory of the existing laws and regulations at the EU level on five vital topics for mobile workers in general and for truck drivers in particular: the role of the EU fundamental freedoms; private international law; the (revised) Posting of Workers Directive including the Enforcement Directive; the EU coordination of social security systems and the European social dialogue in the transport branch. Even though it might come across as if there is a substantial focus oriented at the transport sector, the information presented in this volume is also relevant for other sectors, especially the ones with a cross-border employment element.
Finally, the academic experts from the different partner universities each addressed one crucial topic which resulted in the various chapters of this book. Despite different origin, you will find that the structure of the chapters is substantially aligned. Each chapter starts with some general remarks, following a curriculum outline and specific learning outcomes. The core of the chapters always begin with setting forth the state of the art: the legal instruments that apply, the legal context, the scope of the legal instruments and the general principles. Each chapter also concludes with a list of the most relevant case law of the European Court of Justice and a list of suggested literature, which can be used for additional study for those interested to dwell into the matters further. However, the final chapter on social dialogue has a slightly distinct structure due to the inherent nature of the topic that it maps out.

1.4 How to Use This Book?

First and foremost, this textbook can be used in educational programmes at university level. It can also serve as a resource for post-academic professionals from the transport sector and those interested in the EU legal aspects of mobile workers as such.
Furthermore, this textbook serves as main course material for learners who are enrolled in the course that was launched in the light of this project on online platform Coursera. Those who are interested in taking this free online can find it under the name 'Cross-border road transport in EU law context' on Coursera.[2]
To really get a grasp on the subject and to actively engage in the study of the topic, readers are more than welcome to enrol in this free online course. In addition to the textbook, this online course offers over 30 video knowledge clips explaining the practical application of the rules and what is more, practice quizzes as preparation for the graded assignments prepared by the authors of this textbook. This online

2 www.coursera.org/learn/transport-eu-law.

course is designed as a 7-week programme with suggested due dates to help the participants manage their schedules in order to secure the best learning outcome. However, submitting late will have no consequences, so learners can still participate the course at their own pace if preferred. After each 'week' (the topics of the weeks on Coursera correspond with the chapters in this book), there is an option to test the acquired knowledge by taking a multiple choice test. After completing the course, the participant will be able to solve a sample guide case which resembles a real life scenario example.
Lastly, we would like to add that this book and the online course supplement each other. While studying the textbook, you can either follow the entire online course or choose only the videoclips and practice quizzes that you opt for. In the online course though, you will find out that after each knowledge clip we included a reference to the suggested corresponding reading materials in the textbook to make it easier for you in case you want to use the materials in a complementary manner.
However, whichever way you choose to use this book, we still hope you will find it useful and enjoy reading it!

Amber Zwanenburg & Bartłomiej Bednarowicz
Rotterdam & Antwerp, August 2019

2 The EU Fundamental Freedoms in the Light of Cross-Border Road Transport

Luca Ratti[*]

2.1 Introduction

2.1.1 Curriculum Outline

This chapter will deal with the European legal framework concerning the four fundamental freedoms put by the founders at the basis of the European internal market. Those freedoms have led to autonomous fields of EU law and have been developed by the crucial contribution of the Court of Justice of the European Union (CJEU). Having constitutional importance, the fundamental freedoms pose themselves delicate questions of internal coherence, boundaries, and balance. To the external (i.e. towards other constitutional values), they inevitably put into question the real nature of the process of European integration as such. This is particularly remarkable when considering social rights in the context of international road transport, for the need to establish a levelling playing field for economic actors within the EU.[1]

2.1.2 Specific Learning Outcomes

1. Identify and apply the four fundamental freedoms of the EU in the road transport sector.

---

* Luca Ratti is Associate Professor of European and Comparative Labour Law at the University of Luxembourg.

1 Due to the partial overlap between this chapter and some of the other chapters (concerning in particular free movement of workers in the context of social security, and the freedom of establishment and to provide services in the context of the posting of workers), this chapter will provide general knowledge on the fundamental freedoms at EU level, leaving the detailed analysis of each of them to the subsequent chapters.

2.2 State of the Art

2.2.1 Introduction and Inventory of the Legal Instruments at Stake

All markets need freedom, but need also rules. Since its foundation, the EU has established rules governing the exercise of some, fundamental freedoms. The term 'fundamental freedoms' captures the EU internal market freedoms enshrined in the provisions on free movement of goods, free movement of persons (and workers), services, and capital in Title II and IV of Part Three ('Union Policies and Internal Actions') of the **Treaty on the Functioning of the European Union**.[2] In particular, Article 26 TFEU defines the internal market as 'an area without internal frontiers in which the free movement of goods, persons, services and capital is ensured in accordance with the provisions of the Treaties'. This must be read in the light of the basic provisions contained in the **Treaty on the European Union**,[3] specifically Article 3(2) according to which 'The Union shall offer its citizens an area of freedom, security and justice without internal frontiers, in which the free movement of persons is ensured in conjunction with appropriate measures with respect to external border controls, asylum, immigration and the prevention and combating of crime.', and Article 3(3), where the establishment of the internal market is coupled with 'sustainable development of Europe based on balanced economic growth and price stability, a highly competitive social market economy, aiming at full employment and social progress, and a high level of protection and improvement of the quality of the environment.'

Since 2009, with the entry into force of the Lisbon Treaty,[4] the **EU Charter of Fundamental Rights**[5] has been given constitutional value equal to that of the Treaties. Particular attention must be given to the interaction of the two sources, involving a dichotomy between those freedoms and the discourse on fundamental rights promoted by the Charter. The dynamics of this dichotomy are all but clear, as some, but not all, fundamental freedoms constitute fundamental rights. In this context significant examples come from Article 15 CFREU (Freedom to choose an occupation and right to engage in work), 16 (Freedom to conduct a business), 21 (Non-discrimination), 45 (Freedom of movement and of residence).

In the TFEU the four freedoms are separately defined and regulated in principle: **Articles 28-37** deal with the **free movement of goods**; **Articles 45-48** with the **free movement of workers**; **Articles 49-55** with **freedom of establishment** and

---

2 Consolidated Version of the Treaty on the Functioning of the European Union, pt. 3, tit. II and IV, 30 March 2010, OJ 2010 C 83/47 [hereafter TFEU].

3 Consolidated versions of the Treaty on European Union and the Treaty on the Functioning of the European Union, OJ 2012 C 326/01 [hereafter TEU].

4 Treaty of Lisbon amending the Treaty on European Union and the Treaty establishing the European Community, signed at Lisbon, 13 December 2007, OJ 2007 C 306/1.

5 Charter of Fundamental Rights of the European Union, 18 December 2000, OJ 2000 C 364/ 1 [hereafter CFREU].

Articles 56-62 with the **freedom to provide services**); finally, **Articles 63-75** with the **free movement of capital and payments**.
The development of a specific set of rights inherent to the concept of citizenship of the EU (Articles 18-25 TFEU) must be read as an attribute of the right to free movement of persons protected by Article 21 TFEU.
As far as the **transnational transport** sector is concerned, a number of Treaty provisions apply (Title VI Transport, TFEU). Among them, they must be recalled as relevant:

- Article 90: 'The objectives of the Treaties shall, in matters governed by this Title, be pursued within the framework of a common transport policy';
- Article 91(1): 'For the purpose of implementing Article 90, and taking into account the distinctive features of transport, the European Parliament and the Council shall, acting in accordance with the ordinary legislative procedure and after consulting the Economic and Social Committee and the Committee of the Regions, lay down: (a) common rules applicable to international transport to or from the territory of a Member State or passing across the territory of one or more Member States; (b) the conditions under which non-resident carriers may operate transport services within a Member State; (c) measures to improve transport safety; (d) any other appropriate provisions'.
- Article 92: 'Until the provisions referred to in Article 91(1) have been laid down, no Member State may, unless the Council has unanimously adopted a measure granting a derogation, make the various provisions governing the subject on 1 January 1958 or, for acceding States, the date of their accession less favourable in their direct or indirect effect on carriers of other Member States as compared with carriers who are nationals of that State'.
- Article 95(1): 'In the case of transport within the Union, discrimination which takes the form of carriers charging different rates and imposing different conditions for the carriage of the same goods over the same transport links on grounds of the country of origin or of destination of the goods in question shall be prohibited'.

The constitutional value of the interaction between fundamental freedoms and transnational transport was made clear by the same Court of Justice, while sanctioning the inaction of the Council in the field. On 22 May 1985, on behalf of the European Parliament against the Council, the CJEU decided that the Council had failed 'to ensure freedom to provide services in the sphere of international transport and to lay down the conditions under which non-resident carriers may operate transport services in a member state'.[6]
In the present context a particular stress will be placed on the free movement of workers, freedom to provide services, and freedom of establishment, whose inter-

6 CJEU, 22 May 1985, Case 13/83, *European Parliament v. Council*, ECLI:EU:C:1985:220.

play is crucial to depict a comprehensive legal framework on the rights and guarantees involved in international road transport.

2.2.2 Legal Context

The fundamental freedoms constitute the pillars of the European process of mutual integration. The aim of completing the EU internal market through the enhancement of those freedoms has been put at the core of the legislative concern since the Single European Act (SEA) of 1986. With this document the then president of the Commission Jacques Delors wished to introduce new legal bases for the achievement of a common market without barriers (of physical, technical, and economic nature). Through what is now Article 114 TFEU, the approximation of laws became of pivotal importance to pursue the 'establishment and functioning of the internal market', thus emphasising that the single market was essentially a law-making project. The SEA made clear the need to distinguish between internal market initiatives directed essentially to harmonize legal systems, and mutual recognition of national regulations and standards. These latter may constitute unjustified barriers to trade whenever they are excessive in relation to the mandatory requirements pursued. The SEA repackaged the four freedoms into the renamed internal or single market and set 1992 as the deadline to finally realize it, a date with more political than legal significance.

As noted by Barnard,[7] the term 'single market' appears to be narrower than 'common market', being the former defined by reference to the four freedoms while the latter combines them with flanking measures such as agriculture, competition, and social matters. More than a decade later, the Treaty of Amsterdam introduced the concept of 'area of freedom, security, and justice', referring to fundamental rights and the different legal systems and traditions of the Member States (Article 67(1) TFEU). In particular, the substantive stress on freedom relates to the absence of internal border controls for persons, thus to an entirely free movement of them within the internal borders. The subsequent treaties of Maastricht and Lisbon have added the centrality of an economic and monetary union, and tried to put the bases for a true political union.

The four freedoms' economic aim is to optimally allocate resources for the EU, which is facilitated by allowing the factors of production to move to the area where they are most valued. This implies two forms of legal integration: a *negative integration* for which national rules hindering cross-border trade must be prohibited, and a *positive integration* based on progressive harmonization of domestic legal systems.[8] Such dual integration is often described as the interplay between decentralisation, involving the role of national legislation in affirming non-discrimination, market

7 C. Barnard, *The Substantive Law in the EU. The Four Freedoms* (Oxford: OUP, 2016), 8 ff.

8 P. Craig and G. De Burca, *EU Law: Texts, Cases, and Materials* (Oxford: OUP, 2015), 608.

access, and regulatory competition; and centralisation, relying on a top-down approach towards harmonization.

Decentralisation

The principle of *non-discrimination* on the grounds of nationality is to be seen as the cornerstone of the entire architecture: it requires the same treatment of internal and foreign goods, persons, services, and capital, and presupposes that they can be similarly situated throughout Europe, thus treated in the same way. In this model each Member State is entirely free to regulate how goods are produced and services provided, but they must adopt the same approach towards goods and services coming from other Member States.

The *market access approach* – based on the idea first spelled in *Cassis de Dijon* that goods lawfully produced in one Member State should presumptively have free access in another Member State – goes beyond non-discrimination, testing the legislation of each Member State in order to check whether it is liable to hinder or make less attractive the exercise of a fundamental freedom guaranteed by the treaties. Similarly to the non-discrimination test, market access tolerates exceptions/ justifications, as it goes a long way towards building a single market by removing any unjustified obstacles to trade. The consequence of the market access approach is that it is significantly more intrusive into the legislation of the single Member States, asked to take out its rules even though not discriminatory. In constitutional terms, the market access approach gives the CJEU the significant power to outlaw rules made by democratically elected national Parliaments. An illustrative example in this sense for labour law is the introduction of a legislation on minimum wages: some have argued that it could be challenged under the market access model because it would prevent migrants from working for less than minimum and discourage them from moving to that state.

Regulatory competition relates to the effect of free movement: the legislations of Member States are placed into competition and should make each Member State design better rules to attract and retain valuable assets. As put by Deakin, 'regulatory competition' refers to a process whereby legal rules are selected (and de-selected) through competition between decentralised, rule-making entities (which could be nation states or other units such as regions or localities). Three justifications are normally given for regulatory competition: firstly, it allows the content of rules to be matched more effectively to the preferences or *wants* of the consumers of laws (citizens and others affected); secondly, it promotes diversity and experimentation in the search for effective legal solutions; and thirdly, by providing mechanisms for preferences to be expressed and alternative solutions compared, it promotes the flow of information on effective law making'.

For regulatory competition to function there must be central authorities laying down and enforcing rules, as well as national authorities left free to regulate their assets. This should lead to a race to the top the legislative process, while promoting diversity and experimentation in the search for effective legal solutions. This approach, in reality, has been balanced by a constant attention to public interest issues, such as social, consumer, health, and environmental policies. Such interests are nothing more than justifying factors for Member State legislation, and examples come from the derogations provided for in the same TFEU and from the "mandatory requirements" discussed in *Cassis de Dijon* and the subsequent case-law. The mandatory requirements idea, and its equivalents in the cases of freedom of movement of workers and services and freedom of establishment, allows Member States to set a "floor" to the competitive process, subject, however, to the need to satisfy the test of proportionality. The mandatory requirements principle allows a degree of autonomy by Member States and sets some ground rules for regulatory competition, without the need to resort to centralised standard-setting through harmonisation.

Centralisation/harmonisation

Without any central input towards the single Member States, the decentralised approach may lead to excesses and undesirable results. In the labour law field this is particularly true: reducing labour costs would surely result to be an attractive measure for companies to establish in that Member State, creating short-term advantages for such companies and the Member State itself. In the long run, this would lead to a race to the bottom, lowering the same concept of highly competitive social market economy enshrined in Article 2 TEU. Therefore the EU has always retained some power to regulate some sensitive issues, adopting Regulations and Directives, within the limits of the principles of competence and subsidiarity.

In the light of the legal issues posed by the position of workers in the transnational transport sector, a particular attention must be drawn on the free movement of workers, freedom to provide services, and freedom of establishment.

1) **Free movement of workers** contained in Article 45 TFEU allows the nationals of any Member State to work in another Member State under the same conditions as this latter's nationals.

This freedom entails three different guarantees:

a. the right to participate to the labour market of a Member State different from that of origin: the worker can, in fact, freely access a foreign EU labour market, according to the rules contained in the Regulation No 492/2011 on freedom of movement for workers within the Union and in the Directive 2004/38/EC on citizenship;
b. the prohibition of discrimination based on nationality/citizenship: this aspect is also regulated by Regulation No 492/2011 (Articles 5-9);
c. the prohibition of restrictions according to Article 45 TFEU, as barriers to the free movement of workers are banned unless they can be objectively justified.

The justification method deals with the very nature of the four freedoms, and consists in allowing Member States to introduce or maintain limitations to free movement, only and insofar as they are justified. Restrictions on free movement of workers must always be proportional – appropriate for securing the attainment of

the objective that they pursue and not going beyond what is necessary in order to attain it[9] – and not violate other fundamental rights conferred by EU law.[10]
Article 45 TFEU has direct effect, both in relation to the State[11] and in the horizontal relationship between the worker and her employer,[12] as well as in respect to third parties.[13]
2) **Freedom to provide services** entails the carrying out of an economic activity for a temporary period in a Member State where either the provider or the recipient of the service is not established (Article 56 TFEU). Key norms in this respect are also Articles 61 and 58 TFEU. The former includes in the definition of services all those that 'are normally provided for remuneration, in so far as they are not governed by the provisions relating to freedom of movement for goods, capital and persons.' In practice this includes (a) activities of an industrial character; (b) activities of a commercial character; (c) activities of craftsmen; (d) activities of the professions. Without prejudice to the provisions of the Chapter relating to the right of establishment, the person providing a service may, in order to do so, temporarily pursue his activity in the Member State where the service is provided, under the same conditions as are imposed by that State on its own nationals.
According to the CJEU, the wide definition of services encounters the only limit of service providers establishing their principal residence, on a permanent or anyway almost indefinite duration, in the territory of another Member State, which in practice turns 'the Treaty text on the relationship between the two freedoms on its head'.[14]
There are numerous examples of services to be included in the scope of Article 56, such as: the provision of people by an employment agency; medical services including the termination of a pregnancy; education; the provision of a TV signal; the transmission of programmes and ads from broadcasters in one Member State to cable networks in another; lotteries; judicial recovery of debts.[15]
Specific rules are applicable to certain sectors. In particular, according to Article 58: (1) the freedom to provide services *in the field of transport* shall be governed by the provisions of the Title relating to transport, and (2) the liberalisation of *banking and insurance services* connected with movements of capital shall be effected in step with the liberalisation of movement of capital.

---

9 CJEU, 30 November 1995, Case C-55/94, *Gebhard*, ECLI:EU:C:1995:411, para. 37.
10 CJEU, 26 November 2002, Case C-100/01, *Ministre de l'Intérieur v. Olazbal*, ECLI:EU:C:2002:712, para. 43.
11 CJEU, 4 December 1974, Case 41/74, *Van Duyn v. Home Office*, ECLI:EU:C:1974:133.
12 CJEU, 6 June 2000, Case C-281/98, *Angonese*, ECLI:EU:C:2000:296.
13 CJEU, 16 March 2010, Case C-325/08, *Olympique Lyonnais*, ECLI:EU:C:2010:143.
14 R. Schütze, *European Union Law* (Cambridge, 2018), 664.
15 C. Barnard, J. Snell, *Free movement of legal persons and the provision of services*, in C. Barnard and S. Peers (eds.), *European Union Law* (Oxford: OUP, 2017), Chapter 14.

What is essential for the application of the freedom of services is the *temporariness* of the service provision, which element is to be deducted, more than from the mere existence of an office in a Member State, from the very nature of the economic activity carried out, so referring to its regularity, periodical nature or continuity.
This rule may give rise to abuses, in the event someone runs most of his activities in the territory of a Member State maintaining the place of establishment in another one to evade its professional rules.[16] The CJEU has constantly stated that a Member State 'cannot be denied the right to take measures to prevent the exercise, by a person providing services whose activity is entirely or principally directed towards its territory, of the freedoms guaranteed by the Treaty for the purpose of avoiding the rules which would be applicable to him if he were established within that State'.[17] Of course, those measures must be proportional to the objective pursued.[18] In fact, 'any restriction which, without objective justification, is liable to prohibit, impede or render less attractive the provision of those services must be declared incompatible with EU law'.[19]
3) **Freedom of establishment** is guaranteed by Article 49 TFEU, whose objective is to allow nationals of a Member State or legal persons established in that Member State to set up a secondary establishment in another Member State in order to carry on their business there, and thus to promote economic and social interpenetration within the European Union in the sphere of economic activity other than as an employee. To that end, freedom of establishment is intended 'to allow such nationals or legal persons of the European Union to participate, on a stable and continuing basis, in the economic life of a Member State other than their State of origin and to profit therefrom by actually pursuing, in the host Member States, an economic activity through a fixed establishment for an indefinite period'.[20] The same concept of establishment includes 'actual establishment of the company concerned in that State and the pursuit of genuine economic activity there'.[21]
Article 54 stipulates that 'Companies or firms formed in accordance with the law of a Member State and having their registered office, central administration or principal place of business within the Union shall, for the purposes of this Chapter, be treated in the same way as natural persons who are nationals of Member States.' It further specifies the meaning of "Companies or firms" including 'companies or firms constituted under civil or commercial law, including cooperative societies, and other legal persons governed by public or private law, save for those which are non-profit-making.'

16 CJEU, 3 December 1974, Case 33/74, *Van Binsbergen*, ECLI:EU:C:1974:131; CJEU, 23 November 1999, Case C-376/96, *Arblade*, ECLI:EU:C:1999:575, para. 32.
17 CJEU, 5 October 1994, Case C-23/93, *TV 10*, ECLI:EU:C:1994:362.
18 CJEU, 18 March 1980, Case 52/79, *Debauve*, ECLI:EU:C:1980:83.
19 CJEU, 8 July 2014, Case C-83/13, *Fonnship*, ECLI:EU:C:2014:2053.
20 CJEU, 23 February 2016, Case C-179/14, *Commission v. Hungary*, ECLI:EU:C:2016:108, para. 48.
21 CJEU, 12 July 2012, Case C-378/10, *VALE*, ECLI:EU:C:2012:440, para. 34.

The crucial features of establishment are the stable and continuous basis on which the economic professional activity is carried on and the fact that there is an established professional base within the host Member State. For the provision of services, the temporary nature of the activity is to be determined referring to its periodicity, continuity and regularity; providers of services will not be deemed to be established simply by virtue of the fact that they equip themselves with some form of infrastructure in the host Member State.[22]

Actual exercise of freedom of establishment thus entails, in particular, as a necessary adjunct to that freedom, that 'the subsidiary, agency or branch set up by a legal person established in another Member State must be able, where relevant, and if the activity which it proposes to carry out in the host Member State so requires, to take on workers in that Member State'.[23] It must be recalled that according to the CJEU, Article 49 entails, in principle, 'the freedom to determine the nature and extent of the economic activity that will be carried out in the host Member State, in particular the size of the fixed establishments and the number of workers required for that purpose', as well as 'the freedom subsequently to scale down that activity or even the freedom to give up, should it so decide, its activity and establishment'.[24]

As for the conceptual overlapping between the two freedoms provided for by Articles 49 and 56, the CJEU repeatedly held that unlike the freedom to provide services set out in Article 56 TFEU, which deals with the pursuit of an economic activity by a person in another Member State *without* having the principal or secondary place of business in that State, the freedom of establishment concerns the *permanent* installation in another Member State in order to pursue an economic activity. As prudently suggested by Advocate General Jacobs, however, 'The truth is that the provision of services covers a vast spectrum of different types of activity. At one extreme, it may be necessary for the provider of the service to spend a substantial period of time in the Member State where the service is provided (...); the borderline between services and establishment may be a narrow one, and it is arguable that the Treaty merely requires the abolition of discrimination in such a case.'[25]

The free movement of services, conceived for cross-border performance of the free professionals, has become more markedly an expressive form of enterprise freedom, consisting in companies using their own workers to perform services in foreign countries. Which would make it even more uncertain the fact that the transnational posting of workers, running a service on behalf of the detachable company, may permit their workers to invoke the social rights of the country of destination without incurring any restrictions (prohibited) on the freedom to provide services. This is all the more so where taking into account that a specific feature of the free-

22 CJEU, 11 December 2003, Case C-215/01, *Schnitzer*, ECLI:EU:C:2003:662.

23 CJEU, 10 July 1986, Case 79/85, *Segers*, ECLI:EU:C:1986:308, para. 15.

24 CJEU, 21 December 2016, Case C-201/15, *AGET Iraklis*, ECLI:EU:C:2016:972.

25 Opinion of the Advocate General G. Jacobs, 21 February 1991, CJEU, 25 July 1991, Case 76/90, *Säger*, ECLI:EU:C:1991:72, para. 25.

dom of services, unlike freedom of establishment, is the fact that "contact" with the country where the service is run is only temporary. Therefore, the national treatment that would be extended to the lender of services to reduce dumping, in setting a parameter for legitimizing restrictions on the free movement of services, would not be sufficient to consider the same restrictions as the law of the Union.

2.2.3 Scope

2.2.3.1 Personal Scope

In principle, each of the fundamental freedoms above mentioned has its own scope of application *ratione personae.*

1) The most controversial one is that of Article 45 on **free movement of workers,** for its implications in terms of the extension of labour law protections also to quasi-subordinate workers and self-employed or independent contractors.

EU primary and secondary law had initially avoided any involvement into the definition of the concept of 'worker' for the purpose of free movement. This silence of the EC founding treaties, and of the first few directives adopted in the 1960s and 1970s to confer rights to workers,[26] has been considered particularly surprising given that the regulation of the 'four freedoms', including of course free movement of workers, was one of the main concerns of the Treaty of Rome. This appears to be in contrast with what in the Treaty is said about the concept of 'services' and of natural persons entitled to establish themselves in other Member States.[27]

But since *Hoekstra,*[28] the CJEU decided to advocate the authority to establish a 'Community meaning' for the term 'worker', at least in respect of the EC/EU provisions shaping the rules on 'Free movement of workers'. The Court has since refined its jurisprudence on the concept of 'worker' in this particular field of EU law, relying on three main criteria, to be employed for the purposes of Article 45 TFEU:

a. *subordination*: As noted in *Lawrie-Blum,* 'The essential feature of an employment relationship, however, is that performs *for a certain period of time* a person services *for and under the direction of another*' (emphasis added).[29]
b. *remuneration*: this element requires that work is provided for and under the direction of another, in return for which remuneration is received. The Court has interpreted this requirement broadly in the free movement context, accepting for instance that 'the sole fact that a person is paid a 'share' and that his remuneration may be calculated on a collective basis is not of such a nature as

26 Free movement Directive and Regulation 492/2011.

27 Article 60 of the Treaty of Rome, specifying that 'Services' shall in particular include: (a) activities of an industrial character; (b) activities of a commercial character; (c) activities of craftsmen; (d) activities of the professions.

28 CJEU, 19 March 1974, Case 75/63, *Hoekstra,* ECLI:EU:C:1964:19.

29 CJEU, 3 July 1986, Case 66/85, *Lawrie-Blum,* ECLI:EU:C:1986:284, para. 17.

to deprive that person of his status of worker',[30] and even that services and other benefits in kind provided in lieu of a regular salary, 'may be regarded as being an indirect quid pro quo for their work'.[31] And it may also accept as remuneration payments that do not derive exclusively from the employer but that are 'largely provided by subsidies from public funds'.[32]

c. *genuinity*: for the CJEU the worker must be engaged in 'effective and genuine activities, to the exclusion of activities on such a small scale as to be regarded as purely marginal and ancillary'.[33] The CJEU has further stated that the services provided should not be 'merely a means of rehabilitation' but instead form 'part of the normal labour market',[34] although it has made allowance for 'the fact that the productivity of persons employed ... is low' and that person may be employed under public supported schemes.[35]

From the above one can understand that so far the CJEU's jurisprudence has followed the long-standing binary divide between subordinate employment and autonomous self-employment, deeply rooted in most of Member States' legal traditions. And even with respect to those systems providing for an intermediate category (quasi-subordination, economically dependent self-employment, etc.), the CJEU has been consistent in asserting that 'any activity which a person performs outside a relationship of subordination must be classified as an activity pursued in a self-employed capacity'.[36]

In fact, as the CJEU clarified in the controversial case *FNV Kunsten*,[37] 'the status of 'worker' within the meaning of EU law is not affected by the fact that a person has been hired as a self-employed person under national law, for tax, administrative or organisational reasons, as long as that persons acts under the direction of his employer as regards, in particular, his freedom to choose the time, place and content of his work, does not share in the employer's commercial risks, and, for the

30 CJEU, 14 December 1989, Case C-3/87, *Agegate*, ECLI:EU:C:1989:650, para. 36.

31 CJEU, 5 October 1988, Case 196/87, *Steymann*, ECLI:EU:C:1988:475, para. 12.

32 CJEU, 31 May 1989, Case C-344/87, *Bettray v. Staatssecretaris van Justitie*, ECLI:EU:C:1989:226, para. 15.

33 CJEU, 23 March 1982, Case C-53/81, *Levin*, ECLI:EU:C:1982:105, para. 17; CJEU, 8 June 1999, Case C-337/97, *Meeusen*, ECLI:EU:C:1999:284, para. 13.

34 CJEU, 31 May 1989, Case C-344/87, *Bettray*, ECLI:EU:C:1989:226; CJEU, 7 September 2004, C-456/02 *Trojani*, ECLI:EU:C:2004:488.

35 CJEU, 31 May 1989, Case C-344/87 *Bettray*, ECLI:EU:C:1989:226, para. 15; CJEU, 26 November 1998, C-1/97, *Birden*, ECLI:EU:C:1998:568, paras. 23-32.

36 CJEU, 15 December 2005, Joined Cases C-151/04 and C-152/04, *Durré*, ECLI:EU:C:2005:775, para. 31. See also CJEU, 20 November 2001, Case C-268/99, *Jany and Others*, ECLI:EU:C:2001:616, para. 34 and the decisions cited there.

37 CJEU, 4 December 2014, Case C-413/13, *FNV Kunsten*, ECLI:EU:C:2014:2411, para. 36.

duration of that relationship, forms an integral part of that employer's undertaking, so forming an economic unit with that undertaking'.[38]
As for family members, it must be noted that freedom of movement of workers would be seriously undermined if the migrant worker could not be able to bring the family with her to another Member State. Directive 2004/38 therefore contains a specific provision affirming the right of family members to be granted a right of entry and residence, as well as that of taking up employment (Articles 2(2), 5, 6, and 23, Directive 2004/38). The same rights are granted to those family members who are not EU citizens (Article 10, Regulation No 492/2011).
In principle employment in the public sector is not subject to the free movement of workers, pursuant to Article 45(4) TFEU. The exception based on the expression 'employment in the public sector' has a unitary meaning, otherwise having the effect of impairing the efficacy of EU law, and must be interpreted restrictively. Are therefore excluded from the application of this exception post office workers, railways workers, hospital nurses, plumbers, carpenters, and electricians.[39]
2) A **service** may be carried out by a natural person, acting either as a self-employed or as an employee of a service provider, or by legal persons, being that a company or a non-profit organization, or even by a factual group without legal personality. Services must be normally provided for remuneration (Article 57).
The temporary nature of the service is to be determined both in view of its concrete duration and on the basis of its regularity, periodicity and continuity.
The most controversial issue regarding the personal scope relates to the fact that Article 56 can be used to challenge rules laid down by the host Member State and the home Member State which obstruct the provision of services.
3) Article 49 aims at prohibiting domestic Member State restrictions on the **freedom of establishment**, including primary establishments such as companies as well as secondary establishments (agencies and branch offices). In so far as they are not governed by the provisions relating to freedom of movement of goods, capital or persons, the services mentioned in Article 49 must be considered to be as such, where they are normally provided for remuneration.
The development of the scope of Article 49 has been controversial in the case law of the CJEU. In *Reyners*,[40] one of the earliest cases in this area, a Dutch national, was prohibited from practicing as an advocate in the Belgian courts, for lack of Belgian nationality. The question before the court was whether such discrimination, prohibited by Article 49 (ex Article 43 TEC) and Article 56 TFEU (ex Article 49

38 CJEU, 16 September 1999, Case C-22/98, *Becu and Others*, ECLI:EU:C:1999:419, para. 26. For an overview on the notion of worker in Article 45 TFEU and beyond, see N. Kountouris, 'The Concept of 'Worker' in European Labour Law: Fragmentation, Autonomy and Scope', *Industrial Law Journal*, Vol. 47, No 4, 2018, pp. 192-225.

39 CJEU, 17 December 1980, Case C-149/79, *Commission v. Belgium*, ECLI:EU:C:1982:195.

40 CJEU, 21 June 1974, Case 2/74, *Reyners*, ECLI:EU:C:1974:68.

TEC), was actionable on a directly effective basis. In the light of *Van Gend en Loos* – in which the CJEU stated that a treaty provision is directly effective if it were unconditionally precluding any further Member State implementation – in *Reyners* it was held that Article 49 required directives to give effect, which had not been created at the time. In spite of this the Court held Article 49, and particularly its principle of non-discrimination on the grounds of nationality, to be directly effective allowing the claimant to invoke directly the application of freedom of establishment.

2.2.3.2 Material Scope

Preliminarily it must be recalled that fundamental freedoms are functional to a cross-border situation, that is a situation in which two or more legal systems are involved by the movement: this however must not be understood to mean that a worker may not rely on Article 45 against her home state, as Member States are obliged not to hinder their own citizens from leaving the country in order to take up employment in another Member state (Article 4, Directive 2004/38). The same applies when citizens return to their country of origin. The cross-border limitation means, on the contrary, that purely domestic cases are not to be covered by the relevant Articles of the TFEU.

As for the economic freedoms, the CJEU stated that whether a provision of services falls or not within the free movement principles depends not just (only) by the cross-border element, but also on the fact that the services must be commercial in nature, in that they must be provided for remuneration, even in the case of non-profit organizations. In its case law, the CJEU went further to include the services provided by athletes in the context of a sports association or federation,[41] as well as cases in which the remuneration did not come from the recipient of the services.[42]

The material scope of freedom of services extends also to activities that at national level can be deemed to be immoral or even illegal. This includes gambling, lotteries, prostitution, and other cases, all of which are subject to the proportionality test. A Member State remains free to prohibit them, but the ban must be proportionate and not arbitrary on grounds of nationality or place of establishment.[43]

The justified restrictions to free movement of workers provided for by Article 45 have been progressively extended to the other freedoms, in a way that calls into question the same reasoning. Exceptions of public policy, security and health are admissible when: the restriction is adopted in pursuit of a legitimate public interest, non-incompatible with EU law; it is equally applicable to persons established within the Member State and without discrimination; it is proportionate to the need to observe the legitimate rules in question; and it respects fundamental rights.

41 CJEU, 11 April 2000, Cases C-51/96 and 191/97, *Deliège*, ECLI:EU:C:2000:199, para. 59.

42 CJEU, 26 April 1988, Case C-352/85, *Bond van Adverteerders,* ECLI:EU:C:1988:196.

43 CJEU, 14 October 2004, Case C-36/02, *Omega,* ECLI:EU:C:2004:614.

As for the material scope of freedom to provide services, Articles 56 and 57 apply to activities of industrial character, of commercial character, of craftsmen, and of the professions. According to Article 57, 'services' are those insofar as they are not regulated by other provisions relating to free movement of goods, capitals and persons. To fall within the material scope of application of Article 56, there must be the provision of a service, which needs to have a cross-border element, and is to be provided on a temporary basis for remuneration.

In the specific field of the posting of workers (when regulated by Directive 96/71[44]) the CJEU has held that the aims of preserving the interests of the workers and ensuring good relations on the labour market and to be seen as legitimate aims: therefore, the imposition of a licence requirement is justified so long as it takes into account the relevant evidence and guarantees already furnished by the service provider in the Member State of establishment, thus for example making an unjustified restriction the requirement to obtain a work permit for a company working temporarily in another Member State.[45]

In 2006 the Commission took the stance and introduced a specific set of rules governing the provision of services within the EU. The so-called service directive (Directive 2006/123),[46] after a long and consuming political and legal debate, was adopted with the aim of breaking down barriers to cross-border trade in services between countries in the EU, making it easier for service providers, particularly small and medium sized enterprises, to offer their services to customers in other EU countries. To enhance the rights of services recipients and strengthen their confidence in the internal market, Member States have been asked to remove obstacles for recipients of services supplied by providers established in another Member State, such as obligations to obtain an authorisation, to abolish discriminatory requirements based on the recipient's nationality or place of residence, and to make available general information and assistance on the legal requirements, in particular consumer protection rules and redress procedures applicable in other Member States. According to Article 20, all Member States are obliged to ensure that companies do not discriminate against service recipients by denying access to a service or applying higher prices due to the recipient's nationality or country of residence. Differential treatment is only allowed when the differences are duly justified.

In order to help enhancing these provisions, the Directive envisages a strong cooperation between local administrations, to give mutual assistance in the supervision of service providers by means of an exchange of information and the carrying out of transnational inspections and investigations. This ensures the effective supervision of service providers and guarantees that such supervision does not lead to

44 Directive 96/71/EC of the European Parliament and of the Council of 16 December 1996, concerning the posting of workers in the framework of the provision of services, OJ L 18/01.

45 CJEU, 27 March 1990, Case C-113/89, *Rush Portuguesa,* ECLI:EU:C:1990:142.

46 Directive of the European Parliament and of the Council of 12 December 2006 on services in the internal market, OJ 2006 L 376, p. 36.

additional and unjustified obstacles. As usual, certain requirements can still be imposed by Member States, but only when they are non-discriminatory, justified for reasons of public policy, public security, public health or the protection of the environment and do not go beyond what is necessary to achieve their objective.
The posting of workers constitutes the most important exception to the freedom of services within the EU; the ultimate goal of the relevant Directives has been to enhance the economic dimension of the European market by protecting persons enjoying their right to freely move. This may give rise to a complex set of legal questions, especially regarding conflicting rights of workers and in particular the right to take collective action, all of which fall outside the scope of this chapter.

2.2.4 General Principles

2.2.4.1 Free Movement

Coming to the substantial guarantees provided by the EU legal framework on free movement, Article 45(3) TFEU grants the worker the right to accept job offers actually made, to move freely within the EU to look for a job, to stay in another Member State for the purpose of employment, and to remain in the relevant Member State even after the end of the employment relationship. Secondary law is developed on the basis of Article 46 TFEU, which empowers the European Parliament and the Council to 'issue directives or make regulations setting out the measures required to bring about freedom of movement for workers'. Also Regulation No 492/2011 grants workers moving across the EU an unlimited access to the labour market of another Member State (Article 1-6). Coupled with the right to work, the worker retains the right to enter and reside in the territory of another Member State (Article 45(3)(b), (c), and (d)) TFEU.
The same Article 45(3), in the case of public policy, security, and health reasons, sets out important limitations which, being derogatory from a general rule, must be interpreted restrictively.[47] The public policy exception is furthermore substantiated in secondary legislation, particularly by Directive 2004/38 (Articles 21 et seq.). This means that neither Article 45 nor the relevant secondary legislation preclude Member States from imposing to migrant workers administrative, police measures limiting the worker's right of residence in a specific territory, provided that the action is justified by reasons of public order or public security, that those reasons could otherwise give rise only to a measure prohibiting him to reside in the entire territory of the Member State, and that the conduct is capable to give rise to punitive measures applicable to its own nationals.[48]

47 CJEU, 4 December 1974, Case 41/74, *Van Duyn v. Home Office*, ECLI:EU:C:1974:133, para. 18.
48 CJEU, 26 November 2002, Case C-100/01, *Ministre de l'Intérieur v. Aitor Oteiza Olazabal*, ECLI:EU:C:2002:712.

2.2.4.2 Non-Discrimination

Freedom of movement entails the elimination of any impair treatment based on the person's nationality. In primary law this is reflected by Article 2(1) TEU and Article 45(2) TFEU. Regulation No 492/2011 prohibits discrimination in its Article 7(1), stating that 'A worker who is a national of a Member State may not, in the territory of another Member State, be treated differently from national workers by reason of his nationality in respect of any conditions of employment and work, in particular as regards remuneration, dismissal, and, should he become unemployed, reinstatement or re-employment'. The aims of the prohibition of discrimination relate to the need for the worker not only to enter and start working in another Member State, but also and especially to be treated equally comparably to Member State nationals.

All kinds of discrimination, direct and indirect, are prohibited. It is especially the concept of indirect discrimination that has been interpreted broadly in the case law of the CJEU, including cases in which previous periods of employment abroad were not taken into account,[49] others in which the payment of tide over allowances were paid only to students having completed their secondary education in that Member State,[50] and others where language requirements were deemed to be mandatory to get a job not related to it.[51]

The prohibition of discrimination addresses both Member States as public authorities and associations (such as in the well-known *Bosman* case[52]); it also renders null and void any clause of a collective agreement or any collective regulation concerning eligibility for employment, remuneration, and other conditions of employment or dismissal, insofar as they lay down discriminatory conditions in respect to workers who are nationals of other Member States. This applies in principle also to collective agreements applicable to the public sector.[53]

2.2.4.3 Prohibition of Restrictions

The prohibition of restrictions differs substantially from the principle of non-discrimination as it deals with the existence of single provisions restricting the exercise of the right to free movement either factually or legally without an evident connection to nationality. A pedagogic example could be seen in a national legislation providing for an excessive income tax rating, thus dissuading foreigners to cir-

---

49 CJEU, 23 February 1994, Case C-419/92, *Scholz*, ECLI:EU:C:1994:62; CJEU, 30 November 2000, Case C-195/98, *Österreicher Gewerkschaftsverbund*, ECLI:EU:C:2000:655.

50 CJEU, 12 September 1994, Case C-278/94, *Commission v. Belgium*, ECLI:EU:C:1996:321.

51 CJEU, 6 June 2000, Case C-281/98, *Angonese*, ECLI:EU:C:2000:296.

52 CJEU, 15 December 1995, Case C-415/93, *Union Royale Belge de Société de Football Association v. Bosman*, ECLI:EU:C:1995:463.

53 CJEU, 15 January 1998, Case C-15/96, *Kalliope Schöning-Kougebetopoulo*, ECLI:EU:C:1998:3.

culate. But more in general almost all legal provisions imposing burdens on individuals can be seen as restrictions in the mentioned meaning: being this the case, it is for the national legislation to be assessed by the CJEU applying the proportionality test.

In the settled case law of the CJEU, the concept of 'restriction' covers, for example within the meaning of Article 49 TFEU, 'measures which, even though they are applicable without discrimination on grounds of nationality, are liable to impede the exercise of freedom of establishment or render it less attractive'.[54] In that must be included all those measures taken by a Member State 'which, although applicable without distinction, affect access to the market for undertakings from other Member States and thereby hinder intra-Community trade'.[55]

In the context of the freedom of establishment, the prohibition of restrictions entails the possibility for the CJEU to outlaw a national provision capable of rendering less attractive for a company to move or remain in a Member State different than that of origin. In the words of the CJEU, freedom of establishment, granted by Article 49 TFEU to nationals of the Member States, 'includes the right for them to take up and pursue activities as self-employed persons and to set up and manage undertakings, under the conditions laid down for its own nationals by the law of the Member State where such establishment is effected, entails, in accordance with Article 54 TFEU, for companies or firms formed in accordance with the law of a Member State and having their registered office, central administration or principal place of business within the European Union, the right to exercise their activity in the Member State concerned through a subsidiary, a branch or an agency'.[56] In its case law, the CJEU has gone further and stated that 'freedom of establishment thus covers, in particular, the situation where a company established in a Member State creates a subsidiary in another Member State. The same is true, in accordance with settled case-law, where such a company or a national of a Member State acquires a holding in the capital of a company established in another Member State allowing it or him to exert a definite influence on the company's decisions and to determine its activities'.[57]

In the context of freedom to provide services, restrictions are to be interpreted extensively. According to the jurisprudence of the CJEU, Article 59 of the Treaty 'requires not only the elimination of all discrimination on grounds of nationality against providers of services who are established in another Member State, but also the abolition of any restriction, even if it applies without distinction to national

54 CJEU, 21 April 2005, Case C-140/03, *Commission v. Greece,* ECLI:EU:C:2005:242, para. 27.

55 CJEU, 28 April 2009, Case C-518/06, *Commission v. Italy,* ECLI:EU:C:2009:270, para. 64.

56 CJEU, 13 December 2005, Case C-446/03, *Marks & Spencer*, ECLI:EU:C:2005:763, para. 30.

57 CJEU, 21 October 2010, Case C-81/09, *Idryma Typou,* ECLI:EU:C:2010:622, para. 47.

providers of services and to those of other Member States, which is liable to prohibit, impede or render less attractive the activities of a provider of services established in another Member State in which he lawfully provides similar services'.[58] Restrictions are admitted when they comply with the proportionality test, and more precisely: they are applied in a non-discriminatory way, they are justified by imperative reasons relating to the public interest, they are objectively necessary in order to ensure compliance with professional rules, and they do not exceed what is necessary to attain its objectives.[59]

2.2.4.4 Derogations and Justifications

Once a national rule is qualified as a restriction or an obstacle to one of the freedoms, the TFEU provides for a closed number of justifications that the Member State can put forward. Some of them are expressed in the TFEU itself, and relate to: public policy, public security, and public health (Articles 45(3), 45(4), 52(1), and 62 TFEU).

These derogations must be interpreted strictly, so that their scope cannot be determined unilaterally by the Member State without control by the EU; they cannot be misapplied so as to serve purely economic interests or aims; they must give the individual affected the right to redress; and they are subject to the proportionality test. Barnard and Peers[60] list a number of examples relating to imperative reasons of public interest (also referred to as ORRPI by Directive 2006/123 on freedom of services): combating drug tourism; ensuring road safety; protecting workers; preventing gambling; avoid the risk of crime or fraud; avoid the risk of incitement to spend; preserving press' pluralism; maintaining fiscal cohesion; combating money laundering; protecting the interests of creditors, minority shareholders and employees.

The test to be met in assessing the admissibility of derogations at national level is centred on four conditions: they must be applied in a non-discriminatory manner; they must be justified by imperative requirements of general interest; they must be suitable for securing the attainment of the objective which they pursue; and they must not go beyond what is necessary in order to attain it. In the *Gebhard* case, for example, the CJEU held that 'the possibility for a national of a Member State to exercise his right of establishment, and the conditions for his exercise of that right, must be determined in the light of the activities which he intends to pursue on the territory of the host Member State'.[61] This results in a demonstration on the appropriateness and the necessity of the norm or practice, and the positive answer

58 CJEU, 24 January 2002, Case C-164/99, *Portugaia Construções*, ECLI:EU:C:2002:40, para. 16, citing also CJEU, Case C-76/90 *Säger*, CJEU, Case C-43/93 *Vander Elst*; CJEU, Case C-272/94 *Guiot*, and more importantly both CJEU, Joined Cases C-369/96 and C-376/96 *Arblade and Others* and CJEU, Case C-165/98 *Mazzoleni*.

59 CJEU, 25 July 1991, Case C-76/90, *Säger*, ECLI:EU:C:1991:331.

60 C. Barnard and S. Peers (eds.), *European Union Law* (Oxford: OUP, 2014), 422.

61 CJEU, 30 November 1995, Case C-55/94, *Gebhard*, ECLI:EU:C:1995:411, para. 37.

to the question whether there could be a different wording of the Member State's law or if a decision could be adopted by Member States' authorities that would secure the said interest while having a lower impact in limiting the specific freedom.

2.2.4.5 Recognition of Qualifications and Training

Article 53 TFEU is the constitutional basis for the recognition of qualifications. A different treatment of domestic and foreign qualification would give rise to an infringement of the fundamental freedoms of movement: this applies both in the case of certificates obtained abroad by non-nationals and to be used in a Member State, and in the case of nationals obtaining their own certificates in another Member State.

In the area of the so-called regulated professions, the EU started introducing specific Directives applicable to the various professions: nurses, dentists, veterinarians, pharmacists, doctors, etc. This sectoral harmonization was later abandoned. Since the '80s, the Commission started to sum up all the relevant pieces of legislation into a framework instrument (Directive 89/48), and in the light of the principle of mutual recognition included in the regulation all protected professions, now consolidated in Directive 2005/36.[62]

The purpose of the Directive is to establish that a Member State which makes access to or pursuit of a regulated profession in its territory contingent upon possession of specific professional qualifications shall recognise professional qualifications obtained in one or more other Member States, allowing the holder of the said qualifications to pursue the same profession there, for access to and pursuit of that profession.

The rules for the recognition of qualifications have been supplemented by a code of conduct approved by the group of coordinators for Directive 2005/36/EC (composed of representatives from the Member States), which contains a list of admitted and not admitted national administrative practices.[63]

2.2.4.6 Interim Conclusions

From the jurisprudence of the CJEU it can be inferred that a similar approach on the various freedoms enhanced in the Treaties has been taken, so that any national rule implying an impediment to market access falls within the scope of the free movement rules and requires thus to be justified. Sometimes the CJEU does not even intend to distinguish the two freedoms, and jointly applies both of them.[64]

This conclusion cannot lead to deny the differences between the freedom to provide services and that of establishment, being the former more incline to admit

---

62 Directive 2005/36/EC of the European Parliament and of the Council of 7 September 2005 on the recognition of professional qualifications, OJ L 255/22.

63 A useful tool can be found at: https://ec.europa.eu/growth/single-market/services/free-movement-professionals/qualifications-recognition_en.

64 CJEU, 4 March 2004, Case C-334/02, *Commission v. France*, ECLI:EU:C:2004:129.

objective justification, the boundary being the temporary nature of the service. This led the CJEU to qualify as service within the meaning of Article 56 TFEU the activity of a Portuguese company carrying out plastering in Germany for three years, as "services' within the meaning of the Treaty may cover services varying widely in nature, including services which are provided over an extended period, even over several years, where, for example, the services in question are supplied in connection with the construction of a large building. Services within the meaning of the Treaty may likewise be constituted by services which a business established in a Member State supplies with a greater or lesser degree of frequency or regularity, even over an extended period, to persons established in one or more other Member States, for example the giving of advice or information for remuneration'.[65]

2.2.5 Applicability and Enforcement of Fundamental Freedoms in the Road Transport Sector

2.2.5.1 Preamble: Viking as an Illustrative Case of Clash of Fundamental Rights

All the above mentioned fundamental freedoms are relevant in the case of transnational road transport, involving this situation the movement of workers, services and the establishment of companies in a Member State other than that of origin.

The legal questions arising from that situation can be analysed from many perspectives. In the light of fundamental freedoms, an illustrative case comes from transnational transport by ferry, and involved a Finnish ferry company operating between Estonia and Finland. Seeking to re-flag its ferry Rosella, Viking Line registered it in Estonia with the aim of employing an Estonian crew at local rates and conditions of employment. The Finnish unions opposed the reflagging and involved the ITF (International Transport Workers federation), who called for a refusal to enter any negotiation with Viking, the sanction being the exclusion from the ITF itself. This prevented the Estonian unions and Viking to enter any negotiation. After two years Viking brought a claim asking a British court (where the company was based) to withdraw the ITF circular and ordering them not to interfere with Viking's freedom to move to Estonia.

In brief, the CJEU ruled that collective action initiated by a trade union or a group of trade unions against a private undertaking in order to induce that undertaking to enter into a collective agreement, the terms of which are liable to deter it from exercising freedom of establishment, is not excluded from the scope of that article. Article 49 TFEU is to be interpreted to the effect that 'collective action such as that at issue in the main proceedings, which seeks to induce a private undertaking whose registered office is in a given Member State to enter into a collective work agreement with a trade union established in that State and to apply the terms set out in that agreement to the employees of a subsidiary of that undertaking estab-

65 CJEU, 11 December 2003, Case C-215/01, *Schnitzer*, ECLI:EU:C:2003:662, para. 30.

lished in another Member State, constitutes a restriction within the meaning of that article. That restriction may, in principle, be justified by an overriding reason of public interest, such as the protection of workers, provided that it is established that the restriction is suitable for ensuring the attainment of the legitimate objective pursued and does not go beyond what is necessary to achieve that objective'. In fact, 'the right to take collective action for the protection of workers is a legitimate interest which, in principle, justifies a restriction of one of the fundamental freedoms guaranteed by the Treaty (see, to that effect, *Schmidberger*, para. 74) and that the protection of workers is one of the overriding reasons of public interest recognised by the Court. Further, since the EU has 'not only an economic but also a social purpose, the rights under the provisions of the Treaty on the free movement of goods, persons, services and capital must be balanced against the objectives pursued by social policy, which include, as is clear from the first paragraph of Article 136 EC, inter alia, improved living and working conditions, so as to make possible their harmonisation while improvement is being maintained, proper social protection and dialogue between management and labour'.[66]

Although the outcome of the Viking case was not favourable to the workers and their unions – which brought harsh criticism from scholarship to the CJEU –, the case very well illustrates the Court's approach to the market access test and the sequence of arguments systematically employed by thereby.

2.2.5.2 *Special Rules: Are Those on 'Cabotage' Compatible with Fundamental Freedoms?*

In the sector of international road transport, a preliminary issue is that of promoting fair competition between Member States, in particular fighting illegal practices such as undeclared work or bogus self-employment. As we have seen before, the CJEU is constant in extending the scope of EU labour law and of the fundamental freedoms beyond the binary divide subordinate employees – autonomous self-employed, as well as combating bogus self-employment. A similar anti-abusive move is that of clearly distinguishing freedom of establishment – duly protected and promoted by the treaties – from the illegal practice of the letterbox companies.[67]

A widespread practice is that of *cabotage*, meaning 'the national carriage of goods for hire or reward carried out by non-resident hauliers on a temporary basis in a host Member State'.[68] At EU level, cabotage is regulated by Regulation No 1072/2009. Article 8 of the Regulation provides that every haulier is entitled to perform up to three cabotage operations within a seven days period starting the day

66 CJEU, 11 December 2007, Case C-438/05, *International Transport Workers' Federation -Finnish Seamen's Union v. Viking Line*, ECLI:EU:C:2007:772. *Amplius* see M. Freedland and J. Prassl (eds.), Viking, Laval and Beyond (Oxford and Portland: Hart, 2014).

67 See Chapter 4 on the posting of workers.

68 https://ec.europa.eu/transport/modes/road/haulage/cabotage_en.

after the unloading of the international transport. A haulier may decide to carry out one, two or all three cabotage operations in different Member States and not necessarily the Member State in which the international transport was delivered. In this case only one cabotage operation is allowed in a given Member State to be carried out within three days of entering that Member State without cargo. Article 10(1) provides that 'In the event of serious disturbance of the national transport market in a given geographical area due to, or aggravated by, cabotage, any Member State may refer the matter to the Commission with a view to the adoption of safeguard measures and shall provide the Commission with the necessary information and notify it of the measures it intends to take as regards resident hauliers'.

Cabotage rules are to be seen as restrictions on the fundamental freedoms, as they limit the freedom of companies to provide services wherever they wish across the EU; but they are justified by the aim of protecting the integrity of the internal market by avoiding social dumping among Member States. As companies are required to respect the rules on the posting of workers, the question remains whether the rules introduced or maintained at national level on cabotage may hinder operators' economic freedoms by imposing them excessive burdens.

In a recent action, the EU Commission referred Denmark before the CJEU,[69] for the following reasons:

– The Commission submits that Article 8(2) of Regulation (EC) No 1072/2009 regulates exhaustively how hauliers may to carry out cabotage operations on the terms laid down in that article. The provision does not provide for a maximum number of loading and/or unloading sites within the same cabotage operation. The limit of a maximum of three cabotage operations does not mean that a cabotage operation must include a set number of loading and/or unloading sites.
– Under the Danish rules, cabotage can consist either of a number of loading sites or a number of unloading sites, but not both. The Danish rules preclude non-resident hauliers from carrying out cabotage operations consisting of a number of loading and unloading sites, which constitutes a restriction on how those hauliers may carry out cabotage operations in Denmark as provided for under Regulation (EC) No 1072/2009.

The CJEU held that 'the Cabotage Guidelines provide that a cabotage operation may have several loading points or several unloading points. Therefore, those measures do not limit the number of consignors or principles for the same cabotage operation and impliedly allow a cabotage operation to have several loading points and one unloading point or several unloading points and one loading point. It follows that, according to the Cabotage Guidelines, only cabotage operations having several loading points and several unloading points are prohibited. Therefore, those

69 Action brought on 25 October 2016, Case C-541/16, *European Commission v. Kingdom of Denmark.*

measures do not go beyond what is necessary to achieve the objective pursued by Regulation No 1072/2009. Taking account of the foregoing, it must be held that the Cabotage Guidelines are consistent with the principle of proportionality'.[70]

2.2.5.3 Follows: Is the 'Limosa' Declaration an Admissible Measure in the Light of Article 56 TFEU?

The Limosa declaration is the first step towards legal work in Belgium in accordance with European rules.[71] It is a legal obligation both for workers who habitually work in a country other than Belgium or have been hired in a country other than Belgium, and for independent workers temporarily working in that capacity in Belgium, without residing there on a permanent basis. The obligation to file a Limosa declaration has been in force since 1 April 2007, and its non-compliance may give rise to criminal or administrative sanctions. Belgian law provides an exception for international transport: workers and self-employed people in the international transport sector for passengers and goods are exempt, with the exception of inland transport in Belgium.

This gave rise to an action of infringement brought by the EU Commission towards Belgium, as the provisions laying down the Limosa obligations were suspected to constitute a discriminatory restriction on the freedom of self-employed workers to provide services, the declaration requirement in question applying only to self-employed service providers established or resident in a Member State other than the Kingdom of Belgium.

In the subsequent case before the CJEU, the Court held that 'The formalities implied by the declaration requirement at issue are thus such as to impede the supply of services on the territory of the kingdom of Belgium by self-employed service providers established in another Member State. That obligation thus constitutes an obstacle to the freedom to provide services'.[72] Therefore a justification is required. In order to find out such justification, the CJEU noted that 'the objectives relied on in the present case by the Kingdom of Belgium can be taken into consideration as overriding requirements in the public interest which are capable of justifying a restriction on the freedom to provide services. On that point, it is sufficient to state that the objective of combating fraud, particularly social security fraud, and preventing abuse, in particular detecting 'bogus self-employed persons' and combating undeclared work, can form part not only of the objective of the financial balance of social security systems, but also of the objectives of preventing unfair competition and social dumping and protecting workers, including self-employed service providers.'[73] Nevertheless, a general presumption of fraud is not sufficient to justify a

---

70 CJEU, 12 April 2018, C-541/16, *European Commission v. Kingdom of Denmark*, ECLI:EU:C:2018:251, paras. 58-61.

71 For more details see Chapter 5 on social security.

72 CJEU, 19 December 2012, Case C-577/10, *Commission v. Belgium*, ECLI:EU:C:2012:814, para. 40.

73 Ibid., para. 45.

measure compromising the objectives spelled by the Treaties, and even if it were accepted that self-employed service providers established in a Member State other than Belgium could be subject, in the latter State, to tax and social security obligations, it is established that the application of the declaration requirement at issue is not restricted to cases where there is cause to ascertain that those tax and social security obligations are met. The CJEU concluded then that the Limosa declaration is capable of infringing freedom to provide services ex Article 56 TFEU.
In a subsequent case, the same Limosa declaration was found to be justified by a different reason of public interest. Interpreting Articles 56 and 57 TFEU, the CJEU held that they not preclude a national legislation 'under which the recipient of services performed by workers posted by a service provider established in another Member State is required to declare to the competent authorities, before those workers begin to work, the data identifying those workers who are unable to submit proof of the declaration which their employer should have made to the competent authorities of that host Member State prior to the commencement of that provision of services, since such legislation is capable of being justified as safeguarding an overriding ground of public interest, such as the protection of workers or the combating of social security fraud, on condition that it is established that that legislation is appropriate for ensuring the attainment of the legitimate objective or objectives pursued and that it does not go beyond what is necessary to achieve them, these being matters for the referring court to determine.'[74]

2.3 Case Law

List of the most relevant case law of the Court of Justice of the European Union:

CJEU, 19 March 1974, Case 75/63, *Hoekstra*, ECLI:EU:C:1964:19.
CJEU, 21 June 1974, Case 2/74, *Reyners*, ECLI:EU:C:1974:68.
CJEU, 3 December 1974, Case 33/74, *Van Binsbergen*, ECLI:EU:C:1974:131.
CJEU, 4 December 1974, Case 41/74, *Van Duyn v. Home Office*, ECLI:EU:C:1974:133.
CJEU, 18 March 1980, Case 52/79, *Debauve,* ECLI:EU:C:1980:83.
CJEU, 17 December 1980, Case 149/79, *Commission v. Belgium*, ECLI:EU:C:1980:297.
CJEU, 23 March 1982, Case C-53/81, *Levin*, ECLI:EU:C:1982:105.
CJEU, 22 May 1985, Case 13/83, *European Parliament v. Council*, ECLI:EU:C:1985:220.
CJEU, 3 July 1986, Case 66/85, *Lawrie-Blum*, ECLI:EU:C:1986:284.
CJEU, 10 July 1986, Case 79/85, *Segers,* ECLI:EU:C:1986:308.
CJEU, 26 April 1988, Case C-352/85, *Bond van Adverteerders*, ECLI:EU:C:1988:196.

---

74 CJEU, 3 December 2014, Case C-315/13, *De Clercq and others*, ECLI:EU:C:2014:2408.

CJEU, 5 October 1988, Case C-196/87, *Steymann*, ECLI:EU:C:1988:475.
CJEU, 31 May 1989, Case C-344/87 *Bettray*, ECLI:EU:C:1989:226.
CJEU, 14 December 1989, Case C-3/87, *Agegate,* ECLI:EU:C:1989:650.
CJEU, 27 March 1990, Case C-113/89, *Rush Portuguesa*, ECLI:EU:C:1990:142.
CJEU, 25 July 1991, Case C-76/90, *Säger*, ECLI:EU:C:1991:331.
CJEU, 23 February 1994, Case C-419/92, *Scholz*, ECLI:EU:C:1994:62.
CJEU, 28 March 1994, Case C-272/94 *Guiot*, ECLI:EU:C:1996:147.
CJEU, 9 August 1994, Case C-43/93 *Vander Elst,* ECLI:EU:C:1994:310.
CJEU, 12 September 1994, Case C-278/94, *Commission v. Belgium,* ECLI:EU:C:1996:321.
CJEU, 5 October 1994, Case C-23/93, *TV 1*, ECLI:EU:C:1994:362.
CJEU, 30 November 1995, Case C-55/94, *Gebhard*, ECLI:EU:C:1995:411.
CJEU, 15 December 1995, Case C-415/93, *Union Royale Belge de Société de Football Association v. Bosman*, ECLI:EU:C:1995:463.
CJEU, 15 January 1998, Case C-15/96, *Kalliope Schöning-Kougebetopoulo*, ECLI:EU:C:1998:3.
CJEU, 26 November 1998, Case C-1/97, *Birden*, ECLI:EU:C:1998:568.
CJEU, 8 June 1999, Case C-337/97, *Meeusen*, ECLI:EU:C:1999:284.
CJEU, 23 November 1999, C-376/96, *Arblade and Others*, ECLI:EU:C:1999:575.
CJEU, 15 March 2000, Case C-165/98, *Mazzoleni*, ECLI:EU:C:2001:162.
CJEU, 11 April 2000, Cases C-51/96 and 191/97, *Deliège*, ECLI:EU:C:2000:199.
CJEU, 6 June 2000, Case C-281/98, *Angonese*, ECLI:EU:C:2000:296.
CJEU, 30 November 2000, Case C-195/98, *Österreicher Gewerkschaftsverbund*, ECLI:EU:C:2000:655.
CJEU, 20 November 2001, Case C-268/99, *Jany and Others*, ECLI:EU:C:2001:616.
CJEU, 24 January 2002, Case C-164/99, *Portugaia Construções*, ECLI:EU:C:2002:40.
CJEU, 26 November 2002, Case C-100/01, *Ministre de l'Intérieur v. Olazbal*, ECLI:EU:C:2002:712.
CJEU, 11 December 2003, Case C-215/01, *Schnitzer*, ECLI:EU:C:2003:662.
CJEU, 7 September 2004, C-456/02, *Trojani*, ECLI:EU:C:2004:488.
CJEU, 14 October 2004, Case C-36/02, *Omega*, ECLI:EU:C:2004:614.
CJEU, 21 April 2005, Case C-140/03, *Commission v. Greece,* ECLI:EU:C:2005:242.
CJEU, 13 December 2005, Case C-446/03, *Marks & Spencer*, ECLI:EU:C:2005:763.
CJEU, 15 December 2005, Joined Cases C-151/04 and C-152/04, *Durré*, ECLI:EU:C:2005:775.
CJEU, 11 December 2007, Case C-438/05, *International Transport Workers' Federation - Finnish Seamen's Union v. Viking Line*, ECLI:EU:C:2007:772.
CJEU, 28 April 2009, Case C-518/06, *Commission v. Italy*, ECLI:EU:C:2009:270.
CJEU, 16 March 2010, Case C-325/08, *Olympique Lyonnais*, ECLI:EU:C:2010:143.

CJEU, 21 October 2010, Case C-81/09, *Idryma Typou,* ECLI:EU:C:2010:622.
CJEU, 12 July 2012, Case C-378/10, *VALE,* ECLI:EU:C:2012:440.
CJEU, 19 December 2012, Case C-577/10, *Commission v. Belgium*, ECLI:EU:C:2012:814.
CJEU, 3 December 2014, Case C-315/13, *De Clercq and others*, ECLI:EU:C:2014:2408.
CJEU, 23 February 2016, Case C-179/14, *Commission v. Hungary,* ECLI:EU:C:2016:108.
CJEU, 21 December 2016, Case C-201/15, *AGET Iraklis*, ECLI:EU:C:2016:972.

2.4 Further Reading

2.4.1 Academic Literature

This is a list of suggested bibliography, which can be used for additional study for those interested to dwell into the matters further.

C. Barnard, *The Substantive Law in the EU. The Four Freedoms* (Oxford: OUP, 2016).

C. Barnard and S. Peers (eds.), *European Union Law* (Oxford: OUP, 2017).

C. Barnard and S. Peers (eds.), *European Union Law* (Oxford: OUP, 2014).

R. Blanpain, *European Labour Law*, 14th Edition (Alphen aan den Rijn: Kluwer Law International, 2014).

P. Caro De Sousa, The *European Fundamental Freedoms. A Contextual Approach* (Oxford: OUP, 2015).

D. Chalmers, G. Davies and G. Monti, *European Union Law* (Cambridge: CUP, 2014).

P. Craig and G. De Burca, *EU Law. Text, Cases, and Materials* (Oxford: OUP, 2015).

J. Cremers, 'Economic freedoms and labour standards in the European Union', in *Transfer*, ETUI, 2016, Vol. 22(2) 149-162.

A. Cuyvers, *Freedom of Establishment and the Freedom to Provide Services in the EU,* in: E. Ugirashebuja, J.E. Ruhangisa, T. Ottervanger and A. Cuyvers (Eds.), *East African Community Law: Institutional, Substantive and Comparative EU Aspects* (Leiden Boston: Brill Nijhoff, 2017), 376-391.

M. Freedland and J. Prassl (eds.), *Viking, Laval and Beyond* (Oxford and Portland: Hart, 2014).

G. Thüsing, *European Labour Law* (Munich-Baden-Baden-Oxford: Beck-Hart-Nomos, 2013).

S. Weatherill, 'Viking and Laval: The EU Internal Market Perspective', in M.R. Freedland and J. Prassl, *Viking, Laval and Beyond* (Oxford and Portland: Hart, 2014), 23-39.

2.4.2 Other Documents

'Fundamental rights in the EU', at: www.europarl.europa.eu/atyourservice/en/displayFtu.html?ftuId=FTU_2.1.2.html

'European Union, The Treaty at a Glance', http://europa.eu/lisbon_treaty/glance/index_en.htm.

Websites with additional information:

Website of the European Commission: http://ec.europa.eu/social/main.jsp?catId=849.
Website of the network of legal exports in the field of free movement of workers and social security coordination (FreSsco) (including reports of this network, a regulations database and an e-learning tool): http://ec.europa.eu/social/main.jsp?catId=1098&langId=en.

3 The Analysis of Private International Law in the EU with Regard to EU Cross-Border Road Transport: Competency and Applicable Law

Zef Even, Ruben Houweling, Amber Zwanenburg & Mijke Houwerzijl[*]

3.1 Introduction

3.1.1 Curriculum Outline

Private international law is the legal area made up of mechanisms to facilitate the settlement of international disputes. It designates the rules concerning conflict of laws, and includes the rules concerning the international jurisdiction of the courts and the recognition of foreign judgments.[1] Not all Member States use the term private international law in such a broad sense though. For instance, Germany and Portugal (traditionally) only include the rules concerning conflict of laws.

In practice the first question that needs to be answered in an international dispute is which country's courts have international jurisdiction. Once this has been deter-

* Zef Even is Professor of International and European Labour Law, Ruben Houweling is Professor of Labour Law and Amber Zwanenburg is PhD Researcher and Lecturer in Labour Law, Erasmus University in Rotterdam. Mijke Houwerzijl is Professor of Labour Law at Tilburg University.

1 See Commission, "Green Paper on the conversion of the Rome Convention of 1980 on the law applicable to contractual obligations into a Community instrument and its modernization", COM (2002) 654 final, 36.

mined, this court will decide which law applies to the dispute. It is only when this court has given judgment that the problem of enforcement abroad will arise.
In this chapter, we will focus only on the sub-areas conflict of jurisdiction (which court is competent?) and conflict of laws (which law is applicable?). In situations with a cross-border element, such as employment relations involving cross-border road transport, these questions may arise. Since labour standards are not harmonised within the EU, it can make a major difference which law applies to an international employment relationship and which court has jurisdiction, which court will apply its own national procedural rules.
In the EU, private international law is by and large part of EU law. This chapter focuses on the private international law regimes which have been developed by the European Union institutions, in the form of directives, regulations and case law.
The general academic aim of this chapter is to provide readers with an understanding of private international law in the EU with regard to cross-border road transport. In particular, attention will be given to the rules establishing which court has jurisdiction in cases involving cross-border road transport and which law applies to the employment agreements of the personnel (drivers) working in the cross-border road transport sector.

3.1.2 Specific Learning Outcomes

Readers will be able to determine:
1. the jurisdiction of the courts in employment relationships with a cross-border (road transport) element; and
2. the applicable law in employment relationships with a cross-border (road transport) element.

3.2 State of Art

3.2.1 Which Legal Instruments Apply?

3.2.1.1 Competence of the Courts

In 1968, the Brussels Convention on jurisdiction and the recognition and enforcement of judgments in civil and commercial matters was concluded (the 'Brussel I Convention').[2] This treaty has largely been superseded by Regulation (EC) No 44/2001 on jurisdiction and the recognition and enforcement of judgments in civil and commercial matters (Brussels I)[3] and by Regulation (EU) No 1215/2012 of the European Parliament and of the Council on jurisdiction and the recognition and enforcement of judgments in civil and commercial matters (recast) (Brussels

2 Convention on jurisdiction and the enforcement of judgments in civil and commercial matters, OJ 1968 L388/1.

3 Regulation (EC) No 44/2001 of 22 December 2000 on jurisdiction and the recognition and enforcement of judgments in civil and commercial matters, OJ 2001 L 12/1-23 (hereafter referred to as Brussels I).

I*bis*).[4] Brussel I*bis* applies to legal proceedings instituted on or after 10 January 2015.

3.2.1.2 Applicable Law

When determining which law applies in employment relationships with a cross-border element, the Rome I Regulation (hereinafter 'Rome I')[5] should be applied. Rome I replaces the Convention on the Law Applicable to Contractual Obligations ('Rome I Convention').[6]

Contracts signed after 17 December 2009, must be interpreted according to the rules laid down in Rome I. The difference between Rome I and the Rome I Convention for the purposes of this chapter is negligible.[7] Landmark rulings such as the *Koelzsch* and *Voogsgeerd* cases (ruled on Rome I Convention) are of direct importance for the explanation of Rome I, even though that regulation did not apply to these cases.

3.2.2 Legal Context

Practically speaking, where a court action is to be brought in an international dispute, the first question is which country's courts have international jurisdiction. It is only after the competence of the court has been determined, before this court will decide which law is applicable to the dispute. In this order, we will address both the question which court is competence, and which law is applicable.

3.2.2.1 Competence of the Courts

National rules of private international law and international civil procedures that differ from State to State may hamper the sound operation of the internal market in the European Union. To prevent this, it is essential that there are uniform provisions in the EU in order to determine the competent court. It was in 1968 that the first Convention pertaining jurisdiction rules was concluded (the Brussels Conven-

4 Regulation (EU) No 1215/2012 of the European Parliament and of the Council of 12 December 2012 on jurisdiction and the recognition and enforcement of judgments in civil and commercial matters, OJ 2012 L 351/1 (hereafter referred to as 'Brussels I*bis*').

5 Regulation (EC) No 593/2008 of the European Parliament and of the Council of 17 June 2008 on the law applicable to contractual obligations OJ 2008 L 177/6 (hereafter referred to as 'Rome I').

6 Convention on the Law Applicable to Contractual Obligations, OJ L 266/1 of 9 October 1980 (hereafter referred to as *'Rome I Convention')*.

7 Apart from the codification 'from where'. Compared to the Rome I Convention, the Rome I Regulation had already been extended with the provision that employment contracts are governed by the law of the country where, or failing this, from where the employee in performance of the employment contract habitually carries out his/her work. The Rome I Convention only referred to the habitual place of employment.

tion).[8] On 1 September 1975, the Protocol provided for supervisory jurisdiction of the CJEU entered into force.[9] The CJEU repeatedly used this power ever since.
The original version of the Brussels Convention did not contain specific rules for international employment situations. The preliminary draft of the Convention[10] did have a provision attributing exclusive jurisdiction to the courts of the Contracting State either in which the undertaking concerned was situated, or in which the work was to be or had been performed. After further consideration, the Committee decided to exclude these specific provisions on jurisdiction in this field from the Convention for different reasons. One of these reasons was that, at that time, the Commission of the EEC was working on legislation to harmonize the provisions of labour law in the Member States. The Committee drafting the Brussels Convention ought it desirable that disputes over contracts of employment should, as far as possible, be brought before the courts of the State whose law governs the contract. *Gleichlauf* between the competent judge and the applicable law was thus intended. The Committee wanted to prevent that the rules of jurisdiction it designed might not coincide with those later to be adopted for determining the applicable law. The Committee could in that regard have decided to exclude employment law from the scope of the Brussels Convention, but choose not to do so. It simply drafted a general regime on jurisdiction. These general rules of the Convention applied to contracts of employment as well. According to this regime, in disputes between employers and employees, the following courts have jurisdiction: the courts of the State where the defendant is domiciled (Article 2); the courts for the place of performance of the obligation, if that place is in a State other than that of the domicile of the defendant (Article 5(1)); and any court on which the parties have expressly or impliedly agreed (Articles 17 and 18). Article 5(1) was leading for employment relationships. In the famous *Tessili/Dunlop* and *De Bloos/Bouyer* cases, the CJEU ruled that the 'obligation in question' was the obligation forming the basis is the claim, and the place of performance is determined by reference to the law applica-

8 Convention on jurisdiction and the enforcement of judgments in civil and commercial matters, OJ 1968 L388/1. In the 1980s, the rules of the Brussels Convention were extended to the Member States of the European Free Trade Association (EFTA) by way of an international convention. This Convention, known as The Lugano Convention, was renegotiated once the Regulation Brussels I had been in force for a number of years and this gave rise to a revised Convention. Today, the new Lugano Convention applies in proceedings between the EU Member States and Iceland, Norway and Switzerland.

9 Protocol concerning the interpretation by the Court of Justice of the convention of 27 September 1968 on jurisdiction and the enforcement of judgments in civil and commercial matters 1975 L 204/28.

10 Report by Mr P. Jenard on the Convention of 27 September 1968 on jurisdiction and enforcement of judgments in civil and commercial matters, 1979, C 59/1-65, p. 24.

ble under choice-of-law rules of the forum.[11] Consequently, since multiple obligations can follow from the same employment contract, a variety of courts could have jurisdiction over one employment contract. This would be at odd with the intended *Gleichlauf.*

Apparently, the CJEU held these consequences undesirable and ruled in further case law that the *Tessili/Dunlop* and *De Bloos/Bouyer* cases do not apply to employment disputes.[12] The Court explained that contracts of employment differ from other contracts by virtue of certain particularities. Employment contracts create a lasting bond which brings the worker to some extent within the organisational framework of the business of undertaking or employer.[13] It is for that reason that it is important to take into account the employment contract as a whole, instead of the obligation in question. It is due to those particularities that the court of the place in which the characteristic obligation is to be performed is considered best suited to resolving the disputes to which one or more obligations under such contracts may give rise.

This case law led to an amendment in the Accession Convention, where the following provision was added to Article 5: 'in matters relating to individual contracts of employment, this place is that where the employee habitually carries out his work, or if the employee does not habitually carry out his work in any one country, the employer may also be sued in the courts for the place where the business which engaged the employee was or is now situated'.[14]

After this codification, the CJEU continued ruling in line with the idea of employee protection (case law will be discussed under 3.2.4.). This eventually led to the Brussels I, which entered into force on 1 March 2002.[15] The Brussel I Convention however continues to apply vis-à-vis some overseas territories of certain Member States. Brussels I was revised subsequently and a new – 'recast' – version of the Regulation, the Brussels I*bis,* was adopted in December 2012.[16] The preambles of both Brussels I and Brussels I*bis* ensure continuity with the Brussels I Convention. The same need for continuity applies as regards the interpretation by the

11 CJEU, 6 October 1976, Case C-12/76, *Tessili/Dunlop*, ECLI:EU:C:1976:133 and CJEU, 6 October 1976, Case C-14/76, *De Bloos/Bouyer*, ECLI:EU:C:1976:134.

12 CJEU, 26 May 1982, Case C-133/81, *Ivenel/Schwab*, ECLI:EU:C:1982:199, CJEU, 15 January 1987, C-266/85, *Shenavai/Kreischer,* ECLI:EU:C:1987:11 and Case CJEU, 15 February 1989, C-31/88, *Six Constructions/Humber.*

13 CJEU, 15 January 1987, Case C-266/85, *Shenavai/Kreischer,* ECLI:EU:C:1987:11, para. 16.

14 OJ 1989 L 285/1.

15 Regulation (EC) No 44/2001 of 22 December 2000 on jurisdiction and the recognition and enforcement of judgments in civil and commercial matters, OJ 2001 L 12/1-23.

16 Regulation (EU) No 1215/2012 of the European Parliament and of the Council of 12 December 2012 on jurisdiction and the recognition and enforcement of judgments in civil and commercial matters, OJ 2012 L 351/1.

CJEU of the 1968 Brussels Convention and (for Brussels I*bis*) the Brussels I replacing it.[17]

3.2.2.2 Applicable Law[18]

Traditionally, each Member State has its own national rules of private international law. In 1980, the Member States concluded the 'Rome I Convention'. The Rome I Convention came into effect as of 1991. The CJEU's competence to interpret the Rome I Convention was established in a separate protocol which entered into force on 1 August 2004.[19]

Before the Rome I Convention was adopted as a 'classic international treaty' between Member States,[20] the European Commission had already tried to lay down specific conflict rules for employment contracts in Community Law. Following the adoption of Regulation No 1408/71 on the application of social security schemes to employed persons and their families moving within the Community (see chapter 5 on the EU coordination of the social security systems of the member states and its applicability in cross-border road transport), in 1972 the Commission proposed a Regulation about conflict rules in employment contracts. This proposal was based on the right to free movement of workers. With this proposal, the Commission wanted to make the equal treatment principle in Article 48(2) EEC (now Article 45(2) TFEU) about wages and other employment conditions more concrete. The proposed instrument contained an extensive list of employment conditions for which, at a minimum, the level of protection of mandatory law of the host state would apply (including situations of temporary movement such as what is now called 'posting').[21] Legal scholars, especially those specialised in international private law, were, however, very critical about the proposal: it was supposed to go against the basic principle in contract law, the contractual freedom of the parties. From a labour law perspective, however, great importance was attached to

17 Preamble 19 in Brussels I and Preamble 34 in Brussels I*bis*.

18 This part draws on M.S. Houwerzijl, '"Regime shopping" across (blurring) boundaries', in: S. Evju (ed.), *Regulating Transnational Labour in Europe: The quandaries of multilevel governance* (Oslo: Institut for privatrett), Skrift serie 196, 2014, 95-130.

19 First protocol on the interpretation by the Court of Justice of the European Communities of the Convention on the law applicable to contractual obligations, opened for signature in Rome on 19 June 1980 (89/128/EEC).

20 The Community's founding treaties did not provide European law-makers with a specific legislative competence in the area of PIL. Therefore, Member States were compelled to pursue this goal in the form of conventional international treaties.

21 European Commission, 'Proposal for a Regulation (EEC) of the Council on the Provisions of Conflict of Laws on Employment Relationships within the Community' [1972] OJ C49/26; European Commission, 'Amended Proposal for a Regulation of the Council on the Provisions of Conflict of Laws on Employment Relationships within the Community', COM (75) 653 final.

the stimulation of 'acceptable' (among highly skilled) and the protection against 'unacceptable' (among the less skilled) types of mobility. The motto of the labour law scholar was: national mandatory rules are also international mandatory rules.[22] The extensive list of 'host country law' items was intended to safeguard against influxes of cheap labour by refusing, as far as possible within the boundaries of the private law character of employment contracts, to allow pay discrimination between nationals and non-nationals. The European Commission presented an adjusted proposal in 1976,[23] but when the Rome I Convention was signed in 1980, the proposed Regulation was officially withdrawn. Articles 6 and 7 of the Rome I Convention contain rules for international employment contracts, which limit the key principle of party autonomy enshrined in Article 3.
Since the entry into force of the Treaty of Amsterdam, the European legislator is provided with near to full competences in the field of private international law (hereinafter PIL).[24] This led to 'Europeanisation of PIL', including the adoption of 'Rome I' in 2008.

3.2.3 Scope

3.2.3.1 Competence of the Courts: Brussel Ibis

Material Scope
Brussels I*bis* applies in civil and commercial matters, excluding revenue, customs or administrative matters. It shall not extend, in particular, to revenue, customs or administrative matters or to the liability of the State for acts and omissions in the exercise of State authority (*acta iure imperii*) (Article 1(1)). Furthermore, Brussels I*bis* does not apply to (i.a.) the status or legal capacity of natural persons, bankruptcy, social security and arbitration (Article 1(2)). Employment law in general, when concerning the relationship between the employer and employee, will fall within the scope of Brussels I*bis.*

Formal Scope
The formal scope of Brussels I*bis* includes a geographical element. That is partially implicit and requires that the dispute should be connected to more than one country, i.e. that it should have a genuine international component. The geographical scope of Brussel I*bis* furthermore generally boils down to the concept that the Reg-

22 B. Hepple, 'New Approaches to International Labour Regulation', *Industrial Law Journal*, Vol. 26, No 4, 1976, pp. 353-366.

23 The interference of PIL rules with the equal treatment postulate under Article 45 TFEU was clearly visible in this revised draft Regulation on conflict of laws pertaining to employment relations within the Community (COM (76) 653 final).

24 Article 61(c) in conjunction with Article 65(b) of the Treaty of Amsterdam, currently Article 81(1) and (2)(c) TFEU.

ulation is applicable in case the person being sued, whatever their nationality, is domiciled in a Member State (Articles 4-6). As a result, Brussel I*bis* is applicable in international employment disputes in case:

1. the defendant is domiciled in a Member State;[25] or
2. if the parties have agreed that a court or the courts of a Member State are to have jurisdiction to settle disputes which have arisen or which may arise in connection with a particular legal relationship (hereafter referred to as 'choice of forum clause'). In order for a choice of forum clause in an employment contracts to be valid, special requirements have to be met.

Furthermore, according to Article 6(1) in connection with Article 21(2) Brussels I*bis* applies when:

3. an employer is not domiciled in a Member State, and is sued by the employee:
   a. in the courts for the place where or from where the employee habitually carries out his work or in the courts for the last place where he did so; or
   b. if the employee does not or did not habitually carry out his work in any one country, in the courts for the place where the business which engaged the employee is or was situated.[26]

Time requirement
Brussels I*bis* applies to legal proceedings instituted on or after 10 January 2015 (Article 66).

3.2.3.2 Applicable Law: Rome I
The uniform rules of Rome I apply to contractual obligations in any situation involving a choice between the laws of different countries (Article 1), i.e. in situations in which all the elements are not connected to the legal order of one and the same State. For instance, the parties to the contract may be of different nationality or domiciled in different States, or the contract may be made or performed in different countries or in a country different from that of the court hearing the case. Consequently, Rome I does not apply to purely domestic situations having connecting factors with one single country.

---

25 If an employee enters into a contract of employment with an employer who is not domiciled in a Member State but has a branch, agency or other establishment in one of the Member States, the employer shall, in disputes arising out of the operations of the branch, agency or establishment, be deemed to be domiciled in that Member State. See Article 20(2) Brussels I*bis*.

26 The provision permitting employees to sue a non-EU employer in certain places in the EU was new in Brussels I*bis*: no such provision existed under Brussels I. The reasoning for this broadening of scope, is to ensure the protection of consumers and employees (Preamble 14, Brussels I*bis*).

Material Scope
Rome I applies to all contractual obligations in civil and commercial matters (Article 1 (1)). Article 1(1) states that the Regulation "shall not apply, in particular, to revenue, customs or administrative matters," which matters are regularly considered not to affiliate to civil or commercial law but to public law instead. In Article 1(2 and 3) a number of obligations are excluded. For different reasons, these situations shall not be treated under Rome I.

Formal Scope
Being an EC Regulation, Rome I in principle would be in force in the Member States of the European Union. However, since it has not opted in, Rome I is not in force in Denmark.
Furthermore, Article 2 states clearly that Rome I asks for universal application, meaning that Rome I is not only applicable as among Member States of the Regulation or Member States of the European Union. It also applies in case the law of a Non-Member State is made applicable.

Time Requirement
Rome I applies to contracts which are concluded on or after 17 December 2009.

3.2.4 General Principles

3.2.4.1 Competence of the Courts

Restricted Choice of Forum
Brussels I*bis* explicitly states that in relation to employment contracts, the weaker party should be protected by rules of jurisdiction more favourable to his interests than the general rules.[27] In line with this concept, Brussels I*bis* leaves only limited room for party autonomy departing from these protective rules so as to choose the court in employment disputes. Parties can conclude a choice of forum only in two situations:
1. after the dispute has arisen or
2. if the agreement allows the employee to bring proceedings in courts other than the one which would otherwise be available for the employee under the rules of the Regulation. The clause must therefore widen the choice available to the employee.

The rationale behind these limitations is the protection of the employee as the weaker party by ensuring that the choice offered by the Regulation to the employee as to the courts in which he can sue the employer is not limited and to prevent the

27 Brussels I*bis* Preamble (18).

employer from imposing restrictions on the employee's rights under the Regulation (Article 23).

The CJEU shed its light on the party autonomy to conclude a choice of forum in employment situations in the *Mahamdia* case.[28] Mr. Mahamdia, who had both Algerian and German nationality, was domiciled in Germany. He was employed as a driver for the Algerian Embassy in Berlin with the Ministry of Foreign Affairs of Algeria. The contract of employment contained a choice of forum clause in favour of Algerian courts. Mr. Mahamdia filed a claim against his employer in Germany. The CJEU emphasized that the effect of a choice of forum clause is not to exclude the jurisdiction of the courts which would have jurisdiction in accordance with the rules of the Regulation, but to extend the employee's possibility of choosing between several courts with jurisdiction.

Usually, a choice of forum is explicitly taken up in a clause in the international employment agreement. Nevertheless, a tacit choice of forum is also possible. In general, a court of a Member State before which a defendant enters an appearance, shall have jurisdiction ex Article 26(1) Brussels I*bis*, even though that court may not be competent according to the general rules of Brussels I*bis*. In case the defendant is an employee, however, Article 26(2) Brussels I*bis* obligates the court to ensure, before assuming jurisdiction, that the defendant is informed of his right to contest the jurisdiction of that court and of the consequences of entering or not entering an appearance.

In line with this idea of protection of the employee as the weaker party, Brussels I*bis* differentiates between:

a. claims brought by employees against the employer
b. claims brought by employers against the employee

Claim Brought by the Employee against the Employer

In case of a claim brought by the employee against his employer, the employee can sue the employer:

- at the place of domicile of the employer (or of a deemed domicile of a branch (Article 20(2) and (8)); or
- at the place where the employee habitually carries out his/her work; or
- where the place of habitual work is not situated in any one country, the place where the business which engaged the employee is or was situated.

This means that the employee has a choice to sue the employer at the latter's domicile or at the place where the employee habitually carries out his/her work (or, where there is no such place, at the place where the business which engaged the employee is or was situated).

28 CJEU, 19 July 2012, Case C-154/11, *Mahamdia*, ECLI:EU:C:2012:491.

The Place of Domicile of the Employer

Article 63 Brussels I*bis* provides that the employer (in case it is a company or other legal person) is domiciled at the place where it has its statutory seat; or central administration; or principal place of business. The company is thus domiciled in the EU even when only one of those criteria is fulfilled.

Where an employer is not domiciled in a Member State but has a 'branch, agency or other establishment' in a Member State, the employer shall, in disputes arising out of the operations of that branch, agency or establishment, be deemed to be domiciled there (Article 20(2)). See, for example, the CJEU judgment in the *Mahamdia* case where in a dispute concerning a contract of employment concluded by the embassy on behalf of the sending state, an embassy of Algeria situated in Germany was treated as domiciled in Germany for the purposes of a claim by an employee of the Algerian Embassy in Berlin.

The 'Habitual Place of Work'

The main connecting factor in Brussels I*bis* is the place where the employee habitually carries out his/her work. The habitual place of work is also the main connecting factor for Rome I, the regime for the applicable law. This means that the employee has access to court in the Member State where he/she habitually carries out his/her work and that that Member State's law will generally apply. As the concept is common both to the Rome I and the Brussels I Regulations, it has been interpreted and applied in parallel in the case law.

How did the concept 'habitual place of work' evolve over time?[29] In 1982 the CJEU identified the contract of employment as a 'weaker party contract' meriting special protective PIL rules.[30] In subsequent cases the court specified that "contracts of employment, like other contracts for work other than on a self-employed basis, differ from other contracts - even those for the provision of services - by virtue of certain particularities: they create a lasting bond which brings the worker to some extent within the organizational framework of the business of the undertaking or employer, and they are linked to the place where the activities are pursued, which determines the application of mandatory rules and collective agreements."[31] The 'habitual place of work' was interpreted in a factual manner, referring to the actual performance of the contract rather than the contractual arrangements.[32] Moreover, the CJEU expanded the concept to also include cases in which the worker performed activities in more than one country. According to the case law as

29 For more details see A.A.H. Van Hoek and M.S. Houwerzijl, 'Where do EU mobile workers belong, according to Rome I and the (E)PWD', in: H. Verschueren (ed.), *Residence, employment and social rights of mobile persons: on how EU law defines where they belong* (Cambridge-Antwerp-Portland: Intersentia, 2016), 215-253.

30 CJEU, 26 May 1982, Case 133/81, *Ivenel*, ECLI:EU:C:1982:199.

31 CJEU, 15 January 1987, Case 266/85, *Shenavai*, ECLI:EU:C:1987:11.

32 See for example CJEU, 27 February 2002, Case C-37/00, *Weber*, ECLI:EU:C:2002:122, para. 58.

it currently stands the habitual place of work does not only refer to the place *in which* the work is habitually performed, but also to the place *from which* the employee principally discharges his obligations towards his employer.[33]
In case of a sales representative working in different countries, the national court should try to determine in which place the employee has established the effective centre of his working activities.[34] When the employee carries out a large part of his work in the country in which he has established his office, that country is deemed to be the country *in or from which* the work is habitually performed. However, if a worker is sent to different locations to perform one and the same activity (cooking on oil rigs on the continental shelf for example), no such effective centre of working activities can be determined, nor can any qualitative criterion be used to determine the 'essential' part of the performance. In that case, the relevant criterion for establishing an employee's habitual place of work is the place where he spends most of his working time engaged on his employer's business.[35] In principle the whole duration of the contract should be taken into account, unless there is a clear intention on the side of both parties to change the place of work, in which case only the most recent place of work will be relevant.[36]
As the place where the employee habitually carries out his work is also the main connecting factor under Rome I, the CJEU's case law under Rome I can also be used as guide for the application of this concept under Brussel I*bis*.[37] This chapter will further discuss this case law under 3.2.4.2.

The Place of Business
In case where there is no habitual place of work, the employee can sue his employer at the place where the business which engaged the employee is or was situated. This can be the case if there are two places equally important.[38] For these exceptional situations, the Courts interpretation in the *Voogsgeerd* case is important. In this

33 See Case *Mulox*, paras. 20 and 26. Compare CJEU, Case C-437/00, *Pugliese*, ECLI:EU:C:2003:219, para. 19 which refers to the place where or from which the employee in fact performed the essential part of his duties towards his employer. Neither the text of the Brussels Convention (as changed by the convention of 1989) nor the text of the Brussels I Regulation contain a reference to the place *from which* the work is habitually performed.

34 See CJEU, 9 January 1997, Case C-383/95, *Rutten v. Cross Medical*, ECLI:EU:C:1997:7, para. 23.

35 See CJEU, 27 February 2002, Case C-37/00, *Weber*, ECLI:EU:C:2002:122, para. 50.

36 Ibid., paras. 52-54.

37 See particularly CJEU, 15 March 2011, Case C-29/10, *Koelzsch*, ECLI:EU:C:2011:151 and CJEU, 15 December 2011, Case C-384/10, *Voogsgeerd/Navimer*, ECLI:EU:C:2011:842

38 CJEU, 15 December 2011, Case C-384/10, *Voogsgeerd/Navimer*, ECLI:EU:C:2011:842.

case, the CJEU interpreted the Rome I Convention (for which reason it will be discussed under 3.2.4.2, but this case is also relevant for Brussel I*bis*.

Claim Brought by the Employer Against the Employee
In case of a dispute, an employee domiciled in a EU Member State can be sued by the employer only in the Member State where he/she is domiciled (Article 22(1) Brussel I*bis*). Furthermore, the employer has the right to bring a counter-claim in the court in which, in accordance with Brussel I*bis*, the original claim is pending. In order to determine where the employee is domiciled, the court shall apply its internal law (Article 62(1) Brussel I*bis*).

3.2.4.2 Applicable Law: Rome I[39]

Restricted Choice of Law
Most provisions of Rome I embody the principle of individual party autonomy and the principle of legal certainty. The rules applicable to contractual obligations are in principle neutral to the sort of social-economic interests furthered by (labour) law, since they are based on the assumption that national legal systems are interchangeable. However, for obligations deriving from employment (and consumer) relationships the rules of conflict of laws have partly broken with the presumptions of free choice of law and neutrality in order to protect the, from a social-economic point of view, weaker party in the contractual relationship. In Rome I, Article 8 and 9 contain the rules for international employment contracts. To further *Gleichlauf* between the competent court and the applicable law there is the close link between Rome I and the related instrument in matters of conflicts of jurisdiction, Brussels I*bis*.
Article 8 of the Rome I Regulation harmonizes the conflict rules in Europe on the law applicable to individual contracts of employment. In principle, parties are free to choose the law applicable to their employment contract. But Article 8(1) Rome I limits the effect of a choice of law since such a choice by the parties cannot deprive the employee of the protection afforded to him by mandatory provisions of the law applicable in absence of this choice (the 'objectively applicable law'). According to the majority opinion in literature, this means that the law chosen by the parties applies to the contract in full, except when mandatory rules of the otherwise applicable law would provide the worker better protection.[40] Hence, the employee will

39 This subsection draws on Van Hoek and Houwerzijl (2016).

40 Opinion of Advocate General Trstenjak in CJEU 15 December 2011, Case C-384/10, *Voogsgeerd/Navimer*, ECLI:EU:C:2011:842, para. 48; Opinion of Advocate General Wahl, CJEU, 12 September 2013, Case C-64/12, *Schlecker/Boedeker*, ECLI:EU:C:2013:551, para. 24; O. Deinert, *Internationales Arbeitsrecht* (Tübingen: Mohs Siebeck, 2013),. 96, 102 and 128; Merrett (2011)*, at 215. For an opposing view see inter alia L. Strikwerda, *Inleiding tot het Nederlandse internationaal privaat-*

be protected by the law which offers better protection; if the employer and employee agree on better employment conditions than enshrined in the law applicable in the absence of choice, Article 8(1) Rome I prioritizes the chosen law. By contrast, if the parties agree on worse employment conditions than enshrined in the objectively applicable law, the latter law prevails. This '*favor*-principle' is meant to prevent the employer from abusing his superior bargaining position.
It is important to emphasize that Article 8 has a general regime, applicable to a great variety of international labour situations. This regime is therefore also applicable to the international road transport sector (for the applicability of this regime in the road transport sector, see section 3.2.5).

The Connecting Factors in Article 8(2) and (3)
Since the objectively applicable law acts as a 'floor', a minimum standard of protection, it is always relevant to ascertain the latter law, which can be done following the choice of law rules in Article 8(2)-8(4) Rome I. Rome I provides two connecting factors in Article 8(2) and (3): the 'habitual place of work' and the 'place of business'. In the *Koelzsch* and *Voogsgeerd* case, the CJEU gave guidance in the determination of the applicable labour law in the atypical sector in international transport. These cases will be dealt with in detail under 3.2.5.

The 'Habitual Place of Work'
According to Article 8(2) Rome I, the employment contract is governed in principle by the law of the country in which or, failing that, from which the employee habitually carries out his work in performance of the contract – i.e. the habitual place of work. The country where the work is habitually carried out shall not be deemed to have changed if he is temporarily employed (posted) in another country. By referring to the *habitual* place of work, rather than the *actual* place of work, this provision stabilizes the law applying to the employment contract: during a temporary posting, the law of the home state remains applicable. We will not elaborate on the posting of workers in this part of the chapter, as chapter 4 will focus exclusively on the Posting Directive.
Since Article 8(2) Rome I uses the habitual place of work as its primary connecting factor, it is important to know how to interpret the concept 'habitual place of work'. In the absence of case law on the interpretation of Rome I, similar concepts and criteria in Brussels I*bis* on jurisdiction and the Rome Convention, the treaty which preceded the Rome I Regulation, is still of relevance. In its case law the CJEU has stressed the continuity between the different instruments as well as the

---

recht (Kluwer: Deventer, 2012), 173-175. This would mean that the chosen law only applies in as far as it does not deviate from mandatory provisions of the otherwise applicable law. The CJEU has not taken up a clear position on this issue yet, see CJEU, 15 March 2011, Case C-29/10, *Koelzsch*, ECLI:EU:C:2011:151, para. 35 and CJEU, 15 December 2011, Case C-384/10, *Voogsgeerd/Navimer,* ECLI:EU:C:2011:842, para. 28.

cross-referential character of concepts used therein.[41] Hence, the interpretation of the concept 'habitual place of work' in the Rome Convention is also relevant for the interpretation of the same concept in the Rome I Regulation. In the same vein, the interpretation given in the context of the rules on jurisdiction is also relevant in the context of applicable law.

In *Koelzsch* and *Voogsgeerd*, the CJEU decided to go for a broad interpretation of the workplace principle, for the first time interpreting the Rome Convention in this regard. The CJEU made clear that even in the case of a truck driver working in international transport (*Koelzsch*) or a sailor working on a seagoing vessel (*Voogsgeerd*) the national court should try to establish whether, based on the circumstances as a whole, a country can be identified in which or from which the work is actually performed.[42] These cases were rendered in the context of the application of Article 6 of the Rome Convention, identifying the law applying to the employment contract, more specifically the in international transport situations (for which reason, these cases will be further discussed under 3.2.5). Even though these judgments strictly still concern the Rome I Convention, the regimes of Rome I Convention and Rome I are practically similar. For that reason, and for reasons of readability, from now on, we will only refer to Article 8 when assessing these cases. The main argument for this broad interpretation is that it complies with the objective of Article 8 Rome I (which is to guarantee protection to the employee). The guarantee of protection to the employee is reflected in the idea that the law applied to the employment contract, is the law of the country with which that contract is mostly connected. However, this interpretation must not automatically result in the application, in all cases, of the law most favourable to the worker.[43]

The 'Place of Business'

Article 8(3) Rome I contains an alternative reference rule in case the country where the work is habitually carried out cannot be identified. In that case the contract shall be governed by the law of the country where the place of business through which the employee was engaged is situated. In *Voogsgeerd*, the CJEU clarified that the term 'place of business' should not be interpreted too narrowly. Not only the subsidiaries and branches but also other units, such as the offices of an undertak-

41 For an early reference, with regard to the continuity between the old case law and the new text of Article 5(1) of the Brussels Convention, see CJEU, 9 January 1997, Case C-383/95, *Rutten v. Cross Medical*, ECLI:EU:C:1997:7, para. 21. For a cross-reference between the Brussels I and Rome I Regulations, see CJEU, 15 March 2011, Case C-29/10, *Koelzsch*, ECLI:EU:C:2011:151, para. 33.

42 See CJEU, 15 March 2011, Case C-29/10, *Koelzsch*, ECLI:EU:C:2011:151, paras. 47-49.

43 See CJEU, 12 September 2013, Case C-64/12, *Schlecker/Boedeker*, ECLI:EU:C:2013:551, para. 34.

ing, could constitute places of business, even though they do not have legal personality. However, this undertaking is required to have a degree of permanence.[44]
Taking into account the very broad interpretation of the 'habitual place of work' in Article 8(2) Rome I, it may seem as if there are hardly any situations that will be covered by Article 8(3) Rome I – referring to the place of engagement.[45] The CJEU clarified this concept in the *Voogsgeerd* judgment. As the elements related to the performance of the contract are already taken into account in determining the habitual place of work, the assessment of the place of engagement has a more formal character and focuses on the recruitment procedure: "the courts should take into consideration not those matters relating to the performance of the work but only those relating to the procedure for concluding the contract, such as the place of business which published the recruitment notice and that which carried out the recruitment interview, and it must endeavour to determine the real location of that place of business." Accordingly, this connecting factor does not establish a relevant link to the performance and the life line of the employment contract but is fixed at the very beginning thereof. The connecting factor serves to provide legal certainty in a case in which the primary connecting factor is not able to provide a clear link to any particular jurisdiction.[46] It is - in a sense - a home for the homeless.

Escape Clause in Article 8(4)
Under Article 8(4) Rome I both pre-established connecting factors – habitual place of work and engaging place of business – may be set aside where it appears from the circumstances as a whole that the contract is more closely connected with another country, in which case the law of that other country shall apply.
It might seem like deviation from the habitual workplace and the place of business is not possible given the broad interpretation of the workplace principle in *Koelzsch* and *Voogsgeerd* (and the reasoning for this, being to provide protection for the employee). However, following the CJEU in *Schlecker*, deviation via Article 8(4) is still possible.[47] In *Schlecker* Ms. Boedeker, a German frontier worker, was employed by Schlecker, a German company with branches in a number of Member States. After working in Germany for almost 15 years, she entered into a new

44 See CJEU, 15 December 2011, Case C-384/10, *Voogsgeerd/Navimer,* ECLI:EU:C:2011:842, paras. 54-55.

45 However the provision may remain of or regain relevance for the emerging group of 'hypermobile' workers.

46 See CJEU, 15 December 2011, Case C-384/10, *Voogsgeerd/Navimer,* ECLI:EU:C:2011:842, para. 47. Furthermore, schematic interpretation of Article 6(2)(b) requires the – subsidiary – factor laid down in that provision to be applied when it is impossible to situate the employment relationship in a Member State. Consequently, only a strict interpretation of that subsidiary factor can guarantee the complete foreseeability of the law applicable to the contract of employment.

47 See CJEU, 12 September 2013, Case C-64/12, *Schlecker/Boedeker,* ECLI:EU:C:2013:551.

employment contract when she was sent to a branch in the Netherlands. After working there for 11 years, she received a notification of the abolishment of her function in the Netherlands, as a result of which she had to return to a branch in Germany. Ms Boedeker lodged a complaint against her employer's unilateral decision to change her place of work, claiming i.a. that Dutch law (which was more favourable for Ms. Boedeker) should be applied. Schlecker argued that German law was applicable ex. Article 8(4) as this law was more closely connected to the case. It was clear that the Netherlands should be deemed the habitual place of work, since that was the only place where Ms. Boedeker had been working after entering into her new employment contract. Nevertheless, all the other relevant connecting factors suggested that the employment contract was more closely connected with Germany. Schlecker is a legal person governed by German law; the remuneration was paid in German marks (prior to the introduction of the euro); the pension arrangements were made with a German pension provider; Ms Boedeker had continued to reside in Germany, where she paid her social security contributions; the employment contract referred to mandatory provisions of German law; and the employer reimbursed Ms Boedeker's travel costs from Germany to the Netherlands. The Court ruled that even where an employee carries out the work in performance of the contract habitually, for a lengthy period and without interruption in the same country, the law applicable in that country may be disregarded, if it appears from the circumstances as a whole that the contract is more closely connected with another country. Among the significant factors suggestive of a close connection with a country are, in particular, the country in which the employee pays taxes on his income and where he is covered by a social security scheme and pension, sickness insurance and invalidity schemes. In addition, the national court must also take account of all the circumstances of the case, such as the parameters relating to salary determination and other working conditions.

Overriding Mandatory Provisions

If we apply the Rome I rules to migrant, frontier and seasonal workers in the meaning of Article 45 TFEU in conjunction with Article 7 Regulation No 492/2011, Article 8 Rome I will almost always point to the *lex loci laboris*, being the law of the country where they habitually carry out their work in performance of the contract. In terms of outcome, this means that all mandatory laws and collective agreements in the receiving Member State are applicable to their contracts. Hence, in a system with relatively few mandatory and/or collectively agreed labour law standards, the equal treatment principle enshrined in Article 45 TFEU may suffer from the PIL rules.

However, Article 9(2) Rome I allows courts to apply domestic 'overriding mandatory' provisions (law of the forum), regardless of the (objectively) applicable law. According to Article 9(1): 'Overriding mandatory provisions are provisions the respect for which is regarded as crucial by a country for safeguarding its public interests, such as its political, social or economic organisation, to such an extent that they are applicable to any situation falling within their scope, irrespective of the law otherwise applicable to the contract under this Regulation.' Many labour law rules have an overriding mandatory character, though the Member States traditionally draw the line between *lex causae*[48] rules and overriding mandatory provisions differently.[49] As a result, Article 9 Rome I facilitates labour law systems which rely (sometimes heavily) on overriding mandatory law.

Up until recently the CJEU had no competence to interpret the existing choice of law instruments.[50] This enabled Member States to develop and/or maintain different interpretations of (the interaction between) Article 8 and Article 9 of the Rome I.

3.2.5 Applicability and Enforcement of the Law in the Road Transport Sector

In this section, we will focus further on the applicability and enforcement of the law in the road transport sector. Firstly, we will elaborate on the difficulties faced when applying the general rules on competence of the court and determining the applicable law in the specific circumstances of the international (road) transport sector. Secondly, we will discuss the relevance of this playing field. Why does it make a difference which court is applicable? And does the current legal system of applicable law possibly give rise to social dumping situations in the international road transport sector?

---

48 Lex causae is the law or laws chosen by a forum court from among the relevant legal systems to arrive at its judgment.

49 For a description of the different models of workers' protection in the EU Member States, see A.A.H. van Hoek and M.S. Houwerzijl, 'Comparative Study on the legal aspects of the posting of workers in the framework of the provision of services in the European Union' (2011) and 'Complementary study on the legal aspects of the posting of workers in the framework of the provision of services in the European Union' (2012) *Reports to the European Commission under contract VT/2009/0541* and *contract VC/2011/0096.* Available at: http://ec.europa.eu/social/main.jsp?catId=471&langId=en. Also see A.A.H. van Hoek, 'Private international law: an appropriate means to regulate transnational employment in the European Union?', *Erasmus Law Review,* Vol. 7, No 33, 157-169.

50 The competence to interpret the predecessor of the Rome I Regulation, the Rome Convention, was established in a separate protocol which entered into force on 1 August 2004 (see Case C-29/10, *Koelzsch,* para. 30. The Rome I Regulation only applies to contracts concluded as from 17 December 2009: Corrigendum to Regulation (EC) No 593/2008 of the European Parliament and of the Council of 17 June 2008 on the law applicable to contractual obligations (Rome I) [2008] OJ L 177.

3.2.5.1 Competence of the Courts

The General Regime of Brussel Ibis Applied to the Specific Circumstances of the International (Road) Transport Sector

What determines the jurisdiction of employment contracts where employees work in multiple countries? The CJEU recently has given further guidance in a case concerning mobile workers in the air transport sector. Even though this case does not relate specifically to the international road transport but the air transport sector instead, airline cabin crewmembers, like lorry drivers, work in multiple countries. Determining the 'habitual place of work' (the main connecting factor to determine jurisdiction when the employee is starting the proceedings) for mobile workers, has proven to be a thorny issue.

The (joined) cases revolve around Ryanair. Former Ryanair employees took the view that Belgian law applied to their employment agreements and summoned their former employer Ryanair to pay various heads of compensations with respect to Belgian law. The employees had each sought €20,000 in what they alleged included unpaid wages, unpaid travel expenses and severance pay. When Ryanair refused, they decided to bring their claim before the Belgian court. Ryanair challenged the jurisdiction of the Belgian court, claiming that there is a close and real connection between the dispute and the Irish courts. The question is which country is the habitual place of work: Ireland or Belgium? The answer to this question is also relevant to determine the applicable law, as a result of the repeatedly mentioned '*Gleichlauf*'. To illustrate the relevance of the answer to this question, one can point out the estimation that roughly 60 per cent of Ryanair cockpit and cabin crew are, from the perspective of Ryanair, based in jurisdictions with less favourable labour laws than Ireland.[51] Analysts say that Ryanair could face a € 100 million increase following the CJEU ruling.[52]

The facts of the case can be summarised as follows. Ryanair is an airline having its head office in Ireland. According to the contract, drafted in English, the Irish courts have jurisdiction over possible disputes, and Irish law governs the work relationship between the employees and Ryanair. The contract furthermore stipulated that the work was regarded as being carried out in Ireland, given that the duties were carried out on board aircrafts registered in that country. However, that same contract nominated Charleroi airport (Belgium) as 'home base'. The contract required the employees to live within an hour's journey of the home base that they were assigned to. The employees started their working days at Charleroi airport and ended them there. Similarly, they sometimes had to stay there on standby in

51 Daniel Roeska, of Benstein investment house in an article in the *Financial Times* on 14 September 2017, www.ft.com.

52 'European court ruling could cost Ryanair €100m and swell costs 5%', *The Irish Times* on 14 September 2017, www.irishtimes.com.

order to replace a potentially absent member of staff. The employees were subject to Irish law in the field of tax and social security.
The Belgian court referred the case to the CJEU, basically asking if the concept of the "place where the employee habitually carries out his work" referred to in Article 19(2) of Brussels I (see: Article 21(1) under ii under Brussels I*bis*) must be interpreted as being comparable to the concept of "home base" defined in Annex III to Regulation No 3922/91 (an EU regulation in the field of civil aviation). The CJEU delivered its judgment in this case on 14 September 2017.[53]
As regards the determination of the concept of 'place where the employee habitually carries out his work' the Court refers to its settled case-law, in which it repeatedly held that the concept must be interpreted broadly. When an employment contract is performed in the territory of several countries and where there is no effective center of professional activities, the 'place where the employee habitually carries out his work' covers the place where, or from which, the employee in fact performs the essential part of his duties vis-à-vis his employer. In the present case, that means that the court must identify 'the place from which' the air crew principally discharged their obligations towards their employer.
To determine specifically that place, the national court must refer to a set of indicia. In the transport sector, it is necessary in particular to establish in which Member State: (i) the place from which the employee carries out his transport-related tasks, (ii) the place where he returns after his tasks, receives instructions concerning his tasks and organises his work, and (iii) the place where his work tools are to be found (*Koelzsch,* C-29/10 and *Voogsgeerd*, C-384/10) are situated.
In this case, the place where the aircraft on which the work is habitually performed is stationed must also be taken into account. As regards, more specifically, whether the concept of 'place where, or from which, the employee habitually performs his work' can be equated with that of 'home base', the Court points out that, owing to the circumstantial method and in order to thwart strategies to circumvent the rules, that concept cannot be treated in the same way as any concept referred to in another act of EU law, including that of 'home base', within the meaning of an EU regulation in the field of civil aviation.
Nevertheless, the concept of 'home base' amounts to a significant indicator to determine, in circumstances such as those at issue, the place from which the employee habitually carries out his work. It would only be if, taking account of the facts of each individual case, applications were to display closer connections with a place other than the 'home base' that the relevance of that base in identifying the 'place from which employees habitually carry out their work' would be undermined.
Finally, the Court states that the argument that the concept of 'place where, or from which, the employee habitually performs his work' cannot be equated with any other concept is also true as regards the 'nationality' of aircraft. Thus, nor can

53 CJEU, 14 September 2017, Cases C-168/16 and C-169/16, *Ryanair,* ECLI:EU:C:2017:688.

the Member State from which a member of staff habitually carries out his work be equated with the territory of the Member State of nationality of the aircraft of that company.

Interests at Stake When Determining the Jurisdiction of the Court

Sometimes, a party might favour bringing a claim in the courts of a specific country. This may, besides practical reasons (language, distance etc.), be the case because a court will apply its own national procedural rules (regardless of the law that applies to the employment agreement). Certain national procedural rules might make it harder to bring a claim against certain parties than other national procedural rules. For example, in most Member States, trade unions may provide assistance to their members or act on behalf and in place of their members. Also deadlines for taking legal proceedings vary considerably from one Member State to another.[54] The rules on conflict of jurisdictions create a certain playing field for transnational road transport cases.

3.2.5.2 Applicable Law: Rome I

The General Regime of Rome I Applied to the Specific Circumstances of the International (Road) Transport Sector[55]

As mentioned before, the general regime (in short: a restricted choice of law, two connecting factors and a general 'escape clause') provided in Article 8 Rome I also applies to the international road transport sector. In this sector, lorry drivers are very mobile, working in and across many countries (sometimes only for short periods of time). In these situations, it is not easy to determine the applicable labour law. Therefore, questions rose about the application of Article 8 Rome I in the international (road) transport sector. How to determine the applicable labour law in these atypical employment relationships? In *Koelzsch* and *Voogsgeerd*, Rome I Convention was applied to the specific circumstances of the transport sector.

In the *Koelzsch* and *Voogsgeerd* cases the CJEU made clear that even in the case of a truck driver working in international transport (*Koelzsch*) or a sailor working on a seagoing vessel (*Voogsgeerd*) the national court should still try to establish whether, based on the circumstances as a whole, a country can be identified where or from

54 E. Verhulp, 'Overview of EU principles of labour law and the settlement of labour disputes', Paper presented at the International Conference on Labour disputes Resolution System Shanghai, 15 October 2006.

55 This section draws on A.A.H. Van Hoek and M.S. Houwerzijl, '"Posting" and "posted workers" – The need for clear definitions of two key concepts of the Posting of Workers Directive', in: C. Barnard, M. Gehring and I. Solanke (eds.), *Cambridge Yearbook of European Legal Studies* (Oxford: Hart Publishing, 2012), 419-451.

which the work is actually performed.[56] These cases were rendered in the context of the application of Article 6 of the Rome Convention, identifying the law applying to the employment contract. The CJEU justifies this broad interpretation of the primary connecting factor by referring to the protective character of this provision. Hence, the provision: 'must be understood as guaranteeing the applicability of the law of the State in which [the employee] carries out his working activities (..). It is [there] that the employee performs his economic and social duties and (..), it is there that the business and political environment affects employment activities. Therefore, compliance with the employment protection rules provided for by the law of that country must, so far as is possible, be guaranteed.'[57]
When ascertaining the place of work in case of international transport (including international road transport), the national courts must take account of all the factors which characterise the activity of the employee. These are, in particular:

- the place from which the employee carries out his transport tasks,
- the employee receives instructions concerning his tasks and organises his work, and;
- the place where his work tools are situated.

Additionally, the court must determine:

- the places where the transport is principally carried out;
- where the goods are unloaded and;
- the place to which the employee returns after completion of his tasks.[58]

The habitual place of work is clearly not a connecting factor that is easily applied to so-called 'peripatetic employees'.[59] In the *Koelzsch* case, the Advocate General refers to the need to study the duty roster (*Körselsrapport*) in order to assess the exact time and place of work for each individual employee. This does not only cause problems of proof, but may also lead to a more individualized protection of the workers involved. What might get lost in the process is the collective element of the employment relationship.

56 See CJEU, 15 March 2011, Case C-29/10, *Koelzsch*, ECLI:EU:C:2011:151, paras. 47-49.

57 Ibid., para. 42.

58 Ibid., paras. 48-49 and CJEU, 15 December 2011, Case C-384/10, *Voogsgeerd/Navimer*, ECLI:EU:C:2011:842, paras. 38-39.

59 'Peripatetic' employees (such as airline pilots, international management consultants, sales staff and so on) are in Great Britain distinguished as a category, next to 'expatriate' employees. Interestingly, Advocate General Bot uses the term in his Opinion of 11 June 2015 in the case *Tyco* (Opinion of Advocate General Bot in CJEU, 10 September 2015, Case C-266/14, *Tyco,* ECLI:EU:C:2015:391) at point 32 and point 36, where he considers that 'peripatetic workers may be defined as being workers who are not assigned a fixed or habitual place of work. Such workers are therefore required to work at different premises every day'.

In the *Koelzsch* and *Voogsgeerd* cases, the CJEU stressed the priority of the habitual place of work over the place of establishment of the employer. This was innovative, as in many countries the employment contract of transport workers was deemed to be governed by the law of the place of establishment of their employer. This private international law rule was sometimes reinforced by the rules on admission to the sector by way of transport licensing.[60] In contrast, in the two cases put before the CJEU, the court emphasizes that the reference to the engaging place of business in the Rome Convention is strictly secondary.[61] Only when it is not possible to identify the country in or from which the work is habitually performed, recourse may be had to the second connecting factor, the engaging place of business.[62]
The identification of the habitual place of work in the *Koelzsch* and *Voogsgeerd* cases is left to the national courts. But in both cases it is clear from the facts that there was no relevant link between the actual performance of the contract by the employee and the country of establishment of the employer. The German truck-driver Koelzsch operated from Germany, the Dutch sailor Voogsgeerd from Antwerp (Belgium); both were employed by a Luxembourg company. By focusing on the effective performance of the contract of employment as the connecting factor (which means priority of the habitual place of work over the place of establishment of the employer), the CJEU prevents that a place with no real and relevant connection to the actual performance of the work is designated as the objectively applicable law. Moreover, by specifically denying any priority for the place of establishment of the employer, the court implicitly rejects the existence of a home country control rule with regard to contracts of employment.[63] However, due to the purely

60 It is also interesting to note that in the *Voogsgeerd* case no mention is made of the flag(s) of the ships on which Voogsgeerd performed his work. Admittedly, the flag was not brought forward as a relevant connecting factor by any of the parties to the procedure. Neither was the connection to the habitual place of work, though. See on this issue U. Grušić, 'Should the connecting factor of the "engaging place of business" be abolished in private international law?', *International and Comparative Law Quarterly,* Vol. 62, 2013, 173-92, at 180-1.

61 See CJEU, 15 March 2011, Case C-29/10, *Koelzsch,* ECLI:EU:C:2011:151, paras. 48-49 and CJEU, 15 December 2011, Case C-384/10, *Voogsgeerd/Navimer,* ECLI:EU:C:2011:842, paras. 34-35.

62 See CJEU, 15 December 2011, Case C-384/10, *Voogsgeerd/Navimer,* ECLI:EU:C:2011:842, paras. 32-35.

63 In line with the fierce resistance against the first proposal for what now is Directive 2006/123/EC of the European Parliament and of the Council of 12 December 2006 on services in the internal market, OJ 2006 L 376/36 but in contrast with the effect of the ruling of the CJEU in CJEU, 11 December 2007, Case C-438/05, *Viking,* ECLI:EU:C:2007:772. See more extensively on this issue (with references): A.A.H. Van Hoek and M.S. Houwerzijl, 'Loonconcurrentie als motor van de interne markt? Een tweeluik – Deel 1: De arresten Viking, Laval en Rueffert, verdragsaspecten', *Nederlands tijdschrift voor Europees Recht,* Vol. 14, 2008, 190-205.

secondary relevance of the engaging place of business, it is no longer evident that all workers employed by a single transport company are covered by the same law.[64] In transport by road even a common base from which a group of workers (a 'crew') is employed, might be missing. The fact that the law applying to the employment contract (and hence employment conditions) has to be established on an individual basis, might seriously hamper the possibility for the workers to protect their interests by way of collective negotiations. But the individual character of the assessment may also make other, administrative and collective, modes of protection and enforcement more problematic.[65]

Hence, in the case law of the CJEU, the place of work is deemed to be the primary connecting factor, with the place of engagement only filling a very subsidiary/ancillary role. However, on closer inspection, the habitual place of work is a legal construct which includes elements of *Eingliederung* – embeddedness in an organizational framework. In the transport cases, in determining the habitual place of work, the CJEU attached weight to the place where the worker receives instructions concerning his tasks and organizes his work, as well as to the place where his work tools are situated. These criteria refer – at least in part - to the organizational structure of the employer. In the *Koelzsch* case there seems to have been some kind of collective presence in Germany (the country from which the work was performed) as the workers had established a works council there. In the *Voogsgeerd* case the worker reported to an office in Antwerp, where he received administrative briefings, as well as instructions for the performance of his work. So it could be argued that the CJEU effectively conflated the organizational framework and the actual place of performance into a single connecting factor: the 'place where or from which the work is habitually performed'.

As stated, in *Schlecker* the CJEU shed its light on the escape clause in Article 8(4) Rome I. In this case, which facts are not related to the international road transport sector, the CJEU ruled that the escape clause must be interpreted as meaning that even when an employee carries out work in performance of the employment contract habitually, for a lengthy period and without interruption in the same country, the law applicable in that country may be disregard, if it appears from the circumstances as a whole that the contract is more closely connected with another country. In general, one could ask whether this interpretation benefits legal certainty, as it gives the national court a lot of discretionary power. The fact that there are still

64 Merrett (2011), at 176 describes the importance attached under English common law to the application of one and the same law to all workers employed by a single employer in a single location. This was deemed to be a matter of equality. Also the right to choose the applicable law to the individual contract is assessed critically against this need for equal treatment (ibid. at 214).

65 See for a more detailed discussion on the relevance of public law and collective methods of protection: Van Hoek and Houwerzijl (2011), at 21. See on the impact of collective labour law on the choice of law position taken by individual authors, A.A.H. Van Hoek, *Mobiliteit van werknemers* (Den Haag: Sdu, 2000), 226-227.

possibilities to deviate from the already located habitual place of work, threatens the employee's legal certainty and protection. Some even believe that a different connecting factor is required.[66]
However, this *Schlecker* case concerned a particular frontier worker situation, where the habitual place of work was easily established. For lorry drivers however, it is already difficult to determine the habitual place of work as elements are scattered everywhere. This gives rise to the question whether the *Schlecker* case directly affects the lorry drivers.[67] On the other hand, the CJEU provides some general remarks concerning Article 8(4), so why should *Schlecker* not apply to transport situations? Anyway, in practice this case provides powerful armour to employers who in their argumentation to apply the law of low-wage countries.[68]

Social Dumping Situations in the International Road Transport
It could be lucrative for transport companies in low-wage member States to use the freedom of services to provide cross-border services. They gain serious competitive advantages compared to companies located in high-wage Member States. In order to fight this competitions, transport companies of high-wage Member States can use the freedom of establishment (and subsequently the freedom of services) to establish a (letter-box) company in low wage Member States.[69]
The *Koelzsch* and *Voogsgeerd* cases both accepted a broad interpretation of the workplace principle. Also in cases of transnational transport, the habitual workplace is the main criterion. From a perspective of employee protection, these judgments could be applauded since the CJEU decided to go for this primary linking factor instead of the engaging place of business. Consequently, the sole relocation of a transport company does not automatically mean that the labour of the new place of establishment applies. For that reason, one might say that these judgments make the relocation of companies to low-wage companies less attractive.
However, most facts in transport cases are not that easy. In *Koelzsch* for example, many factors could be linked to Germany. But how should we deal with constructions in the road transport that were set up to avoid the applicability of a specific Member State's labour law? In cases in which it is a lot harder to determine the 'habitual workplace', it should be kept in mind that the consequences of failing to determine a habitual place of work is unfavourable to lorry drivers: the regime of

66 J. Beulens and L. Michielsen, 'Social Dumping: A Sympton of the European Construction', in J. Beulens and M. Rigaux (eds.), *From Social Dumping to Social Competition* (Cambridge-Antwerp-Portland: Intersentia, 2016), 48 and F. van Overbeeke, 'Do we need a new conflict-of-laws rule in the European road transport sector? Yes we do', in Beulens and. Rigaux (2016), 107-122.

67 V. van Den Eeckhout, 'De ontsnappingsclausule van art. 6 lid 2 EVO. Hoe bijzonder is de zaak Schlecker?', *TRA* 2014/31; Van Overbeeke (2016), 119-120.

68 Van Overbeeke (2016), 119-120.

69 See more extensively on this issue Beulens and Michielsen (2016), and Van Overbeeke (2016).

Article 8 then points to the law of the country where the place of business through which the employee was engaged is situated Article 8(3).

3.3 Case Law

List of the most relevant case law of the Court of Justice of the European Union:

Competency of the Court
CJEU, 9 January 1997, C-383/95, *Rutten v. Cross Medical*, ECLI:EU:C:1997:7.
CJEU, 27 February 2002, C-37/00, *Weber*, ECLI:EU:C:2002:122.
CJEU, 10 April 2003, C-437/00, *Pugliese*, ECLI:EU:C:2003:219.
CJEU, 22 May 2008, C-462/06, *Glaxosmithkline*, ECLI:EU:C:2008:299.
CJEU, 19 July 2012, C-154/11, *Mahamdia*, ECLI:EU:C:2012:491.
CJEU, 10 September 2015, C-47/14, *Holterman Ferho Exploitatie e.a.*, ECLI:EU:C:2015:574.
CJEU, 14 September 2017, C-168/16 and C-169/16, *Ryanair*, ECLI:EU:C:2017:688.

Applicable Law
CJEU, 15 March 2011, C-29/10, *Koelzsch*, ECLI:EU:C:2011:151.
CJEU, 15 December 2011, C-384/10, *Voogsgeerd/Navimer*, ECLI:EU:C:2011:842.
CJEU, 12 September 2013, C-64/12, *Schlecker/Boedeker*, ECLI:EU:C:2013:551.

3.4 Further Reading

3.4.1 Academic Literature
O. Deinert, *International Labour Law under the Rome I Convention* (Baden: Nomos Verlagsgesellschaft, 2017).

A.A.H. van Hoek, 'Private international law: an appropriate means to regulate transnational employment in the European Union?', *Erasmus Law Review*, Vol. 7, No 3, 2014, 157-169.

F. Van Overbeeke, 'Do we need a new conflict-of-laws rule in the European road transport sector? Yes we do', in: J. Buelens and M. Rigaux, *From Social Competition to Social Dumping* (Cambridge – Antwerp – Portland: Intersentia, 2016).

3.4.2 Other Documents
Practice guide on jurisdiction and applicable law in international disputes between the employee and the employer, to be found at: http://ec.europa.eu/justice/civil/files/employement_guide_en.pdf.

4 The Analysis of the Posting of Workers Directive(s) with a Specific Focus on EU Cross-Border Road Transport

Mijke Houwerzijl[*]

4.1 Introduction[1]

4.1.1 Curriculum Outline

Most EU citizens working in an EU member state other than their home state do so by using free movement of workers' rights enshrined in Article 45 TFEU. However, EU workers qualifying as 'posted workers' rely on their employer who may use cross-border service rights available to businesses established in the EU (the freedom to provide services, laid down in Article 56 TFEU). By using this freedom, companies established in one EU member state may win contracts to provide services in other member states and 'post' EU workers across member state borders to perform the work on a temporary basis.

The classification of 'posted worker' has proven controversial as a distinct category of worker in EU law. Service providers who post workers to another member state only have to guarantee their workers a basic package of working conditions applicable in the host state, instead of full equal treatment with local workers. Therefore, it costs much less to engage a posted worker from a low-wage EU member state such as Portugal or Poland, than to employ a worker directly in a high-wage EU member state such as Belgium or Germany. In this way, the EU-wide 'services

* Mijke Houwerzijl is Professor of Labour Law at Tilburg University.

1 The text of this chapter draws on earlier work of the author and on M. Houwerzijl & H. Verschueren, 'EU free movement of (posted) workers and applicable labour and social security law', in: T. Jaspers, F. Pennings and S. Peters (Eds.), *European Labour Law* (Cambridge-Antwerp-Portland: Intersentia 2019 (forthcoming)), Chapter 2.

market to post workers' creates commercial opportunities for cross-border service providers to make use of a strong competitive advantage by posting. One of the sectors where posting has become 'a business model' is said to be the road transport sector.

However, such a competitive advantage based on legal differences in labour costs across member states is apparently not lucrative enough, since in practice posting companies often fail to pay their posted workers the accurate wage levels. There is evidence that, in a number of cases, posted workers have been exploited and left e.g. without payment of wages or part of the wages they are entitled to. Such abuses are often facilitated by so-called letterbox companies, which seems to be prominent issue in e.g. the road transport sector.

Central to this chapter are the Posting of Workers Directive, the Posting of Workers Enforcement Directive, and the revised Posting of Workers Directive. The general academic aim of this chapter is to provide readers with an understanding of issues concerning the 'posted workers directives', with specific attention to cross-border road transport. In particular, we will examine the rules enshrined in the Posting of Workers Directive (Directive 96/71/EC, hereinafter PWD) and the Posting of Workers Enforcement Directive (Directive 2014/67/EU, hereinafter PWED). Moreover, the interaction between the PWD and Private International Law (hereinafter: PIL), as laid down in the Rome I Regulation will be briefly addressed, as well as the revised PWD (Directive 2018/957).

4.1.2 Specific Learning Outcomes

Readers will gain a general understanding of the rules enshrined in the PWD and the enforcement of these rules. More specifically they will know:

1. How to apply the rules of the PWD in relation to employment relationships with a cross-border (road transport) element and what changes the revised PWD will bring.
2. Which problems occur in assessing whether a situation of 'genuine' posting exists (e.g. in relation to the road transport sector).
3. Which 'tools' Inspectorates and other stakeholders may use to enforce the rights of genuine posted workers and/or to detect situations of non-genuine posting.

4.2 State of the Art

4.2.1 (Applicable or to Be Implemented) Legal Instruments

4.2.1.1 The Posting of Workers Directive (PWD)

The Posting of Workers Directive 96/71/EC[2] provides rules regarding the working conditions of workers, posted by their EU-based employer to carry out a cross-border service in the framework of the free provision of services (on the basis of Article 56 TFEU), in another Member State than where they normally work.

4.2.1.2 The Posting of Workers Enforcement Directive (PWED)

Rules to facilitate the information exchange, monitoring and enforcement of the PWD, are laid down in the Posting of Workers Enforcement Directive.[3]

4.2.1.3 The Revised Posting of Workers Directive (Revised PWD)

The revised PWD[4] revises a number of provisions of the PWD 1996, in order to ensure the smooth functioning of the single market and to stop 'unfair competition' on wage costs and working conditions.

4.2.2 Evolution and Legal Context

As early judgments of the Court of Justice in the cases *Manpower* and *Van der Vecht*[5] show, employee posting was already a phenomenon in the late 1960s and early 1970s. The practice of hiring (temporary agency) workers from a country with a 'cheaper' social security scheme, with the sole purpose of posting them to a Member State with a more expensive social security regime, was at that time labelled abusive and 'social dumping'. In the first half of the 1990s, in the context of the Delors' project 'Europe 1992', the proposal for a Directive on the Posting of Workers led to fierce debates in European Parliament and Council.[6] It was only

2 Directive 96/71/EC of the European Parliament and of the Council of 16 December 1996 concerning the posting of workers in the framework of the provision of services, OJ 1997, L 18, 1 (hereafter 'PWD').

3 Directive 2014/67/EU of the European Parliament and of the Council of 15 May 2014 on the enforcement of Directive 96/71/EC concerning the posting of workers in the framework of the provision of services and amending Regulation (EU) No 1024/2012 on administrative cooperation through the Internal Market Information System ('the IMI Regulation'), OJ 2014, L 159, 11 (hereafter 'Enforcement Directive').

4 Directive (EU) 2018/957 of the European Parliament and of the Council of 28 June 2018 amending Directive 96/71/EC concerning the posting of workers in the framework of the provision of services, OJ 2018, L 173, 16.

5 CJEU, 5 December 1976, Case 19/67, *Van der Vecht*, ECLI:EU:C:1967:49 and CJEU, 17 December 1970, Case 35/70, *Manpower*, ECLI:EU:C:1970:120.

6 See for instance OJ 15, C 166/123.6.95, No 4-464/204 and No 4-464/206.

after a six-year process of negotiations, deadlock and amended proposals that the PWD (Directive 96/71/EC, of 16 December 1996) was finally adopted. The debates focused in particular on the extent to which Member States must be allowed, or should be required, to apply their mandatory wage provisions and other working conditions to workers posted to their territory. Another issue concerned the legal basis of the Directive, which was found in the Treaty provisions establishing the freedom to provide services.

4.2.2.1 Legal Base PWD and the Development of Two Lines of Case Law

The legal base of the PWD adopted was legitimised by the argument that in order to promote a true single market, a framework of rules for posted workers would have to be created in order to avoid unfair competition. From a political point of view, the undoubted merit of this legal basis is that it facilitated a qualified majority vote. Without this, the PWD proposal would probably have stranded.[7] Still, from a legal point of view, the disadvantage of the choice of (only) this legal base is that it suggests that the PWD is purely intended to facilitate the cross-border provision of services. That it also serves to protect employees and to create a level playing field (and no unfair competition) is by no means evident from its legal base.

In fact, the landmark judgment in the case *Rush Portuguesa* of 1990 paved the way for this legal base. In this case, the CJEU ruled (at para. 15) that 'an undertaking established in one Member State providing services in the construction and public works sector in another Member State may move with its own work-force which it brings from its own Member State for the duration of the work in question.' Hence, the revolutionary aspect of the ruling was that third country nationals who do not have the right to freely move to another EU country to work without a work permit, acquired a right to movement derived from their EU-based employer, albeit a 'passive' one.[8] With regard to the terms and conditions of employment of the posted worker, the CJEU stated (at para. 18) that 'Community Law does not preclude Member States from extending their legislation, or collective labour agreements, to any person who is employed, even temporarily, within their territory, no matter in which country the employer is established.'[9]

---

7 See about the political circumstances of the early 1990s (in which the British Conservative Government tried to veto almost everything that had to do with social policy) that influenced the political fate of the posting directive, M. Biagi, "The 'Posted Workers' EU Directive", in: R. Blanpain (ed.), *The Bulletin of Comparative Labour Relations in the European Union* (1998), 175.

8 In this chapter, the position of third country national workers will not be dealt with in further detail.

9 CJEU, 27 March 1990, Case C-113/89, *Rush Portuguesa*, ECLI:EU:C:1990:142, para. 18, with reference to Joined Cases 62/81 and 63/81 *Seco SA and Another v. EVI* and confirmed subsequently, albeit amended with the crucial restriction to minimum wages, by CJEU, 9 August 1994, Case *Vander Elst*, ECLI:EU:C:1994:310; CJEU, 28 March 1996, Case C-272/94, *Guiot*, ECLI:EU:C:1996:147; CJEU, 23 November

With regard to both considerations in the *Rush Portuguesa* judgment, two – separate - lines of case law were developed: (1) The first one (building on para. 15) concerned the unjustified restrictions on the freedom of a service provider established in a Member State to post workers possessing a third- country nationality to another Member State. In this regard, the CJEU ruled that the authorities of the host state may not impose conditions relating to obtaining work permits, since posted workers who are regularly employed by the service provider and only temporarily in the host country for the duration of the service are not deemed to enter the labour market of that state. However, a duty to notify the presence of a posted worker to the host state authorities was allowed, under certain conditions.[10] This line of case law was not influenced by the adoption and consequent implementation of the PWD, as the Directive does not regulate the presence of (third country national) posted workers but only coordinates which hard core of mandatory host state labour standards should be applicable to workers.

(2) The second line of case law (building on para. 18) concerns conflicts involving the wages and other working conditions of posted workers. Many aspects were touched on, but the main approach in these judgments starts with a comparison of labour law protection in the host state and that in the state where the worker allegedly is normally employed. If the protection is the same or 'in essence' the same, the social protection of the latter state has priority. A precondition for the application of host-state law is that it offers the posted worker a genuine and effective advantage and that it does not disproportionally restrict the free movement of services.[11]

1999, Cases C-369/96 and C-376/96 *Arblade and Leloup*, ECLI:EU:C:1999:575; CJEU, 15 March 2001, Case C-165/98 *Mazzoleni*, ECLI:EU:C:2001:162; CJEU, 25 October 2001, Case C-49/98 et seq. *Finalarte*, ECLI:EU:C:2001:564; CJEU, 24 January 2002, Case C-164/99 *Portugaia*, ECLI:EU:C:2002:40.

10 See CJEU, 9 August 1994, Case C-43/93, *Vander Elst*, ECLI:EU:C:1994:310; CJEU, 19 January 2006, Case C-244/04, *Commission v. Germany*, ECLI:EU:C:2006:49; CJEU, 21 October 2004, Case C-445/03, *Commission v. Lux*, ECLI:EU:C:2004:655; CJEU, 21 September 2006, Case C-168/04, *Commission v. Austria*, ECLI:EU:C:2006:595.

11 See ECJ judgments in CJEU, 24 January 2002, Case C-164/99, *Portugaia*, ECLI:EU:C:2002:40; CJEU, 15 March 2001, Case C-165/98, *Mazzoleni*, ECLI:EU:C:2001:162; CJEU, 25 October 2001, Case C-49/98 et seq., *Finalarte*, ECLI:EU:C:2001:564; CJEU, 23 November 1999, Cases C-369/96 and C-376/96, *Arblade and Leloup*, ECLI:EU:C:1999:575 and CJEU, 28 March 1996, Case C-272/94, *Guiot*, ECLI:EU:C:1996:147. In all these rulings the facts of the case date from the period that the PWD was not adopted yet or still subject to implementation and thus not (fully) applicable.

4.2.2.2 *Objectives of the PWD*

The position of workers who are posted to another Member State in the framework of the provision of services has thus been a European concern for a considerable time. The PWD is a tangible results of this concern. The PWD aims to reconcile the exercise of companies' fundamental freedom to provide cross-border services under Article 56 TFEU (old Article 49 EC), on the one hand, with the need to ensure a climate of fair competition and respect for the rights of workers (Recital 5). In order to achieve these aims, it identifies which national mandatory rules of the host state must apply to posted workers (see in more detail below). According to the Preamble of the PWD (Recital 7-11), the Directive thus makes the optional character of Article 7 Rome I Convention (now Article 9 Rome I Regulation) obligatory, by defining those subjects of employment law in which the national mandatory rules must be seen as 'overriding mandatory provisions'.

According to the Explanatory Memorandum: 'The national differences as to the material content of working conditions *and the criteria inspiring the conflict of law rules* may lead to situations where posted workers are applied lower wages and other working conditions than those in force in the place where the work is temporarily carried out' (emphasis added). 'This situation would certainly affect fair competition between undertakings and equality of treatment between foreign and national undertakings; It would from the social point of view be completely unacceptable'.[12]

Notably, the position of posted workers is characterized by the fact that they maintain their employment relationship with their own employer established in another Member State during the posting in the host Member State. As a rule, the employment contracts of posted workers are governed by the law of their habitual country of work instead of that of the host country. This contractual perspective reveals an important aspect of the legal position of the posted worker: the employment contract of a posted worker is typically influenced by more than one legal system, as the employment contract is concluded in one Member State (home state) and the performance of the service takes place in another Member State (host state). The interface with private international law is discussed more in detail below.

4.2.2.3 *Interaction Between Rome I and the PWD*

The PWD, aiming to reconcile the exercise of companies' fundamental freedom to provide cross-border services under Article 56 TFEU with the need to ensure a climate of fair competition and respect for the rights of workers (preamble, paragraph 5), uses in essence the same technique as Article 9 Rome I to achieve its aims. In Article 3, the PWD identifies which national mandatory rules of the host state must apply to posted workers. In this manner a hard core of clearly defined terms and conditions of work and employment for minimum protection of workers (laid down in Article 3(1)a-g) is established, that must be complied with by the service provider in the host Member State. According to the Preamble of the PWD (Reci-

12 COM (91)230 final, p. 11, under point 12.

tal 7-11), the Directive thus makes the optional character of (now) Article 9 Rome I obligatory, by defining those subjects of employment law in which the national mandatory rules must be seen as 'overriding mandatory provisions'. Hence, the rules on mandatory protection laid down in the PWD can be understood to form an application of Article 9 Rome I.

The PWD can and should not be read in isolation from Article 8 Rome I. Indeed, from the perspective of the host state, the PWD fills in the 'gap'[13] that Article 8 Rome I would create for the territorial application of labour law. Accordingly, Article 3(1) PWD states that: 'Member States shall ensure that, *whatever the law applicable to the employment relationship* (emphasis added), the undertakings referred to in Article 1(1) PWD guarantee workers posted to their territory the terms and conditions of employment covering the following matters...' Thus, it is made clear that the law applying to the employment contract is regulated by PIL rules, but the PWD superimposes – if necessary – the minimum protection of the law of the host state upon the protection already offered under the law applying to the contract by virtue of Article 8 Rome I.

An indication for the complementary character of the PWD in relation to Article 8 Rome I may also be found in Article 3(7) PWD. Article 3(7) first sentence PWD allows the *application* of better protection to posted workers than the minimum provided for by the Directive.[14] In the *Laval* and *Rüffert* judgments the CJEU made it clear that this provision only refers to the more favourable terms and conditions of employment which those workers already enjoy pursuant to the law or collective agreements in the Member State of origin, or agreed voluntarily by the employer.[15]

If one reads the case law on the posting of workers in the context of the free provision of services from a lens of searching the applicable law to the contract between the parties involved, it seems as if the underlying assumption is that posted workers (always) ordinarily work in the country of establishment of their employer and therefore will be covered by the law of their (employer's) home state ('the country of origin'). This reading would however submit the posted worker to the laws of

13 Article 8(2) Rome I stipulates that the country where the work is habitually carried out shall not be deemed to have changed if a worker is temporarily employed (posted) in another country.

14 Recital 17 of the PWD also refers to *application* of more favourable terms and conditions to posted workers. For the embodiment of the 'favor principle' in pre-PWD case law: see M.S. Houwerzijl and F.J.L. Pennings, 'Double Charges in Case of Posting of Employees: The Guiot Judgment and its Effects in the Construction Sector', *The European Journal of Social Security*, Vol. 1, No 1, 1999, 102.

15 See Judgment in CJEU, 18 December 2007, Case C-341/05, *Laval un Partneri*, ECLI:EU:C:2007:809, paras. 79-81, 120 and in CJEU, 3 April 2008, Case C-346/06, *Rüffert*, ECLI:EU:C:2008:189, paras. 32-34. More in detail: S. Evju, 'Posting Past and Present The Posting of Workers Directive – Genesis and Current Contrasts', *Formula WP 8*, 2009, 32.

the country of establishment of his employer and disallow the application of more favourable provisions contained in the law applicable by virtue of Article 8 Rome I.[16] Admittedly, the reference to the 'country of origin' or 'home country' in the court's case law may cause confusion if the Member State where the employee is recruited or where he will habitually perform his work is not the same as the Member State where the employer is established. However, it seems more logical that 'country of origin' or 'home country' should be read to refer to the country whose law is objectively applicable in light of Article 8 Rome I. This will most often be the country in which the work is normally or habitually performed, rather than the country of establishment of the employer.[17] Support for this reading may also be found in Article 4(1) of Directive 91/533 which, under the heading 'expatriate employees', gives rules on information requirements in situations where the employee is required to work in one or more countries other than *the Member State whose law and/or practice governs the contract or employment relationship abroad* (emphasis added).[18]

---

16 See e.g. M. Fornasier and M. Torga, 'The Posting of Workers: The perspective of the Sending state – The Judgment of the Civil Chamber of the Estonian Supreme Court of 16 January 2013 No 3-2-1-179-12', *Europäische Zeitschrift für Arbeitsrecht (EuZA)*, Vol. 3, 2013, 356-365 at 364.

17 In *Vander Elst*, the Court refers to the applicable law of the country of establishment of employer, but from a private international law perspective (currently in the Rome I Regulation No 593/2008), it depends on the individual situation of the posted worker whether the law of 'the (common) country of origin' applies or the law of another country. The main connecting factor is supposed to be 'the habitual country of work'. See A. Van Hoek and M. Houwerzijl, 'Where do EU mobile workers belong, according to Rome I and the (E)PWD', in: H. Verschueren (ed.), *Residence, employment and social rights of mobile persons: on how EU law defines where they belong*, Social Europe Series, Vol. 36 (Cambridge-Antwerp-Portland: Intersentia, 2016); see also A. Van Hoek, 'Re-embedding the transnational employment relation-ship – can the Commission proposal deliver?', Amsterdam Law School Legal Studies Research Paper No 2016-69. Available at: https://papers.ssrn.com/sol3/papers.cfm?abstract_id=2886430.

18 Directive 91/533 was adopted a few months after the first draft was presented by the Commission for what has become the PWD. See COM(91)230. The interrelationship between Directive 91/533 and the PWD (Directive 96/71) was emphasized during the implementation process of the latter Directive. In the transposal stage, the Commission expressed its belief that compliance with the requirements laid down in Directive 91/533 (in particular Articles 2 and 4) should facilitate the implementation of the PWD and in particular the process of comparing the home state's and host state's provisions on minimum wages and paid holidays. See *Report Working Party on the transposal of the Directive concerning the posting of workers, Brussels*: European Commission, Employment & Social Affairs, 1999, p. 13. Also in case law, the linkage between the two Directives has been at issue. See judgments in CJEU, 23 November 1999, Cases C-369/96 and C-376/96, *Arblade and Leloup*, ECLI:EU:C:1999:575, paras. 61, 65,

So far, the CJEU never had to decide on the applicable law to the contract of a posted worker and this may explain why it never paid attention to the underlying contractual position of the parties. Until now, the case law has focused on establishing whether the application of host state law during the period of posting would (disproportionally) infringe the free provision of services. In this respect, as is common ground, the posting of workers in the context of the free provision of services opposes the interests of host state employers and workers to the interests of the company performing the cross-border service (and - according to some[19] – even the interests of the posted workers themselves). But it also pitches the interests of high cost host states against those of low cost sending states.[20] This makes the topic highly controversial.

4.2.3 Scope

4.2.3.1 Material Scope PWD

Pursuant to Article 3(1) PWD Member States are to ensure that undertakings falling within the scope of the Directive guarantee workers posted to their territory the terms and conditions of employment laid down by mandatory law including collective agreements which have been declared universally applicable insofar as they concern the construction sector referred to in the Annex of the PWD. Hence, Article 3(1) PWD determines the nature of the labour standards that the Member States must ensure but not the substance of these standards. Also, the PWD has an influence on the way the minimum level of protection should be established – e.g. by law or generally applicable collective agreement. Moreover, additional protection is allowed in case of employment through temporary work agencies (Article 3(9) PWD).

The terms and conditions to be guaranteed to posted workers in the host state include law on the duration of the work, rest periods and holidays, minimum rates

67-68, 70, and CJEU, 19 June 2008, Case C-319/06, *Commission v. Luxembourg*, ECLI:EU:C:2008:350, paras. 39-41.

19 Often their employers, i.e. the service providers. For the first time this argument was put forward in CJEU, 25 October 2001, Case C-49/98 et seq., *Finalarte*, ECLI:EU:C:2001:564. More recently, this (presumed) point of view of the workers from the new member states is defended in literature by inter alia D. Leczykiewicz, 'Conceptualizing conflict between the economic and social in EU law after Viking and Laval', in: M. Freedland and J. Prassl (eds.), *EU law in the Member States: Viking, Laval and beyond*, (Oxford: Hart Publishing, 2015) and D. Kukovec, 'Hierarchies as law', *Columbia Journal of International Law*, Vol. 21, 2014, 131-193 at 142. An illuminating description of the different perspectives on justice contained in the different viewpoints is given by A. Somek, 'From Workers to Migrants, from Distributive Justice to Inclusion: Exploring the Changing Social Democratic Imagination', *European Law Journal*, Vol. 18, 2012, 711-726.

20 See Fornasier and Torga (2013) at 358; Leczykiewicz (2015).

of pay, health, safety and hygiene at work, the conditions of hiring-out of workers, protective measures for pregnant women, for women who recently gave birth, for young people and children, and equality of treatment between men and women (Article 3(1) PWD). By establishing this so-called 'hard core' of minimum protection by mandatory law in the host state for posted workers, the PWD tries to balance the interests involved. However, this balance shifted towards the aim to further the provision of services, when the CJEU interpreted the PWD in the notorious 'Laval-tryptich' as to also limit the application of host state labour law to the areas mentioned in the Directive, unless the rule to be applied is considered to be part of public policy. In other words: the PWD contains not only a minimum but also a maximum rule on application of host state law in the context of intra-EU provision of services.

The 'Laval-Tryptich'

The judgments of the CJEU in the *Laval, Rüffert* and *Commission v. Luxembourg* cases in 2007 and 2008, all fuelled intense scholarly and public debate.[21]

As stated in its Recital 5, the PWD means to reconcile the exercise of companies' fundamental freedom to provide cross-border services under Article 56 TFEU, on the one hand, with the need to ensure a climate of fair competition and respect for the rights of workers, on the other. However, in *Rüffert* the CJEU seems to have created a priority between the three goals, emphasizing that the objective of the Directive is 'in particular to bring about the freedom to provide services' (para. 36). Moreover, the material scope of the PWD got a strict interpretation by the CJEU in all three cases.

In *Laval*, the main focus of the CJEU's judgment was whether the collective action in the form of a blockade taken by trade unions in this case was compatible with the EU rules on the freedom to provide services (Article 56 TFEU). Moreover, the setting of minimum wages (and other work related benefits) for posted workers by collective bargaining by trade unions in the host State was cast into doubt. The relevant collective agreement in this case provided for more favourable conditions than those envisaged by the PWD. The Court, therefore, considered whether the collective action taken was justifiable in light of its objective, namely, to force a service provider to grant more favourable conditions to its workers than those prescribed by the PWD.

In its ruling, the CJEU did not accept the method of implementation of the PWD in Sweden where the applicable rates of pay are negotiated on a case by case basis between employer and the Swedish trade unions in a collective agreement without

21 CJEU, 18 December 2007, Case C-341/05, *Laval un Partneri*, ECLI:EU:C:2007:809; CJEU, 3 April 2008, Case C-346/06, *Rüffert*, ECLI:EU:C:2008:189; CJEU, 19 June 2008, Case C-319/06, *Commission v. Luxembourg*, ECLI:EU:C:2008:350. The cases, together with the CJEU, 11 December 2007, Case C-438/05, *Viking*, ECLI:EU:C:2007:772, gave rise to numerous conferences among scholars and policymakers and led to a 'tsunami' of (working) papers and articles in academic journals.

universal applicability: it concluded that this leads to a climate of unfair competition between national and posted service providers (paras. 71 and 80-81). Furthermore, the Court pointed out that the PWD does not allow the host Member State to make the provision of services in its territory conditional on the observance of terms and conditions of employment which go beyond the mandatory rules for minimum protection, as laid down in Article 3(1) PWD (para. 80). It is this consideration that the phrase often used in literature, the 'floor' of minimum labour conditions in the host state has (also) become 'a ceiling', stems from.[22] Clearly, the Court considers the PWD to be about protection of workers only in a secondary sense, noting that the minimum protection in force, in the host state, enables the posted workers 'to enjoy better terms and conditions of employment in the host member state' (paras. 76-77). The *Laval* judgment has been heavily criticised for its potential to limit trade unions' rights to take collective action and for its failure to take into account the successful and flexible system of collective bargaining prevalent in Sweden.[23]

According to Article 3(10) first indent of the PWD, the host Member States may add public policy provisions on other subjects than those explicitly listed in Article 3(1) PWD. This was part of the delicate political compromise needed to get the PWD adopted. We know now that the CJEU, with the judgment in *Commission v. Luxembourg*, has chosen a restrictive interpretation of this provision, by cutting back the margin of appreciation the Member States have in defining what is to be understood under public policy. The CJEU has pointed out that the concept of public policy, first, comes into play where a genuine and sufficiently serious threat affects one of the fundamental interests of society and, second, that it must, as a justification for a derogation from a fundamental principle of the Treaty, be narrowly construed (para. 50).

22 S. Evju, 'Posting Past and Present The Posting of Workers Directive – Genesis and Current Contrasts', *Formula WP 8*, 2009, 32, n. 15.

23 After amendments, the Swedish Posting of Workers Act states that unions are subject to more restrictive regulations in order to take collective action with the aim of regulating posted workers' employment conditions (M. Rönnmar, 'Laval returns to Sweden: the final judgment of the Swedish Labour Court and Swedish legislative reforms', *Industrial Law Journal*, Vol. 39, No 3, 280-287). As a consequence, the position of Swedish unions in relation to posting companies has become weaker and the number of signed collective agreements with foreign construction companies has dropped dramatically (D. Seikel, 'Class struggle in the shadow of Luxembourg. The domestic impact of the European Court of Justice's case law on the regulation of working conditions', *Journal of European Public Policy*, Vol. 22, No 8, 1175-6). See K. Kall & N. Lillie, *Protection of Posted Workers in the European Union: Findings and Policy Recommendations based on existing research*, PROMO briefing paper (Finland: University of Jyväskylä, 2017), 22.

Matters Belonging to the 'Hard Core' of Host State Protection for Posted Workers

As mentioned above, Article 3(1) of the PWD includes in the hard nucleus of protection maximum work periods and minimum rest periods, minimum paid annual holidays and minimum rates of pay. These elements each have a distinct function in the overall protection of workers. However, they are closely correlated when considered from the perspective of fair competition. Especially when wages are calculated at the monthly or weekly rate, it is crucial to know how many hours a week/month the worker actually performs work in order to qualify for full pay. Likewise, holidays constitute direct wage costs and hence determine the actual cost per hour worked.[24] So, beyond doubt, the inclusion of minimum rates of pay, working time and paid holidays in the subjects regulated by the host country was seen as important to prevent unfair competition. Although health & safety rules were not addressed in the Explanatory Memorandum,[25] the character of these rules makes it difficult to opt for a non-territorial application.[26]

However, regarding minimum wages and paid holidays *unconditional* application of host state law was deemed to infringe the free provision of services and the freedom of contract too much. Hence, if the applicable law to the employment contract offers equivalent or even better protection, there is no need to set aside the normal rule of conflict enshrined in Article 8 Rome I. This seems to be the rationale behind Article 3(7) PWD (first sentence) which is also supported by the early pre-PWD case law of the CJEU on avoiding 'double burdens' for service providers in relation to their posted workers.[27]

Operationalization of the Favour-Principle

It is easier to pay lip-service to the favour-principle, than to operationalize it. For instance, how to interpret the minimum rates of pay in the host state and how to compare this with the level of wage actually paid by the service provider to his pos-

---

24 Compare CJEU, 15 March 2001, Case C-165/98, *Mazzoleni*, ECLI:EU:C:2001:162, para. 39: "Second, in order to ensure that the protection enjoyed by employees in the Member State of establishment is equivalent, they must, in particular, take account of factors related to the *amount of remuneration and the work-period to which it relates* (emphasis added), as well as the level of social security contributions and the impact of taxation."

25 Nor the other items in the list included in Article 3(1), such as protection to specific (vulnerable) groups of workers, equal treatment m/f and provisions relating to conditions for hiring out of workers, in particular the supply of workers by temporary agencies.

26 Often the national rules do not apply to work performed outside the territory. The rules are enforced by public law bodies and may carry criminal sanctions in case of breach.

27 See Houwerzijl and Pennings (1999), at 91-112.

ted workers? While there is some case law on the latter issue,[28] the first issue remained unclear for a long time. In this respect, the last sentence of Article 3(1) stipulates that the concept of minimum rates of pay referred to in paragraph 1(c) is defined by the national law and/or practice of the host state. Does this mean that Member States are entirely free in the way they define 'minimum rates of pay'?[29] Can the host state impose only a single (statutory or collectively agreed) minimum wage (flat rate)[30] or rather a set of rules determining the minimum rate of pay in the individual case (wage structure / job ladder)? The CJEU confirmed the latter interpretation in his judgment in the Finnish preliminary reference case *Sähköalojen ammattiliitto*.[31] Notably, the CJEU specifically points out that 'the minimum wage calculated by reference to the relevant collective agreements cannot be a matter of choice for an employer who posts employees with the sole aim of offering lower labour costs than those of local workers'.[32]

Moreover, in this judgment the CJEU gave a broad interpretation of the freedom for host states to include in the minimum rates of pay specific allowances such as a daily allowance intended to ensure the social protection of workers 'making up for the disadvantages' of the posting 'as a result of the workers being removed from their usual environment', and a compensation for daily travelling time (paras. 48-52, 54-56). Regarding the coverage of the cost of accommodation (as obliged in the Finnish collective agreement) and meal vouchers (in accordance with the contract of employment between service provider and posted worker) the CJEU ruled

28 CJEU, 14 April 2005, Case C-341/02, *Commission v. Germany*, ECLI:EU:C:2005:220. Confirmed in CJEU, 7 November 2013, Case C-522/12, *Isbir*, ECLI:EU:C:2013:711.

29 Apart from the guidance provided in Article 3(1)(c) regarding overtime charges (which are explicitly deemed to form part of the 'minimum rates of pay' to be applied to posted workers) and contributions to supplementary pension schemes (which are specifically excluded from the minimum rates of pay).

30 For a long time, this seems to have been the prevailing opinion in Germany, which was codified in the German implementation Act of the PWD (AEntG) prior to its amendment in 2009. See more in detail about the German situation M. Kullmann, *Enforcement of Labour Law in Cross-Border Situations. A Legal study of the EU's Influence on the Dutch, German, and Swedish Enforcement systems* (PhD Thesis), (Deventer: Kluwer, 2015), at 80.

31 CJEU, 12 February 2015, Case C-396/13, *Sähköalojen ammattiliitto Ry*, ECLI:EU:C:2015:86, para. 43. Also, the Court clarified that host state rules may determine whether the calculation of the minimum wage must be carried out on an hourly or a piecework basis (para. 40) and that holiday pay constitutes part of the minimum wage (paras. 66-69).

32 Ibid., para. 41. The Court also seems to slightly restates the purpose of the PWD as well as the objective of a nucleus of mandatory rules for minimum protection guaranteed to posted workers. See paras. 28-30, emphasizing the double aim of preventing unfair competition and ensuring the social protecting of the workers concerned.

that these should be regarded as compensation for expenses in line with Article 3(7) (second sentence), which does not permit such expenditure to be taken into account in the calculation of their minimum wage.
Consequently, the service provider cannot take these costs into account when comparing the actual wage paid with the prescribed level of minimum rates of pay in the host country. Hence, if other host Member States would follow the example set by the Finnish collective agreement (on the conditions explicated by the CJEU in *Sähköalojen ammattiliitto*), the status of the posted worker may (in some respects) eventually approximate the expat contract, which is (also) characterized by the special arrangements made to compensate for the expatriation of the worker, such as travel arrangements, housing facilities and expat allowances.

Matters Kept Outside the 'Hard Core' of Host State Protection for Posted Workers

But what about the other side of the coin? When and why may the law applicable to the employment contract continue to be adhered to in the case of cross-border posting? As explained in the Explanatory Memorandum, the designation and application of the mandatory rules to be observed by foreign service providers in the host state, has to be compatible with the temporary nature of the performance of work in the host country and consistent with the PWD's stated aims and objectives. Against that background, it was decided that 'mandatory rules concerning the form, suspension, alteration and termination of the contract of employment and workers' rights on information, consultation and participation are not dealt with'.[33]
Hence, the selection of said subject-matters which were kept outside the 'hard core' of Article 3(1) PWD, seems to be based either on considerations concerning the organisation of the work (second line of ordering), such as employee co-determination rights, or on considerations relating to the continuation of the employment relationship, such as in the case of dismissal law (third line of ordering). Indeed, in genuine cases of (short term) posting an overriding interest to apply host states' dismissal law is absent, since the labour market of the host country may be regarded as not-involved in such situations. In case of dismissal, a genuine posted worker (with a habitual country of work) will usually fall back on the labour market in the home country. Likewise, the host state has no (or only a limited interest) in regulating the co-determination rights within the foreign company. From the perspective of internal market law, giving effect to mandatory host country rules on dismissal and co-determination rights may be seen as a violation of the free movement of services and of the freedom of contract, not justified by overriding interests of a public policy nature.

33 COM(91)230 final, p. 15, under point 25, third indent and p. 13 under point 19, third indent.

Posted Workers Belong to Both Host and 'Home' Country

So, depending on the subject matter of their labour law entitlements, as defined in Article 3(1) PWD, (genuine) posted workers belong both to host and 'home' country. Regarding wages, working time, safety at work and other (minimum) labour standards which influence the day to day performance of the contract, the posted workers clearly is deemed to belong to the host country. Here, preference is given to the actual place of work instead of the habitual one. Regarding the other labour law entitlements,[34] including dismissal law, the posted worker continues to 'belong' to the labour market on which he habitually works. However, this preference of the habitual over the actual place of work is by definition 'finite': the precondition is that the posting should remain an exceptional circumstance of *limited duration* within a contract habitually performed in another country. Therefore, the PWD only covers workers who fulfil the definition of posted worker in Article 2 PWD. And it is to this personal scope of the PWD that we now turn.

4.2.3.2 Personal Scope PWD

In order to avoid stretching the scope of application of the PWD (in interaction with the Rome I Regulation) to non-genuine situations of posting, the concepts of 'posting' and 'posted worker' are crucial.

PWD: Concept of 'Posting'

With regard to the concept of cross-border 'posting', the PWD covers different types of posting which are described in Article 1 PWD and include service contracts in the context of subcontracting, intra-company transfers and temporary agency work. For these three situations of posting covered by the PWD, Article 1(3) states that there must be a link to a cross-border service provision that is temporary in nature. The requirement has two related aspects:

- The posting should be connected to provision (by the posted worker) of a cross-border service in the meaning of Article 56 of the TFEU (as defined in Article 1(1) of the PWD).
- In two of the three situations of posting there seems to be required a service contract between the employer and a recipient established or active in the country where the service is performed. This requirement is mentioned in Article 1(3)(a) and (c), but does not seem to be a prerequisite in case of intra-company postings (Article 1(3)(b) PWD).

In respect of the latter aspect, it is important to note that the provision of services is not the sole context in which posting (secondment) might take place. A worker may also be posted/seconded in the framework of a project for the account of his own employer. Here, we may think of the activities of film crews, employees who are sent abroad on business trips or for research projects, to attend seminars or per-

34 According to the Explanatory Memorandum, this concerns 'the bulk of labour law' COM(91)230 final, p. 13, under point 19, third indent.

form harvesting activities.[35] As a result, instead of coming within the scope of the PWD, this group of seconded workers will be covered by Article 45 TFEU in interaction with Article 8 (and 9) of Rome I. Apart from the fact that the PWD does not cover all cross-border postings, it should be noted that it does not contain a full coordination of cross-border services either.[36] Moreover, it does not even fully coordinate all employment in this context. For example, it would seem from the facts of the cases *Voogsgeerd* and *Koelzsch*, that neither Mr Voogsgeerd nor Mr Koelzsch were posted workers in the meaning of the PWD – even though their employer was a cross-border service provider.[37] Hence, the status of the employing company – as cross-border service provider – can and should be separated from the status of the worker – posted, migrant or otherwise.

PWD: Concept of 'Posted Worker'

With regard to the concept of 'posted worker', in Article 2(1), the PWD defines the posted worker as a worker "who, for a limited period, carries out his work in the territory of a Member State other than the State in which he *normally* works" (emphasis added). This phrasing closely resembles Article 8(2) of the Rome I Regulation, although the PWD uses the word 'normally', whereas the Rome I Regulation refers to a 'habitual' country of work. For a long time, it was unclear whether there is a difference in meaning between the two concepts; whereas the Rome I Regulation seems to focus on the habitual place of work *under the contract*, the concept of the PWD may also be applied when the work in the country of origin is performed for more than one employer. Thus, a purely literal reading of Article 2(1) PWD would fit with the posting rule with regard to social security: here, previous insurance in the country of origin is required, not necessarily previous engagement with the posting undertaking. However, a contextual interpretation would be more in line with the aims of the PWD.

The difference between the two possible interpretations is important in the situation that workers are hired solely for the purpose of posting. In that case there will be no habitual place of work in the country of 'origin', at least not under the contract. So, according to the contextual interpretation of Article 2(1) PWD, such a situation would not qualify as a genuine posting within the meaning of the PWD.[38] The Enforcement Directive seems to endorse the contextual approach:

35 In contrast, Article 4 Directive 91/533 seems to encompass both groups of posting, more closely resembling the notion of posting in Article 12 Regulation No 883/04 (see chapter 5 on Coordination of Social Security).

36 The coordination of cross-border services is regulated (inter alia) by the Services Directive. Labour law is specifically excluded from the fields coordinated by this directive; see preamble paragraphs 14 and 86-87 and Article 1(6) of Directive 2006/123.

37 See for these facts Chapter 3 on Private International Law.

38 This approach is sometimes taken in national case law. See for example a Dutch case (Rechtbank Midden Nederland, 22 juli 2015, ECLI:NL:RBMNE:2015:5393) between Portuguese and English subsidiaries of the notorious Atlantco Rimec group

Article 4(3)(c) of the EPWD makes an explicit link between the concept of posting in the PWD and the 'habitual country of work' under the Rome I Regulation.[39]

What Is Temporary?

A controversial issue which was eventually clarified by the revised PWD, is the interpretation of 'a limited period' in Article 2(1) PWD. It is remarkable that neither case law nor legislation based on Article 56 TFEU regarding the freedom to provide services, gives a practicable definition of 'temporary'. In *Rush Portuguesa* the CJEU stated that a service provider 'may move with its own work-force which it brings from its own Member State for the duration of the work in question'.[40] Hence, the temporary character of posting seems to be linked to the duration of the service abroad. So far, in this general case law on services *no limitation in time* to the temporariness of a service provision has been accepted.[41] As stated in *Gebhard*, the temporary nature of the activities has to be determined in the light, not only of the duration of the provision of the service, but also of its regularity, periodical nature or continuity.[42] In *Schnitzer*,[43] application of these criteria made the CJEU conclude that Article 56 TFEU includes services such as construction projects involving large building works which are provided over an extended period, up to several years. On the other hand, the CJEU held in *Trojani* that an activity carried out on a permanent basis or without any foreseeable limit would not be considered a service within the meaning of Article 56 TFEU.[44] Also, it was ruled that a construction company exclusively focused on a different country than that of

on the one hand and the Dutch parties to the collective labour agreement in the construction industry on the other hand. The 'posted' workers involved were, according to their employment contracts, explicitly and solely hired for a specific construction project in the Netherlands. Therefore, according to the Dutch court, their 'habitual' country of work under the contract was the Netherlands. As a consequence, Dutch law was deemed to be objectively applicable to the employment contracts of the workers pursuant to Article 8(2) Rome I.

39 Albeit only as an indicative factor in the overall assessment of whether a posted worker temporarily carries out his or her work in a Member State other than the one in which he or she normally works.

40 CJEU, 27 March 1990, Case C-113/89, *Rush Portuguesa v. Office national d'immigration*, ECLI:EU:C:1990:142, paras. 17 and 19.

41 CJEU, 26 January 2006, Case C-514/03, *Commission v. Spain*, ECLI:EU:C:2006:63, para. 22.

42 CJEU, 30 November 1995, Case C-55/94, *Gebhard*, ECLI:EU:C:1995:411, para. 27; CJEU, 13 February 2003, Case C-131/01, *Commission v. Italy*, ECLI:EU:C:2003:96, para. 22.

43 CJEU, 11 December 2003, Case C-215/01, *Schnitzer*, ECLI:EU:C:2003:662, para. 30.

44 As shown by the very wording of Article 57 TFEU, in contradistinction to the permanent nature of the activity carried out by an economic operator who is established in a

establishment cannot be considered a service provider by the CJEU.[45] Notably, the distinction between Article 56 and Article 49 is in reality difficult to operationalize. In the words of A-G Léger in his Opinion in *Gebhard*: 'On the strictly legal level, this distinction is a tricky one, in so far as it is the upshot of a combination of criteria, closely depends on the factual circumstances in question and has never been precisely and systematically defined.'

Labour Market Access?

In the case *Rush Portuguesa*, the CJEU made a distinction between EU workers, who enter the labour market of the host member state by making use of the free movement of workers within the EU (Article 45 TFEU), and posted workers, who generally do not. The employer of a posted worker makes use of the free movement of services (Article 56 TFEU). In that context, the posted worker does not need to avail himself of the free movement of workers, because he does, according to the CJEU, not seek access to the labour market of the host Member State, but will instead immediately return to the state where he normally works once the service is carried out. This 'passive movement' (namely because the employer assigns him to) may be illustrated by the fact that the posted worker has concluded an employment contract with his employer governed by the law of the habitual country of work. Another indicator of such passive movement, often used in the context of PIL, is the provision or reimbursement of travel, board and lodging costs by the employer.[46] Notably, in its judgment *Sähköalojen ammattiliitto*, the CJEU brought the status of the posted worker (in this respect) closer to the traditional expatriate employee, by ruling that such special arrangements should be regarded as compensation for expenses in line with Article 3(7) (second sentence) PWD.

The distinction based on labour market access is crucial in case the posted worker does not enjoy free movement himself, for instance because he is covered by a transitional regime or when he has a third country nationality.[47] But the distinction between 'Article 45 TFEU mobility' and 'Article 56 TFEU mobility' also has an

Member State (observation of Advocate General Lèger, Opinion in CJEU, 30 November 1995, Case C-55/94, *Gebhard*, ECLI:EU:C:1995:411, para. 32).

45 This clearly follows from the judgment in CJEU, 9 November 200, Case C-404/98, *Plum*, ECLI:EU:C:2000:607, situated in the context of what is now Regulation No 883/04.

46 This indicator is made explicit in Article 4(2)(d) of the PWED.

47 This may be different when the worker is send abroad by a temporary work agency: see CJEU, 10 February 2011 Case C-307/09-309/09, *Vicoplus*, ECLI:EU:C:2011:64. For third country nationals working and residing legally in a Member State the distinction makes it possible to post them to another Member State. See judgment in CJEU, 9 August 1994, Case C-43/93, *Vander Elst*, ECLI:EU:C:1994:310, confirmed in CJEU, 11 September 2014, Case C-91/13, *Essent Energie Productie*, ECLI:EU:C:2014:2206; CJEU, 14 November 2018, C-18/17, *Danieli & C. Officine Meccaniche and Others*, ECLI:EU:C:2018:904.

impact on the labour law protection of the workers involved. The PWD intends to provide a significant but not a full level of host state protection for posted workers, who may be vulnerable given their situation (temporary employment in a foreign country, difficulty in obtaining proper representation, lack of knowledge of local laws, institutions and language). As Kilpatrick observes:[48] 'Socially, it is not difficult to imagine that long-stretches of life in a (typically more expensive) host-state on a minimum skeleton of host-state labour standards can seem exploitative to posted workers and host-state inhabitants alike.'

The differences in labour costs attached to both 'gateways' for cross-border worker mobility seem to have been used more and more strategically by firms ('posting as a business model') in order to gain this 'comparative advantage', which are from a 'fair competition' point of view most often referred to as 'social dumping practices'. Labour law is but one of the points to be taken into consideration; social security and tax law being at least as important. Intermediaries in other Member States are used with the sole purpose of turning (temporary or seasonal) migration into posting. When, for example, a TWA recruits Polish workers for jobs in Sweden, the actual circumstances may not change according to whether the TWA is Polish or Swedish, but the legal situation does. Therefore, blurring regulatory concepts and criteria also generate ample opportunities for non-compliance, resulting in violation of labour law and other (fundamental) rights of migrant workers.

4.2.4 PWED & the Revised PWD

4.2.4.1 Issues of Information, Monitoring and Enforcement

Problematic in this context, is that the PWD does not put specific requirements on national governments to regulate the nature or level of monitoring and enforcements of the rights of posted workers. Although Article 4, 5 and 6 PWD provide some guidance, each Member State decides in accordance with its own specific national system of labour law on how to organize its information, monitoring and enforcement activities.

According to Article 4(3) of the PWD, monitoring authorities in the host state have responsibilities to provide information to the general public on posted workers' rights laid down in law and (generally binding) CLAs. In practice, the dissemination of information is mainly provided through national websites by the responsible authorities. For a long time however, these websites focused on the statutory core labour standards that have to be guaranteed to posted workers only, whereas core labour standards laid down in generally binding CLAs were much more difficult to find. Also, said websites were not always easily accessible nor regularly kept up-to-date or sufficiently precise. This is problematic, e.g. from the perspective of transparency and accessibility of host state requirements for foreign service providers. First and foremost, foreign companies should be able to estimate their labour

48 C. Kilpatrick, 'British Jobs for British Workers? UK Industrial Action and Free Movement of Services in EU Law', *LSE Legal Studies Working Paper* No. 16/2009, at 27.

costs in advance, in order to be able to tender for service contracts in another Member State then where they are established. Moreover, and pursuant to Article 4 of Directive 91/533 (the written statement Directive), foreign employers have a duty to inform their posted workers in advance about some core labour standards in the host state (in addition to the obligation stemming from Article 2 to notify an employee in writing of the essential aspects of the contract or employment relationship including level of remuneration).[49] To comply with this duty towards their employees it is self-evident that they are in need of clear and easy-to-find information about the applicable labour standards in the host country.
At the same time and in accordance with Article 5 PWD, national authorities of the host state may impose information duties on service providers and others, such as the service recipient. Most Member States have therefore imposed notification requirements on foreign service providers in order to enable the responsible government agencies to fulfil their monitoring and enforcement tasks. Often, Member States also impose other and/or additional requirements, such as the need to request prior authorization or to keep employment documents available for the authorities, or to appoint a representative, which may in certain cases be in breach of EU law. To strengthen the 'empowerment' of posted workers, Article 6 of the PWD stipulates that the posted worker must have the opportunity to institute judicial proceedings against his employer in the host Member State. Hence, all Member States in their role as a host state must ensure that possibility for workers posted to their territory, covered by the Directive. Moreover, some Member States enacted joint & several or chain liability measures. For instance, in Germany, the liability for wages and paid holiday contributions applies to the whole chain, so that each subcontractor up to the principal contractor might be held liable in the case of misconduct in these fields.[50]
The European Commission has regularly monitored the implementation and enforcement of the PWD to assess whether the aims of the PWD were being met. A comprehensive monitoring exercise launched in 2006 by the European Commission led to the assessment that the PWD's main shortcomings, could be traced to a range of issues relating to its implementation, application and enforcement in practice.[51] This situation was caused by the virtual absence of administrative cooperation, unsatisfactory access to information, and cross-border enforcement problems,

49 Currently, this information duty is limited to postings lasting longer than 1 month.

50 See M. Houwerzijl & T. Wilkinson, 'The Effects of EU Law on the Social and Economic Goals of Europe 2020: A Decision Theoretic Approach to Wage Liability Regimes in Modern Europe', *German Law Journal*, Vol. 14, 2013, available at: www.germanlawjournal.com/index.php?pageID=11&artID=1587.

51 See the Commission Communication, *Guidance on the posting of workers in the framework of the provision of services*, SEC(2006) 439/COM(2006)0159 final, followed by the Communication, *Posting of workers in the framework of the provision of services: maximising its benefits and potential while guaranteeing the protection of workers*, SEC(2007) 747/COM(2007)0304 final.

all of which were provided for in the Articles 4,5 and 6 PWD but did not work in practice.

The exercise in 2006, must be situated against the debate about the then draft Services Directive.[52] With regard to the possible tension between the application of internal market rules and the need to respect the protection of the rights of workers by means of administrative requirements and control measures, guidelines were adopted to clarify the prevailing Community law.[53] Directive 2006/123/EC, as adopted, does not deal with labour law or the posting of workers within the EU, since these were deemed matters that were specifically to be dealt with in the PWD and the Rome I Convention.[54] The controversies surrounding what was commonly referred to in the popular press as the 'Bolkestein Directive', together with the EU's enlargements in 2004, 2007 and 2013 with Central and Eastern European countries, have played an important role in drawing attention to the limited impact of the PWD.[55]

4.2.4.2 Gap Between 'Law on Paper' and 'Law in Practice'

In the aftermath of the 'Laval judgments', it became increasingly clear that there is, in practice, a huge lack of control, monitoring, and cooperation among Member States, and that enforcement of minimum terms and conditions of employment is poor, e.g. on wages, working time, and costs of housing and transport.[56]

Contentious cases in the media often relate to situations which may not deemed to be 'proper' posting because the worker does not normally work in another state

52 See for instance 14 February 2006 Commissioner Charlie McCreevy's Statement on the Services Directive at the European Parliament Plenary session of February 2006; SPEECH/06/84.

53 COM(2006)159, "Guidance on the posting of workers within the framework of the provision of services" and the accompanying Staff Working Document SEC(2006)439. These guidelines were partly based on deleted proposals for restricting national possibilities to monitor and enforce the PWD in the draft Services Directive.

54 This non-applicability of the Services Directive also includes national monitoring rules regarding posting of workers, see CJEU, 13 November 2018, C-33/17, *Čepelnik*, ECLI:EU:C:2018:896, para 36.

55 See for an account of the 'integration fatigue' and '(single) market fatigue' in the old Member States in western Europe due to the enlargements and the unemployment and discrediting of financial capitalism in the credit crisis, the report of M. Monti, *A new strategy for the single market, at the service of Europe's economy and society*, May 2010. See: http//:ec.europa.eu/bepa/pdf/monti_report_final_10_05_2010_en.pdf.

56 See A.A.H. van Hoek and M.S. Houwerzijl, 'Comparative Study on the legal aspects of the posting of workers in the framework of the provision of services in the European Union', *Reports to the European Commission under contract VT/2009/0541* (2011); J. Cremers, 'In search of cheap labour in Europe', *CLR studies* 6 (2011); J. Cremers, *In Search of Cheap Labour in Europe: Working and living conditions of posted workers* (Brussels: CLR/EFBWW/International Books, 2011).

than the host state, because the employer is not genuinely established in another state or because an employment relationship between employer and worker is missing. In the popular press there is (almost) no awareness of the fact that there are different migration modalities, let alone that these are governed by different legal regimes. Clearly, the distinction, explained above, between 'active' labour mobility covered by Article 45 TFEU and 'passive' posted workers mobility covered by Article 56 TFEU, as stemming from Rush Portuguesa, is often poorly understood. This may be explained by the fact that all these modalities seem to lead to very similar actual work patterns and problems, such as underpayment, excessive deduction of costs for lodging and travel, violations of health & safety and working time regulation.

Some cases relate to letter box companies opened only for the purpose of posting. The worker might actually be made to work under the direct supervision of the user undertaking, thus creating a situation of bogus subcontracting or illicit provision of manpower. The absence of genuine activities in the country of origin may be combined with repeated postings, in which the 'posted' worker is working in a specific Member State on an (almost) permanent basis. Other cases describe situations of rotational posting in which the worker is posted consecutively to different Member States or, with an unpaid leave in-between, to the same Member State again and again. Anecdotic evidence from media is confirmed and elaborated upon by empirical research. Studies of (e.g.) Wagner and Berntsen based on interviews with workers situated at the building sites of the European Central Bank in Germany and the 'Eemshaven' in the Netherlands, as well as in workplaces in the meat sector and the supermarket distribution centers, clearly show that the workers concerned most often do not know their legal status.[57]

Exploitation and Social Dumping

Hence, political concern grew about abuses of the freedoms granted by the EU internal market. In between 2010 and 2014, it had become abundantly clear that posting regulations are misused systematically and do create competition on wage levels in host state labour markets. Especially in the area of provision of manpower,

57 L.E. Berntsen, *Agency of labour in a flexible pan-European labour market: A qualitative study of migrant practices and trade union strategies in the Netherlands Groningen* (PhD Thesis) (Groningen: University of Groningen, SOM research school,2015) and I. Wagner, *Posted Work and Deterritorilization in the European Union: A study of the German Construction and Meat Industry*, (PhD Thesis) (Groningen: University of Groningen, SOM research school, 2015). They conducted micro-level research (based on interviews) regarding migrant/posted workers strategies and union strategies at two big building sites, in the supermarkets branch and in the meat sector in the Netherlands and Germany. See also, N. Lillie, I. Wagner and L. Berntsen, 'Posted Migration, Spaces of Exception, and the Politics of Labour Relations in the European Construction Industry', in: M. Hauptmeier and M. Vidal (eds.), *Comparative Political Economy of Work* (Basingstoke: Palgrave Macmillan, 2014), 312–331.

the problem of combating illegal activities is encountered. However, these forms of abuse are not specific to posting (nor for provision of manpower). The illegal temporary work agencies may be established both in the country of recruitment (leading to posting) or in the county of work (leading to migration). Several reported cases of abuse concerned migrant workers or even (bogus) self-employed.[58] These cases involve social dumping in its purest form – with no respect for either the protective system of the country of origin or that of the host country.

For trade unions and enforcement authorities it is difficult to trace and combat the situations mentioned above; the fluidity in the cross-border context with firms often disappearing across borders or going bankrupt, complicate their efforts to enforce (and execute) local labour standards. Moreover, the employer-arranged migration context leads to isolation of migrants, as they often have limited knowledge of host state law and institutional structures. They are also segregated spatially and socially from their host surroundings because of the way they are housed near the place of work. And if trade unions and host state institutions succeed in reaching the workers, they experience enormous practical difficulties in establishing exactly which conditions (should) apply to a specific individual employment relationship, because the rules are so complicated in cross-border situations.[59]

A different, more ambiguous, situation arises when the employment conditions do conform (more or less) to the standards of the home state but not to those of the host state. As becomes apparent from several empirical studies, in such cases the workers may not have an incentive to claim the extra rights awarded to them under the law of the host state. They seem to be happy with the job opportunity and do not want to put that in danger by claiming host state entitlements. As Berntsen puts it: 'the commodified employment context tends to disempower migrants, at the same time it enables them to live better lives then they would if they opted not to participate in this European market context'.[60] Nevertheless, as noted by Bernaciak, although in the short-term posted workers may profit from dumping strategies, in the long run dumping practices not only lead to the erosion of employ-

58 The European Agency on Fundamental Rights (FRA) called for 'zero tolerance for severe forms of labour exploitation', in its report on *Severe Labour Exploitation: Workers Moving within or into the European Union, States' Obligations and Victims' Rights* (Brussels, 2015).

59 See Berntsen (2015), at 170-175; Kullmann (2015), at 211-225, 266-290; Wagner (2015), at 70-76.

60 Berntsen (2015), at 171. A long quotation from a Polish scaffolder, 28 years old, shows that the sense of belonging to the 'home country' may also be lost: 'I don't see my future in Poland. I see my future where there is work, because without work...you know how it is over there [in Poland], it is difficult to get a job'. Berntsen (2015), at 24.

ment protection systems in the host states, but might also hinder the gradual improvement of wages and working conditions in the poorer sending countries.[61] On the short term however, the harm of the passive attitude of posted workers in claiming their rights is (felt to be) done to third parties, and – more abstractly – to the social structure of the host state, rather than to one of the parties to the individual contract. In extreme cases the workers will even operate in cohort with the employer to evade the law of the host state.[62] In such cases the law of the host state will only be enforced if enforcement is entrusted to host state authorities or interested third parties (such as social funds or the unions in the host state).

4.2.4.3 The Posting of Workers Enforcement Directive (PWED)

Against this background of exploitation of posted workers and increasing resistance against social dumping practices in host states, the long debated PWED was adopted in May 2014,[63] which had to be implemented in the Member States by 18 June 2016. The PWED focuses on those elements of the PWD that were considered as problematic by stakeholders and that pertain to enforcement of compliance, improvement of legal certainty and strengthening administrative cooperation. The PWED's overall objective is to ensure that posted workers actually enjoy the minimum protection offered by the PWD, whilst also facilitating the free provision of services. To achieve its aims, the PWED sets a common framework of measures and control mechanism. Its most important measures include the following:

- a non-exhaustive list of indicative factual elements to help competent authorities such as Labour Inspectorates in determining whether there is a genuine establishment of the posting company in the sending state (Article 4(2) PWED) and in assessing whether a posted worker is only temporarily carrying out his or her work in a Member State other than the one in which he or she normally works (Article 4(3) PWED);
- a stricter framework for improving access to information in host Member States, relevant for the posting of workers (Article 5 PWED) to enhance legal certainty for service providers;
- a framework for enhancing administrative cooperation between authorities and other stakeholders across countries (Articles 6 and 7 PWED);
- a (non-limitative) list of justified and proportionate administrative requirements and control measures that *might* be applied by the Member States (Article 9 PWED);

61 See M. Bernaciak, 'Social Dumping? Political catchphrase or threat to labour standards', *ETUI WP* 2012/06, 26.

62 See Van Hoek and Houwerzijl (2011).

63 COM(2012)131. The controversial character may also be deduced from the large number of amendments (833) which were submitted for the draft report on the enforcement directive of the committee on employment of the EP (procedure file 2012/0061/COD).

- an obligation upon Member States to ensure effective mechanisms for posted workers to lodge complaints and institute juridical/administrative proceedings (also through trade unions) against their employers also in the Member State where they are posted (Article 11 PWED);
- a subcontracting liability arrangement for wages (Article 12 PWED). Regarding the construction sector this is phrased in mandatory wording, stipulating that posted construction workers can hold the contractor in a direct subcontractor relationship liable for any outstanding net remuneration corresponding to the minimum rates of pay, in addition to or in place of the employer. Nevertheless, Member States can escape the liability arrangement through implementation of 'equivalent measures' in a direct subcontracting relationship, to tackle fraud and abuse in situations when workers have difficulties in obtaining their rights (see Article 12(5) PWED). On the other hand, Member States are allowed to take more stringent liability measures, such as chain liability affecting all subcontractors in the chain;[64]
- additional measures to ensure that administrative penalties and fines imposed on service providers by one Member State's enforcement authorities for failure to respect the requirements of the PWD can be enforced and recovered in another Member State.

Clearly, the PWED facilitates and stimulates better information, monitoring and enforcement of the PWD in some respects, but the effectivity of its measures depend on a real effort with budgetary implications and strong political will at the level of the host Member State. Ensuring that the rights of posted workers are adequately protected requires comprehensive cooperation – like joint visits to work sites of posted workers, enhanced information exchange – of different national actors (depending on national system these can be inspectorates, other state bodies, social partners). Moreover, enforcers of host state rights of posted workers (e.g. trade unions, labour inspectorates) do not have the competences to act beyond their own national jurisdictions. Although cross-border cooperation has increased during the last decade, procedures are long and time-consuming and host state sanctions are often too weak. Some enhancement may be expected from the PWED which links the inspectorates' information exchange to the so-called Internal Market Information System (IMI), however, the reliability and compatibility of the information itself needs improvement as well.

64 The most well-known and far-reaching example of chain liability was established in Germany in 1995 for the construction sector and since then extended to several other sectors. In the CJEU, 12 October 2004 Case C-60/03, *Wolff & Müller GmbH & Co. KG v. José Filipe Pereira Félix*, ECLI:EU:C:2004:610, the CJEU ruled that the German chain liability system was in line with EU law. Its restrictive impact on the free movement of services was justified by the additional protection it provides to posted workers.

Stricter registration rules (like notification systems, dissuasive penalties for not following the rules, making service recipients co-responsible for registration) for service providers posting their workers have been introduced in several Member States in order to enhance the quality of data collection on postings and to facilitate monitoring and enforcing the rights of posted workers. The Belgian LIMOSA scheme is one of the first and certainly the most well-known and advanced notification system. Since 2007, all service providers who want to perform a temporary economic activity in Belgium have to register online and notify their activities and posted workers through the LIMOSA system before they start the activity. At the same time, it is also a highly contested notification system, from the perspective that it would limit the free provision of services too much. The system has been subject of several procedures before the CJEU, with mixed outcomes.[65] More recently, LIMOSA has been acknowledged as a very interesting tool from the perspective of collecting statistic information. Its extensive information collection about posted workers is rather unique and provides currently the most accurate data source about postings. The advantages of the advanced LIMOSA database were highlighted by statistical research, making reliable estimates of the extent to which posting in the Belgian construction sector has resulted in displacement of local labour.[66]

4.2.4.4 Launch of a 'Fair Mobility Package'; Towards a Revised PWD

The adoption of the PWED left largely unaffected a number of persisting problems, pinpointed at in the impact assessment for the European Commission as well as in the different studies undertaken in its preparation.[67] In particular, the PWED does not address the unequal labour standards of posted and local workers, nor the 'Laval-judgments', that were interpreted as setting a ceiling of protection (rather

65 Belgium had e.g. to reduce the amount of information they collected initially because according to the CJEU the scheme unjustifiably restricted the free movement of services. See CJEU, 7 October 2010, Case C-515/08, *dos Santos Palhota and others*, ECLI:EU:C:2010:589; CJEU, 19 December 2012, Case C-577/10, *Commission v. Belgium*, ECLI:EU:C:2012:814; CJEU, 3 December 2014, Case C-315/13, *De Clercq and others*, ECLI:EU:C:2014:2408.

66 F. De Wispelaere & J. Pacolet, *The size and impact of intra-EU posting on the Belgian economy. With a special focus on the construction sector* (HIVA KU Leuven, 2017), 12.

67 See notably the studies on study on the legal aspects of the posting of workers in the framework of the provision of services in the European Union by Van Hoek and Houwerzijl (2011 and 2012); Fondazione Giacomo Brodolini (FGB), *Study on wage setting systems and minimum rates of pay applicable to posted workers in accordance with Directive 96/71/EC in a selected number of Member States and sectors*, Final report, November 2015, Report to the European Commission; F. De Wispelaere & J. Pacolet, *An ad hoc statistical analysis on short term mobility – economic value of posting of workers. The impact of intra-EU cross-border services, with special attention to the construction sector* (HIVA KU Leuven, European Commission, 2016).

than a floor of rights) for posted workers. Combined with an ever growing number of (not always genuinely) posted workers being sent from new to old Member States, this led to waves of protest across old Member States against cheap labour originating from new Member States.

Figures published by the European Commission indicate that between 2010 and 2014, the number of postings from one EU State to another increased by almost 49% to a total of approximately 1.9 million. Some 86% of the postings are to the EU-15 Member States with Germany, France and Belgium receiving the largest share. Poland, Germany and France accounted for the three largest senders of posted workers in 2014. Postings involve 0.7% of the total EU workforce although there are wide variations in different sectors. Some 42% of total postings occur in the construction sector but posting of workers is also important in the manufacturing industry (21.8%), and in other service sectors such as personal services (education, health and social work, 13.5%) and business services (administrative, professional, and financial services, 10.3%).[68]

It should be noted however that these statistics are far from perfect. The European Commission uses information provided by administrative forms (so-called A1-forms) issued by the social insurance authority of the posted workers' country of origin. But significant gaps arise between national and EU figures and there is a lack of precise data. Still, it is clear that the number of workers who are sent from one Member State - in which they supposedly normally work - to another for a limited period of time has increased sharply, whereas these so-called posted workers often earn substantially less than local workers for the same work. Moreover, concerns about posted workers being vulnerable to fraudulent activities such as undeclared work practices have also grown.

As mentioned, the PWED attempts to address some of the issues surrounding effective enforcement of the PWD, but it does not alleviate many of the concerns raised. Against this background, the European Commission launched, as part of a 'fair mobility package', a proposal for a targeted revision of the PWD in March 2016.[69] According to the Explanatory Memorandum, the main aims for the revision are ensuring the smooth functioning of the single market and stopping 'unfair competition' on wage costs and working conditions, reflected in the mantra 'same pay for the same work in the same place'.

Diverging Interests of 'Host' and 'Sending' Member States

The response to the proposed Directive by national parliaments clearly showed the diverging interests between Member States.[70] Whereas the French parliament criti-

---

68 J. Pacolet and F. De Wispelaere, *Posting of workers: report on A1 portable documents issued in 2014,* (Network Statistics FMSSFE, European Commission, 2015).

69 COM(2016)128 final of 8 March 2016.

70 Individual Member State opinions are available here: http://ec.europa.eu/dgs/secretariat_general/relations/relations_other/npo/index_en.htm For a more detailed discussion see: M. HOUWERZIJL & A. SCHRAUWEN, 'From Competing to Aligned

cised the proposal for not providing sufficient protection for equality of treatment of posted workers, parliaments from Central and Eastern European Member States objected to the proposal since, according to their view, the European Commission had to wait and see what the impact of the PWED would be. Furthermore, they argued that a right to equal pay would harm competitiveness; 'the alignment of wages across Member States should come as a consequence of further economic development and not from the Union's legislative action.'
As of 10 May 2016, fourteen chambers from eleven Member States (ten from Central and Eastern Europe, and Denmark) had made use of the Subsidiarity Control Mechanism to raise subsidiarity concerns and thereby triggered a 'yellow card'[71] On 20 July 2016, the European Commission published a Communication which concluded that the proposed revision of the PWD did not breach the subsidiarity principle.[72]

Main Features of the Revised PWD

After fierce debates and considerable amendments to the Commission's proposal by Parliament and Council, the revised PWD was finally adopted on 28 June 2018. As its Preamble (e.g. Recital 4), makes clear: 'More than 20 years after the adoption of the PWD', it was time to reset 'the right balance between the need to promote the freedom to provide services and ensure a level playing field on the one hand and the need to protect the rights of posted workers on the other'. In Recital 10, the need to ensure greater protection for workers is stressed, in order 'to safeguard the freedom to provide, in both the short and the long term, services on a fair basis, in particular by preventing abuse of the rights guaranteed by the Treaties'. According to its Recital 16: 'In a truly integrated and competitive internal market, undertakings compete on the basis of factors such as productivity, efficiency, and the education and skill level of the labour force, as well as the quality of their goods and services and the degree of innovation thereof'.[73]

Narratives on (Posted) Mobile Workers Within the EU?', in T. de Lange and C. Rijken (eds.), *Towards a Decent Labour Market for Low Waged Migrant Workers* (Amsterdam: AUP 2018), 81–108.

71 See www.euractiv.com/section/social-europe-jobs/news/national-parliaments-invoke-yellow-card-in-response-to-revised-posted-workers-directive/. This is the third time that such a procedure has been triggered.

72 Communication from the Commission on the proposal for a Directive amending the Posting of Workers Directive, with regard to the principle of subsidiarity, in accordance with Protocol No 2 COM(2016)55 final.

73 Moreover, the principle of equal treatment, equal pay and the prohibition of any discrimination on grounds of nationality in Union law is emphasized (recital 6) and recital 3 refers expressly to Article 3 of the Treaty on European Union, establishing that the Union is to promote social justice and protection and Article 9 TFEU, emphasizing that the Union takes in defining and implementing its policies and activi-

Member States will have to implement the new Directive 2018/957 ultimately on 30 July 2020 and therefore Directive 96/71/EC will remain applicable until that date. The revised PWD is to amend the PWD and to complement the PWED, rather than to replace these Directives. The revised PWD focuses on three main areas: rules on temporary work agencies,[74] the remuneration of posted workers where it introduces the principle of equal pay for equal work, and rules applying to long-term posting.[75]

Almost Full Equal Treatment in Case of Postings of Longer Duration

The revised PWD enhances the protection of workers, posted for a longer duration. It stipulates that 'where the effective duration of the posting exceeds 12 months', posted workers should be guaranteed 'all the applicable terms and conditions of employment which are laid down' in the host state' (except for formalities and conditions for the conclusion and termination of contracts, non-compete clauses and supplementary pension schemes).[76] The reference period of 12 months may be extended to 18 months if the service provider submits a motivated notification. In such cases, for the obligation to ensure equal working conditions to arise, the duration of the posting must exceed 18 months.

In contrast to the reasoning of the CJEU in *Rush Portuguesa*, the introduction of extended rights in relation to postings of longer duration as defined by a temporal criterion, implies a recognition that, after a certain defined period of time, posted workers *do enter the labour market* of the host state.[77]

Extension of the 'Hard Core' of Host Labour Standards and Strengthening of 'Transparency Requirements'

Secondly, regarding the 'hard core' of labour standards that remain applicable for all workers posted less than one year, it is emphasized that these should be guaranteed by the host state on the basis of equality of treatment. This amendment builds

ties, into account requirements linked to e.g. the guarantee of adequate social protection.

74 The revised PWD links the protection of posted agency workers to the 'equal treatment provision' of the Temporary Agency Work Directive 2008/104 (Article 5), stipulating equal treatment of temporary agency workers in the user company. Full equal treatment is optional, see Article 1(2)(e) revised PWD, amending Article 3(9) PWD. Article 1(1)(c) of the revised Directive adds to the protection of temp agency workers in specific situations.

75 The current PWD does not define when a posting ceases to be 'temporary'.

76 Article 1(2)(b) of the revised Directive, adding a paragraph 1a to Article 3 PWD.

77 See recital 9: 'Posting is of a temporary nature and the posted worker usually returns to the country of origin after the completion of the work for which he has been posted. However, in view of the long duration of certain postings, and *in acknowledgment of the link between the labour market of the host country and the workers posted for such long periods*, it is necessary to provide that…,' (emphasis added by the author).

on the case law of the CJEU in *Sähköalojen ammattiliitto Ry*. The minimum wage guarantee is deemed no longer enough to protect a level playing field, and is therefore replaced by a guarantee of equal remuneration, including all elements of remuneration that are mandatory in the host state (both in statutory law and in generally binding CLAs) apply to both local and posted workers.[78] This means that employers have to apply all the rules of the host country in relation to pay/remuneration, as laid down by law or by universally applicable collective agreements, and not just the minimum rates of pay. Constituent elements of remuneration include e.g. thirteenth month allowances, travel expenses, or compensation for work during public holidays or night work.[79] Moreover, conditions of workers' accommodation and allowances or reimbursements for travel, board and lodging cost for workers away from home for professional reasons, are added as matters belonging to the hard core of host labour standards.[80]

To foster legal certainty and law enforcement, Member States are obliged to publish 'without undue delay and in a transparent manner' information on the constituent elements of remuneration on their single official national website, next to the other information as referred to in Article 5 PWED, as well as information on the additional set of terms and conditions of employment applicable to postings exceeding 12 or, where applicable, 18 months. It is emphasized that each Member State should ensure the information on the single official national website is accurate and is updated on a regular basis. Failure to comply with this obligation shall be taken into account when determining the fines applicable for infringement of the national provisions adopted pursuant to the (revised) PWD, 'to the extent necessary to ensure the proportionality thereof'.

78 Article 1(2)(a) of the revised PWD, amending Article 3(1) of the PWD. The explicit exclusion of supplementary occupational retirement pension schemes remains.

79 According to recital 18: 'when comparing the actual remuneration paid to a posted worker and the remuneration due in the host Member State, the gross amount of remuneration should be taken into account, rather than the individual constituent elements of remuneration which are rendered mandatory as provided for by this Directive. Nevertheless, in order to ensure transparency and to assist the competent authorities and bodies in carrying out checks and controls it is necessary that the constituent elements of remuneration can be identified in enough detail. Unless the allowances specific to the posting concern expenditure actually incurred on account of the posting, such as expenditure on travel, board and lodging, they should be considered to be part of the remuneration and should be taken into account for the purposes of comparing the total gross amounts of remuneration'.

80 The latter point shall apply exclusively to travel, board and lodging expenditure incurred by posted workers where they are required to travel to and from their regular place of work in the Member State to whose territory they are posted, or where they are temporarily sent by their employer from that regular place of work to another place of work.

Other Measures

In the revised PWD, also some other surveillance and control measures are further developed. In particular, it complements the PWED by establishing an obligation for the host state to create a sanctioning regime. Last but not least, the revised PWD has specific implications for the road transport sector, to which we will turn in the following, final section.[81]

4.2.5 Applicability and Enforcement of the PWD in the Road Transport Sector

4.2.5.1 The PWD and Cross-Border Work in the Road Transport Sector

The PWD does not exclude specific branches of industry from its scope of application with the exception of the seagoing personnel of merchant navy undertakings (Article 1(2)). Nevertheless, comparative research of 2011, commissioned by the European Commission, revealed that the system of the PWD is ill-fitted to deal with the kind of cross-border labour mobility characteristic for the international transport sector. At the time, with the most prominent exception of France,[82] the implementing statutes and regulations of the Member States did – implicitly – cover international transport but did not contain any specific rules concerning this sector.

This topic received ample attention for the first time during political debates on necessary revisions of the transport regulations for the internal road haulage market. With the opening up of the national markets to ***cabotage*** (see below for an explanation), the need to apply a minimum level of protection to the workers performing the cabotage service became more pressing, as was acknowledged during the negotiations on what is now transport regulation 1072/2009.[83] The end result of the discussions in 2008/09 was the inclusion of a consideration in the preamble which states that the provisions of the PWD apply to cabotage activities.[84] In prac-

81 See in detail on this thorny issue; F. van Overbeeke, 'The Commission's proposal to amend the Posting of Workers Directive and private international law implications', NIPR 2017, 178-194; F. van Overbeeke, 'Do we need a new conflict-of-laws rule in the European road transport sector? Yes we do', in: J. Buelens (ed.), *From social competition to social dumping*0(Cambridge-Antwerp-Portland: Intersentia, 2016), 107-122.

82 See Van Hoek and Houwerzijl (2011), section 3.2.

83 See preamble paras. 17 and 18 of Regulation No 1072/2009 and Draft recommendation for second reading on the Council common position for adopting a regulation of the European Parliament and of the Council on common rules for access to the international road haulage market (recast) A6-0211/2009 (11788/1/2008 – C6 0014/2009 – 2007/0099(COD)) Committee on Transport and Tourism, 15/16.

84 Para. 17 of the preamble of Regulation No 1972/2009 on common rules for access to the international road haulage market, OJ L 300/72 confirms the application of the PWD to cabotage activities.

tice, however, the practical effect thereof seems to have been minimal due to the short time span of the cabotage activities.[85]

What Is Cabotage?

Currently, cabotage operations are allowed to a limited extent only, purely in the course of an international transport operation. Cabotage is a term that refers to transportation of goods in a country by a vehicle registered in another country. Cabotage improves the efficiency of road freight transport by reducing empty trips after the unloading of international transport operations. Hence, in the case of cabotage a service is provided in the host state.[86] This implies that cabotage could be subsumed under posting as defined in Article 1(3)(a) PWD: 'posting of workers to the territory of a Member State on the account and under the direction of the undertaking making the posting, under a contract concluded between the undertaking making the posting and the party for whom the services are intended, operating in that Member State, provided there is an employment relationship between the undertaking making the posting and the worker during the period of posting'.
However, this also implies that there has to be a contract between the transport company and a service recipient operating in the state where the cabotage takes place. In Sweden such a contract is deemed to be absent when the contract with the transport company was entered into by a forwarding or freighting agency established outside the country of cabotage. This (debatable) conclusion draws attention to the fact that the definition of 'type a posting' may pose problems in cases where the end user of the service has no contract with the employer.

Other Modalities of 'Posting'

Other modalities of 'posting' are also used in international transport.[87] Regarding ***transit operations***, the situation seems most clear. Transit means that in the course of an international transport operation between Member States A and B, there is a transit through Member State C: in such situations no posting is involved.
Regarding ***international transport***, it is a reality that the big haulage companies in Western Europe often have subsidiaries in Eastern European countries, but in

85 Article 8 of Regulation No 1072/2009, stipulates that in the course of an international operation concerning the transport of goods by road, cabotage is permitted to a limit of three operations within seven days from unloading of the cargo in the host state.

86 However, the same seems to be true of an international transport operation ending in the host state. The place of performance of a transport service can be deemed to be situated in both the country of origin and the country of destination. Compare Commission Decision C(2008)8458 final and CJEU, 9 July 2009, C-204/08, *Peter Rehder v. Air Baltic Corporation*, ECLI:EU:C:2009:439, para. 29 ff., for the place of performance of the service under the Brussels I Regulation. In the case of cabotage, both places are located within the same state. On compatibility of cabotage rules with fundamental freedoms, see CJEU, 12 April 2018, C-541/16, discussed in Chapter 2.2.5.2.

87 See also the overview of media cases in section 3.5 and Annex 1, PWD I study.

many cases only with the aim of providing drivers for transport abroad. Such arrangements are often characterised as intra-group posting (defined in Article 1(3)(b) PWD; 'type b posting'). Also posting through temporary agency firms (defined in Article 1(3)(c) PWD; 'type c posting') is often invoked in practice.
For example, a Dutch transport company contracts with a Polish (daughter or independent) company for the provision of Polish truck drivers. This may be qualified as intra-group posting or temporay agency posting. Moreover, when the Polish worker used for the services regularly works from the Netherlands[88] rather than Poland, his employment contract has a close link with the Dutch labour market. This would merit protection according to Dutch labour standards. However, pursuant to Article 2 of the PWD, it is necessary to have a normal country of work other than the country of posting. Clearly, in our example this is not the case and therefore such a driver would probably not be considered genuinely posted.
Moreover, even if the truck driver would be deemed to have a habitual country of work other than the host Member State, his situation would still not fit easily into the PWD when the transport service itself is largely performed outside the 'host country' (in our example the Netherlands). Because its system is based on the premise that posted workers are working temporarily *in* another country than the one *in* which they normally work, it is unclear whether the PWD can be applied by analogy to situations in which someone is working *from* a country, as is the case in international transport (as a rule covered by Article 8(2) Rome I).

4.2.5.2 The Role of 'Letterbox-Companies'

In June 2015, Commisioner for Transport Violetta Bulc launched a 'Social Agenda for Transport'. There, she acknowledged that social dumping had become a critical issue in particular in the road transport sector:

> "…. the current economic situation has led to increased competition and pressure to reduce costs, and the development of dubious employment practices such as letter box companies or fake self-employment. *Too often, truck drivers like Radu, 30, from Bucarest, are hired through* ***a very complex mix of companies, subsidiaries, agencies based in different EU Member States, some of which have no real existence****. As a result, they are hired at the lowest possible cost and they are not protected whenever problems arise."* (emphasis added by the author)[89]

88 In practice, drivers from 'cheap' sending states are often brought by train, car, bus or plane to the host state, where they will start their working schedule in their truck, parked in the host state, from where they go *en route* to one or several other EU Member States to load and unload goods. They may be away from their home in the sending state for a couple of months and most often take their rest and sleep in their cabins.

89 Speech Violeta BULC (EU Commissioner DG Move): 4 June 2015.

According to Bulc, one of the main causes for tension between low-wage and high-wage countries in the internal market for road transport is the establishment of so-called 'letterbox' companies and so-called 'forumshopping' or 'regulatory arbitrage'. In an ex-post evaluation support study for the European Commission, it was estimated that there were at least 430 letterbox companies in 2012 in the EU. Although the absolute number of companies infringing the requirement of stable and effective establishment being detected is relatively low (below 1% of companies investigated), these figures do not capture companies that were able to avoid detection.[90] Also, specific cases of letterbox companies have been brought to the attention of the Commission. For example, in 2014 the Belgian authorities requested the Commission to intervene on their behalf in order for the Slovak authorities to investigate suspected letterbox subsidiaries set up by Belgian hauliers in Slovakia. The Slovak authorities carried out on-site inspections concerning 42 companies. Several companies were found not to comply with the establishment provisions of Regulation No 1071/2009. In one case, the authorisation had already been withdrawn and for nine other companies the respective authorisations were withdrawn following the inspections. In March 2017, there was an investigation by the Belgian authorities into Belgian hauliers having established letterbox companies in Portugal and Slovakia. The Belgian authorities found 25 letterbox companies registered in the same address in Slovakia, 3 people were arrested and the estimated unpaid social contributions in Belgium amounted to €6-€7 million.[91]

Cost Advantages

According to the ex-post evaluation of road transport regulations, the cost advantage of setting up a letterbox company for hauliers is 31% in relation to a properly-established company. Within a highly competitive industry such as road transport, this level of cost differential is very significant. The fiscal loss per vehicle per year for the Member State where the company should be established (where the haulier actually operates) was deemed to be around €6,000. Labour-related losses per driver per year for the Member State where the drivers should be paying social contributions were deemed to be in the range of €30,000-€40,000.[92] Hence, the negative impacts of letterbox companies appear to be disproportionately large due to

90 Moreover, 75 (43%) of respondents to an open public consultation considered that the setting up of letterbox companies to be a widespread practice, whilst only 9% (16) considered this to be only a minor issue. 88% of respondents from associations representing road transport workers (29 out of 33) considered that this was a widespread practice, a much greater percentage than from any other respondent category (mostly between 25-44%).

91 COM(2017)277; COD 2017/0123: ex-post evaluation support study for the European Commission.

92 Ibid., 15: For example, a French driver's salary costs are up to 2.4 times higher than those of a Polish driver. If it is assumed that letterbox companies employ, on average, the same number of workers as legally-established hauliers (5 workers per haulier).

the cost advantage they have over competing firms which comply with the legislation.[93]

Illegal Cabotage

The available statistics suggest that the level of illegal cabotage detected by checks might not be of a significant size in most Member States for which data are available. However, there have been significant concerns expressed over the low levels of effectiveness of cabotage checks, which could affect the detection of illegal cabotage and underestimate the respective share. According to the post-evaluation study, the calculations based on the cost differentials suggest that currently illegal cabotage represents 0.56% of cabotage activity at the EU aggregate level, but that it will continue to affect some Member States more than others (with illegal cabotage rates ranging from close to zero, up to 6.4%).

While the prevalence of illegal cabotage and letterbox companies may seem relatively limited based on the data mentioned above, these illegal practices have wider-reaching consequences. Several Member States have adopted national uncoordinated measures to fight illegal cabotage and letterbox companies, such as the systematic application of the national minimum wage laws to hauliers providing international transport services and cabotage in their territory. These national measures have significant consequences on the internal market in terms of high costs for non-resident hauliers.[94] Moreover, in February 2017, eight western European member States (France, Germany, Italy, Denmark, Austria, Luxembourg, Belgium, Sweden) signed in Paris a common declaration where they oppose themselves to further liberalisation of the road transport market, through liberalisation of cabotage operations.

4.2.5.3 The Revised PWD and the "Road Mobility Package"

To tackle the complex set of problems sketched above, the European Commission launched a comprehensive set of measures under the heading 'road mobility pack-

93 According to the results of the open public consultation, 63% of respondents (110) felt that the presence of letterbox companies leads to a competitive disadvantage for hauliers established in some Member States, which have to compete with other hauliers operating in the same Member State but illegally established elsewhere. There is a clear divide between EU-15 respondents (77% indicating very important or significant impact) and EU-13 (31% indicating very important or significant impact).

94 The European Commission has launched infringement procedures against such anti-social dumping measures of Germany, France and Austria (2016/17). To combat social dumping, these countries have started to apply their minimum wage law to certain international transport operations, in particular in case trucks upload or unload goods on their territory. According to the Commission, said national measures create disproportionate administrative barriers, hampering the free movement of services and goods.

age' on 31 May 2017.[95] This package includes a proposal to amend a Directive concerning social legislation relating to road transport activities (Directive 2006/22), which is currently mainly concerned with (enforcing) driving and rest times. The proposal adds to this legal instrument specific rules and enforcement requirements, including whether host labour rules should apply to truck drivers on foreign trips and how many pick-ups and drop-offs drivers can do outside their home country. Therefore the proposal impacts on the relevance of the PWD and the PWED in the road transport sector.

Anticipating on said pending proposal, Article 3(3) of the revised PWD stipulates that it will only apply to the road transport sector from the date of application of a legislative act amending Directive 2006/22/EC. In this regard, Recital 15 of the revised PWD explains that, 'because of the highly mobile nature of work in international road transport, the implementation of this Directive [the revised PWD] in that sector raises particular legal questions and difficulties, which are to be addressed, in the framework of the mobility package, through specific rules for road transport also reinforcing the combating of fraud and abuse'.

However, the road mobility package is subject of a fierce political battle and on 4 July 2018, the European Parliament rejected three Commission proposals on the social aspects of this Mobility Package including the proposals on posting of drivers, working and rest time and cabotage.[96]

So, what does this mean in relation to the posting of truck drivers? For the time being, at least for cabotage (type a posting), it is clear that the so-called Common EU rules for access to the international road haulage market are still relevant. As mentioned, in Recital 17 of the preamble to the regulation 1072/2009, the PWD is explicitly deemed applicable to transport undertakings performing a cabotage operation.

Moreover, the PWD may be applied to situations of intra-group 'postings' (type b posting) and/or 'postings' of drivers by temporary agency firms (type c posting). Unless assessments made by national authorities or other stakeholders would cast in doubt the genuine character of such postings, many truck drivers as well as their employers may still act as if they are in situations of posting. Since the PWD does not exclude the road transport sector from its scope, this all seems perfectly legal, at least until the revised Directive enters into force in mid 2020. From then on, the road transport sector will be excluded from the scope of the posting of workers rules. Future inclusion will depend on the fate of the proposal to amend Directive 2006/22.

Ultimately by 30 July 2023, the European Commission has to submit an evaluation report on the application and implementation of the revised PWD to the European Parliament and the Council, which shall include an assessment of

95 Mobility Package, 'Europe on the Move' Occupation and Market Access, COM(2017)281 - 1071/2009/EC; 1072/2009/EC; COM(2017 282 - 2006/1/EC.

96 www.europeantransportforum.eu/mediaroom/meps-reject-trucking-rules-in-setback-for-eu-mobility-package/.

whether further measures to ensure a level playing field and protect workers are required, in particular in light of the developments concerning the envisaged amending of Directive 2006/22/EC.[97]

4.3 Case Law

Judgments of the Court of Justice of the European Union (CJEU) regarding the Posting of Workers (Directive) concern the following cases:

CJEU, 27 March 1990, Case C-113/89, *Rush Portuguesa*, ECLI:EU:C:1990:142.
CJEU, 9 August 1994, Case C-43/93, *Vander Elst*, ECLI:EU:C:1994:310.
CJEU, 28 March 1996, Case C-272/94, *Guiot*, ECLI:EU:C:1996:147.
CJEU, 23 November 1999, Cases C-369/96 and C-376/96, *Arblade*, ECLI:EU:C:1999:575.
CJEU, 9 March 2000, Case C-355/98, *Commission v. Belgium*, ECLI:EU:C:2000:113.
CJEU, 15 March 2001, Case C-165/98, *Mazzoleni*, ECLI:EU:C:2001:162.
CJEU, 25 October 2001, Case C-49/98 et seq., *Finalarte*, ECLI:EU:C:2001:564.
CJEU, 24 January 2002, Case C-164/99, *Portugaia*, ECLI:EU:C:2002:40.
CJEU, 12 October 2004 Case C-60/03, *Wolff & Müller*, ECLI:EU:C:2004:610.
CJEU, 21 October 2004, Case C-445/03, *Commission v. Luxembourg*, ECLI:EU:C:2004:655.
CJEU, 14 April 2005, Case C-341/02, *Commission v. Germany*, ECLI:EU:C:2005:220.
CJEU, 19 January 2006, Case C-244/04, *Commission v. Germany*, ECLI:EU:C:2006:49.
CJEU, 21 September 2006 Case C-168/04, *Commission v. Austria*, ECLI:EU:C:2006:595
CJEU, 18 July 2007, Case C-490/04, *Commission v. Germany*, ECLI:EU:C:2007:430.
CJEU, 18 December 2007, Case C-341/05, *Laval un Partneri*, ECLI:EU:C:2007:809.
CJEU, 3 April 2008, Case C-346/06, *Rüffert*, ECLI:EU:C:2008:189.
CJEU, 19 June 2008, Case C-319/06, *Commission v. Luxembourg*, ECLI:EU:C:2008:350.
CJEU, 7 October 2010, Case C-515/08, *dos Santos Palhota and others*, ECLI:EU:C:2010:589.
CJEU, 10 February 2011, Case C-307/09-309/09, *Vicoplus*, ECLI:EU:C:2011:64.
CJEU, 19 December 2012, Case C-577/10, *Commission v. Belgium*, ECLI:EU:C:2012:814.
CJEU, 7 November 2013, Case C-522/12, *Isbir*, ECLI:EU:C:2013:711.

97 As stipulated in Article 2(2)(b) of the revised PWD.

CJEU, 11 September 2014, Case C-91/13, *Essent Energie Productie*, ECLI:EU:C:2014:2206.
CJEU, 18 September 2014, Case C-549/13, *Bundesdruckerei*, ECLI:EU:C:2014:2235.
CJEU, 3 December 2014, Case C-315/13, *De Clercq and others*, ECLI:EU:C:2014:2408.
CJEU, 12 February 2015, Case C-396/13, *Sähköalojen ammattiliitto Ry*, ECLI:EU:C:2015:86.
CJEU, 18 June 2015, Case C-586/13, *Martin Meat*, ECLI:EU:C:2015:405.
CJEU, 17 November 2015, Case C-115/14, *RegioPost*, ECLI:EU:C:2015:760.
CJEU, 13 November 2018, Case C-33/17, *Čepelnik*, ECLI:EU:C:2018:896.
CJEU, 14 November 2018, Case C-18/17, *Danieli & C. Officine Meccaniche and Others*, ECLI:EU:C:2018:904.

4.4 Further Reading

4.4.1 Academic Literature

C. Barnard, 'Internal market v. labour market: a brief history', in: M. de Vos (ed.), *European Union Internal Market and Labour law: Friends or Foes* (Cambridge-Antwerp-Portland: Intersentia, 2009).

M. Bernaciak, 'Social Dumping? Political catchphrase or threat to labour standards,' *ETUI Working Paper 2012/06.*

L.E. Berntsen, *Agency of labour in a flexible pan-European labour market: A qualitative study of migrant practices and trade union strategies in the Netherlands*, Groningen (PhD Thesis) (Groningen: University of Groningen, SOM research school, 2015).

J. Cremers, *In Search of Cheap Labour in Europe: Working and living conditions of posted workers* (Brussels: CLR/EFBWW/International Books, 2011).

J. Cremers, J. E. Dølvik, and G. Bosch, 'Posting of workers in the single market: attempts to prevent social dumping and regime competition in the EU', *Industrial Relations Journal*, 2007, 524-541.

S. Evju (ed.), *Regulating Transnational Labour in Europe: The quandaries of multilevel governance* (Oslo: UiO Institutt Privatrett, 2014): www.jus.uio.no/ifp/english/research/projects/freemov/publications/books/196.pdf.

M. Fornasier and M. Torga, 'The Posting of Workers: The perspective of the Sending state – The Judgment of the Civil Chamber of the Estonian Supreme Court of 16 January 2013 No 3-2-1-179-12', *Europäische Zeitschrift für Arbeitsrecht* (*EuZA*), Vol. 3, 2013, 356-365.

M. Freedland and J. Prassl (eds.), *EU law in the Member States: Viking, Laval and beyond* (Oxford: Hart Publishing, 2015).

A. van Hoek, 'Re-embedding the transnational employment relationship: A Tale about the Limitations of (EU) Law?', *Common Market Law Review*, Vol. 55, No 2, 2018, 449–87.

A. van Hoek & M. Houwerzijl, 'Where do EU mobile workers belong, according to Rome I and the (E)PWD?', in: H. Verschueren (ed.), *Residence, Employment and Social Rights of Mobile Persons. On How EU Law Defines Where They Belong*, Social Europe Series, Vol. 36 (Cambridge-Antwerp-Portland: Intersentia 2016), 215-253.

M. Houwerzijl, 'Regime shopping across (blurring) boundaries', in: S. Evju (ed.), *Regulating Trans-national Labour in Europe: The quandaries of multilevel governance* Oslo: Skriftserie nr. 196 (2014).

M. Houwerzijl & A. Schrauwen, 'From Competing to Aligned Narratives on (Posted) Mobile Workers Within the EU?', in: T. de Lange and C. Rijken (eds.), *Towards a Decent Labour Market for Low Waged Migrant Workers* (Amsterdam: AUP, 2018), 81-108.

M. Houwerzijl & H. Verschueren, 'EU free movement of (posted) workers and applicable labour and social security law', in: T. Jaspers, F. Pennings and S. Peters (eds.), *European Labour Law* (Cambridge-Antwerp-Portland: Intersentia 2019 (forthcoming)), Chapter 2.

M. Houwerzijl & T. Wilkinson, 'The Effects of EU Law on the Social and Economic Goals of Europe 2020: A Decision Theoretic Approach to Wage Liability Regimes in Modern Europe', *German Law Journal* Vol. 14, 2013, available at: www.germanlawjournal.com/index.php?pageID=11&artID=1587.

K. Kall & N. Lillie, *Protection of Posted Workers in the European Union: Findings and Policy Recommendations based on existing research*, PROMO briefing paper, (Finland: University of Jyväskylä, 2017).

C. Kilpatrick, 'British Jobs for British Workers? UK Industrial Action and Free Movement of Services in EU Law', *LSE Legal Studies Working Paper* No. 16/2009.

D. Kukovec, 'Hierarchies as law', *Columbia Journal of International Law*, Vol. 21, 2014, 131-193.

M. Kullmann, *Enforcement of Labour Law in Cross-Border Situations. A Legal study of the EU's Influence on the Dutch, German, and Swedish Enforcement systems* (PhD Thesis), (Deventer: Kluwer, 2015).

D. Leczykiewicz, 'Conceptualizing conflict between the economic and social in EU law after Viking and Laval', in: M. Freedland and J. Prassl (eds.), *EU law in the Member States: Viking, Laval and beyond*, (Oxford: Hart Publishing, 2015).

N. Lillie, I. Wagner and L. Berntsen, 'Posted Migration, Spaces of Exception, and the Politics of Labour Relations in the European Construction Industry', in M. Hauptmeier and M. Vidal (eds.), *Comparative Political Economy of Work* (Basingstoke: Palgrave Macmillan, 2014), 312–331.

F. van Overbeeke, 'Do we need a new conflict-of-laws rule in the European road transport sector? Yes we do', in: J. Buelens (ed.), *From social competition to social dumping* (Cambridge-Antwerp-Portland: Intersentia, 2016), 107-122.

F. van Overbeeke, 'The Commission's proposal to amend the Posting of Workers Directive and private international law implications', *NIPR* 2017, 178-194.

Z. Rasnaca, 'Identifying the (dis)placement of "new" Member State Social Interests in the Posting of Workers: The Case of Latvia', 2018 *European Constitutional Law Review* 2018 (14), 150.

M. Rönnmar, 'Laval returns to Sweden: the final judgment of the Swedish Labour Court and Swedish legislative reforms', *Industrial Law Journal*, 2010, 280-287.

A. Somek, 'From Workers to Migrants, from Distributive Justice to Inclusion: Exploring the Changing Social Democratic Imagination', *European Law Journal*, Vol. 18, 2012, 711-726.

H. Verschueren, 'Cross-border workers in the European internal market: Trojan horses for Member States' labour and social security law?', *International Journal of Comparative Labour Law and Industrial Relations*, Vol. 24, 2008, 176.

I. Wagner, *Posted Work and Deterritorialization in the European Union: A study of the German Construction and Meat Industry*, (PhD Thesis) (Groningen: University of Groningen, SOM research school, 2015).

R. Zahn, 'Revision of the Posted Workers Directive: a Europeanisation Perspective', *Cambridge Yearbook of European Legal Studies* 2017 (5).

4.4.2 Other Documents

Webpage European Commission DG Employment, Social Affairs & Inclusion on posting of workers: http://ec.europa.eu/social/main.jsp?catId=471.

European Commission, *Revision of the Posting of Workers Directive-frequently asked questions* (Strasbourg, 2016). Available at: http://europa.eu/rapid/press-release_MEMO-16-467_en.htm.

European Agency on Fundamental Rights, *Severe Labour Exploitation: Workers Moving within or into the European Union, States' Obligations and Victims' Rights* (Brussels, 2015).

Fondazione Giacomo Brodolini (FGB), authored by J.-P. Lhernould, M. Coucheir, S. Fisker, P. Madsen and E. Voss, *Study on wage setting systems and minimum rates of pay applicable to posted workers in accordance with Directive 96/71/EC in a selected number of Member States and sectors*, Final report, November 2015, Report to the European Commission.

K. Mcgauran, *The impact of letterbox- type practices on labour rights and public revenue* (Amsterdam: SOMO, commissioned by the ETUC: June 2016).

A.A.H. van Hoek and M.S. Houwerzijl, *Comparative Study on the legal aspects of the posting of workers in the framework of the provision of services in the European Union*, Report to the European Commission (2011).

M. Houwerzijl, E.d Traversa and F. Henneaux, *A Hunters game: How policy can change to spot and sink letterbox-type practices* (Brussels: ETUC, December 2016).

M. Monti, *A new strategy for the single market, at the service of Europe's economy and society* (2010). Retrieved from: http//:ec.europa.eu/bepa/pdf/monti_report_final_10_05_2010_en.pdf.

F. De Wispelaere & J. Pacolet, *An ad hoc statistical analysis on short term mobility – economic value of posting of workers. The impact of intra-EU cross-border services, with special attention to the construction sector* (HIVA KU Leuven, European Commission, 2016).

F. De Wispelaere & J. Pacolet, *The size and impact of intra-EU posting on the Belgian economy. With a special focus on the construction sector* (HIVA KU Leuven, 2017).

5 The EU Coordination of the Social Security Systems of the Member States and Its Applicability in Cross-Border Road Transport

Herwig Verschueren & Bartłomiej Bednarowicz[*]

5.1 Introduction

5.1.1 Curriculum Outline

This chapter will deal with the EU coordination of the social security systems of the Member States. It will explain the objectives, the scope and the main features of this coordination system. It will discuss in more detail the rules determining which national social security legislation is applicable in cross-border situations and analyse these rules in the context of international road transport highlighting specific issues of their implementation in this field. Specific attention will be paid to the relevant case law of the Court of Justice of the European Union (CJEU).

5.1.2 Specific Learning Outcomes

1. Teaching the basic characteristics of the EU social security coordination system set up by Regulation No 883/2004 and Regulation No 987/2009.
2. Understanding the rules of this coordination system on the determination of the applicable legislation in cross-border situations.

* Herwig Verschueren is Professor of International and European Labour and Social Security Law and Bartłomiej Bednarowicz is PhD Researcher and Teaching Assistant, University of Antwerp.

3. Unravelling the impact of this coordination system on the social security rights of workers in international road transport, in particular the implementation of the rules on the determination of the applicable legislation.
4. Analysing the most relevant case law of the European Court of Justice with an impact on the rights of international road transport workers.
5. Familiarising readers with official documents of the EU institutions and with academic and other relevant literature in this field.
6. Analysing the implementation of these EU rules at national level.
7. Enabling readers to solve cases with regard to the implementation of these rules.
8. Letting them benefit from mutual learning opportunities and teaching them to find problem solving solutions.

5.2 State of the Art

5.2.1 Which Legal Instruments Are Applicable?

The first EU social security coordination system was established as early as 1958 by Regulations 3 and 4. From 1972 to 1 May 2010 this was regulated by Regulation (EEC) No 1408/71[1] and Regulation (EEC) No 574/72.[2]

Currently, the EU social security coordination rules are laid down in Regulation (EC) No 883/2004[3] and Regulation (EC) No 987/2009.[4] Meanwhile, Regulation No 883/2004 has been amended by Regulation (EC) No 988/2009,[5] Regulation (EU) No 1244/2010,[6] Regulation (EU) No 465/2012,[7] Regulation (EU) No 1244/2012,[8] Regulation (EU) No 517/2013,[9] Regulation (EU) No 1372/2013[10] and Regulation No 1368/2014.[11] Regulation No 987/2009 has been amended by

1 Regulation (EEC) No 1408/71 of the Council of 14 June 1971 on the application of social security schemes to employed persons and their families moving within the Community (hereafter 'Regulation No 1408/71').
2 Regulation (EEC) No 574/72 of the Council of 21 March 1972 fixing the procedure for implementing Regulation (EEC) No 1408/71.
3 Regulation (EC) No 883/2004 of the European Parliament and of the Council of 29 April 2004 on the coordination of social security systems, OJ 2004, L 200/1 (corrigendum OJ 2004, L 200/1), (hereafter 'Regulation No 883/2004).
4 Regulation (EC) No 987/2009 of 16 September 2009, OJ 2009, L 294/1 (corrigendum OJ 2016, L 288/58) (hereafter 'Regulation No 987/2009').
5 OJ 2009, L 284/43.
6 OJ 2010, L 338/35.
7 OJ 2012, L 149/4.
8 OJ 2012, L 349/45.
9 OJ 2013, L 158/1.
10 OJ 2013, L 346/27.
11 OJ 2014, L 366/15.

Regulation (EU) No 465/2012,[12] Regulation (EU) No 1244/2012,[13] Regulation (EU) No 1372/2013,[14] Regulation No 1368/2014,[15] and Regulation (EU) No 2017/492.[16]

5.2.2 Legal Context

5.2.2.1 Social Security as a Matter for the Member States

Under the terms of the EU Treaties, the Member States retain, at least in principle, the sovereign power to define their own social security systems. The starting point of EU law and EU policy is indeed that the Member States are entirely free to organise their internal social protection systems as they see fit. Insofar as social protection is concerned, the European Treaties assign hardly any harmonising powers to the European institutions. The current Article 153(1)(c) TFEU does entitle the Union to support and complement the activities of the Member States in the field of "social security and social protection of workers", including laying down minimum requirements by means of directives. However, the Union has never used this competence, nor is it likely to do so in the short to medium term. The only harmonising initiatives that have been taken are a number of directives concerning the equal treatment of men and women in matters of social security.[17]

5.2.2.2 Treaty Mandate to Coordinate the Social Security Systems of the Member States

In the absence of harmonisation, it is for each Member State to determine the features of its own social security system, including which benefits are provided, the conditions for eligibility, how these benefits are calculated, the level of contributions to be paid by insured persons and the income to be taken into account when calculating social security contributions. However, when exercising their power in the field of social security, Member States must comply with EU law.[18] The most relevant area of EU law in this respect is the internal market law. In particular, the application of the Member States' social security legislation must not create unjus-

12 OJ 2012, L 149/4.

13 OJ 2012, L 349/45.

14 OJ 2013, L 346/27.

15 OJ 2014, L 366/15.

16 OJ 2017, L 76/13.

17 See, e.g. Council Directive (EEC) 79/7 on the progressive implementation of the principle of equal treatment for men and women in matters of social security OJ 1979, L6/24.

18 See, *inter alia*: CJEU, 28 April 1998, Case C-158/96, *Kohll*, ECLI:EU:C:1998:171, para. 19; CJEU, 9 March 2006, Case C-493/04, *Piatkowski*, ECLI:EU:C:2006:167, para. 33; CJEU, 3 April 2008, Case C-103/06, *Derouin*, ECLI:EU:C:2008:185, para. 25 and CJEU, 14 March 2019, Case C-134/18, *Vester*, ECLI:EU:C:2019:212, paras. 30-31.

tified obstacles to the exercise of the EU rights of free movement of persons and services.[19] In this context, the Treaty of Rome of 1957 already mandated in its Article 51 the EU legislator to adopt the necessary measures in the field of social security to provide freedom of movement for workers (now Article 48 TFEU). This Treaty provision refers to measures such as the aggregation, for the purpose of acquiring and retaining the right to benefits and of calculating the amount of benefits, of all periods taken into account under the laws of the various countries and the payment of benefits to persons residing in the territories of the Member States. Meanwhile, the TFEU not only guarantees the right of European citizens to seek employment, to work, to pursue self-employed activities or to provide services in another Member State[20] but it also guarantees, in general, every EU citizen's right to move and reside freely within the territory of the Member States, irrespective of the exercise of an economic activity.[21] In addition, the prohibition of discrimination on grounds of nationality as laid down in Articles 18 and 45 TFEU, must also be respected by the Member States in their social security systems.

It is not the intention of this coordination system to harmonise or approximate the systems of the Member States in any way. Its purpose is to coordinate the social security systems of the Member States in such a manner as to eliminate any negative consequences for the migrating individual that may arise from differences between the various systems. It does not affect the material and formal differences between the social security regimes of the various Member States and therefore does not affect the divergent rights of the individuals working or residing in those States.[22] This implies, amongst other things, that (labour) migration between the Member States may give rise to a more extensive or less extensive social protection, depending on the system that is in place in the Member State where the individual concerned is working or residing.[23]

---

19 See for instance: CJEU, 5 October 1994, C-165/91, *van Munster*, ECLI:EU:C:1994:359, para. 27; CJEU, 22 November 1995, Case C-443/93, *Vougioukas*, ECLI:EU:C:1995:394, para. 39; and more recently: CJEU, 21 January 2016, Case C-515/14, *Commission v. Cyprus*, ECLI:EU:C:2016:30, para. 38.

20 Articles 45, 49 and 56 TFEU.

21 Article 21 TFEU as introduced by the Maastricht Treaty in 1992.

22 See, e.g.: CJEU, 15 January 1986, Case C-41/84, *Pinna*, ECLI:EU:C:1986:1, para. 20; CJEU, 30 January 1997, Case C-340/94, *de Jaeck*, ECLI:EU:C:1997:43, para. 18; CJEU, 9 March 2006, Case C-493/04, *Piatkowski*, ECLI:EU:C:2006:167, paras. 19-20; and CJEU, 16 July 2009, Case C-208/07, *von Chamier-Glisczinski*, ECLI:EU:C:2009:455, para. 84.

23 See, e.g.: CJEU, 19 March 2002, Joined Cases C-393/99 and C-394/99, *Hervein and others*, ECLI:EU:C:2002:182, paras. 50-51; CJEU, 9 March 2006, Case C-493/04, *Piatkowski*, ECLI:EU:C:2006:167, para. 34; CJEU, 16 July 2009, Case C-208/07, *von Chamier-Glisczinski*, ECLI:EU:C:2009:455, para. 85; and CJEU, 14 March 2019, Case C-134/18, *Vester*, ECLI:EU:C:2019:212, para. 32.

The objective of the EU social security coordination is twofold: first, to contribute to the establishment of the greatest possible freedom of movement for persons;[24] second, to prevent that individuals would lose their social security rights or have their benefits reduced by making use of the right of freedom of movement within the EU.[25]

5.2.2.3 The Currently Applicable Rules

The European legislature has tried to attain these goals by adopting an elaborate social security coordination system. In 1958, it had already adopted Regulations 3 and 4 which were replaced by Regulation No 1408/71 and Regulation No 574/72 in 1971 and 1972. In their turn these regulations were applicable until 1 May 2010, when they were replaced by Regulation No 883/2004 and Regulation No 987/2009.

Regulation No 883/2004 contains the basic rules (it is also called the Basic Regulation (BR)) which are further implemented by procedures laid down in Regulation No 987/2009 (also called the Implementing Regulation (IR)). Title I of Regulation No 883/2004 defines the concepts used in this regulation (Article 1), its personal and material scope (Articles 2 and 3) and lays down its general principles. The coordination system is governed by the principle of equality of treatment for all persons and benefits covered by the Regulation with regard to the social security rights enshrined in the legislation of the Member States (Article 4 Regulation No 883/2004). Furthermore, the coordination system contains rules with regard to the waiving of residence clauses in the allocation or preservation of social security benefits (Article 7 Regulation No 883/2004). It also establishes a number of rules with regard to the aggregation of periods of insurance, employment and residence (e.g. Article 6). The purpose of this aggregation is to avoid that by dividing a person's insurance career between different Member States he/she would suffer a reduction in or loss of rights.

A central element in this coordination regime is the determination of which Member State's social security legislation is applicable in a cross-border situation. These rules are laid down in Title II of Regulation No 883/2004. The underlying principles of the rules that determine the applicable legislation are the State-of-employment principle for economically active persons and the State-of-residence principle for economically non-active persons.

Title III of Regulation No 883/2004 contains detailed rules on the different social security branches, more specifically on the way of calculation and on how Member

24 CJEU, 30 June 2011, Case C-388/09, *da Silva Martins*, ECLI:EU:C:2011:439, para. 70; and CJEU, 21 January 2016, Case C-515/14, *Commission v. Cyprus*, ECLI:EU:C:2016:30, para. 34.

25 CJEU, 12 February 2015, Case C-114/13, *Bouman*, ECLI:EU:C:2015:81, para. 39; CJEU, 21 January 2016, Case C-515/14, *Commission v. Cyprus*, ECLI:EU:C:2016:30, para. 34; and CJEU, 14 March 2019, C-134/18, *Vester*, ECLI:EU:C:2019:212, para. 33.

States shall take into account situations occurred or occurring in another Member State, such as periods of insurance (payment of contributions), employment or residence.
Finally, a detailed system of collaboration was established between the social security institutions to facilitate the application of said regulation for insured persons who have ties with more than one Member State. These rules are to be found in Title IV of Regulation No 883/2004 as well as in the implementing Regulation No 987/2009. Regulation No 883/2004 has set up an "Administrative Commission" to deal with all administrative questions and questions of interpretation and to foster and develop cooperation between Member States (Article 72).
These regulations have been subject to numerous judgments of the Court of Justice which applied and interpreted the provisions of these regulations in the light of the general objectives laid down in the Treaties. This case law forms an integral part of the EU coordination system.
The EU social security coordination is a highly complex and technical piece of legislation. This is due, first of all, to the complexity of and great diversity in the national social security systems and legislation which the European regulations need to coordinate. Without the detailed regulation provisions, the general principles of the Treaties on which they are founded would have no legal expression. Indeed, the mandate which the Treaty accords in this field to the EU legislator (now Article 48 TFEU) is very generally worded and offers very little guidance in terms of the legal techniques to be used in legislation with a view to attaining the general goals.[26] Hence, intervention by the EU legislator was absolutely indispensable for the establishment of this system of coordination.

5.2.3 Scope

5.2.3.1 Personal Scope

In principle, the EU social security coordination regulations are only applicable to nationals of an EU Member State, an EEA State[27] or Switzerland. The regulations also cover refugees or stateless persons residing in a Member State. In addition, they are also applicable to the members of the families and survivors of these persons as well as to survivors of non-EU nationals when these survivors are nationals of a Member State or stateless persons or refugees residing in one of the Member States. These regulations only apply as far as these persons are of have been subject to the social security legislation of one or more Member States (Article 2).

26 The CJEU confirmed that Article 48 TFEU itself has no direct effect and cannot, as such, confer rights on individuals which those individuals might be able to rely on before their national courts, see: CJEU, 10 March 2011, Case C-379/09 *Casteels*, ECLI:EU:C:2011:131, paras. 15-16.

27 Norway, Iceland and Liechtenstein. Any reference hereafter to an EU national, also refers to nationals of these States as well as of Switzerland. References to an EU Member State also refer to these States.

This nationality clause is linked to the legal context of these regulations: the promotion of the free movement of EU citizens in general and of EU workers more specifically (Articles 21 and 45 TFEU). Since such a right to free movement is limited to the nationals of the Member States, the social security coordination regulations based on these provisions (and in particular Article 48 TFEU) must also be limited to these persons.[28]

However, a number of non-EU nationals are directly as well as indirectly covered by these regulations. This is the case for persons holding the (recognised) status of refugee or stateless person[29] as well as for the members of the family of EU citizens. Under the legislation of the Member States, the latter category often derives rights from another person, irrespective of their nationality. The status of family member may for instance be relevant for the right to family benefits as well as for benefits in case of sickness and for widow/widower or survivors' benefits.[30] In addition, Regulation No 1231/2010[31] extends this personal scope to all third-country nationals as far as they are legally residing in a Member State and the situation of the person concerned is not in any way confined to a single Member State.[32] The main reason for this extension is the fact that a large number of third-country nationals are already present in the EU and covered by the social security system of the Member State in question.[33] Their social security rights need to be coordinated once they

28 CJEU, 11 October 2001, Joined Cases C-95/99, C-98/99 and C-180/99, *Khalil et al.*, ECLI:EU:C:2011:532.

29 The inclusion of these persons in the scope of the regulations is the result of the Member States' international obligations that stem from the international conventions on the protection of these persons (The Geneva Convention of 1951 and the New York Convention of 1954), see: CJEU, 11 October 2001, Joined Cases C-95/99, C-98/99 and C-180/99, *Khalil et al.*, ECLI:EU:C:2011:532.

30 The concept of family member is defined by Article 1(i) Regulation 883/2004 by referring to the definitions thereof in the relevant legislation of the Member States.

31 Regulation (EU) No 1231/2010 of the European Parliament and of the Council of 24 November 2010 extending Regulation (EC) No 883/2004 and Regulation (EC) No 987/2009 to nationals of third countries who are not already covered by these Regulations solely on the ground of their nationality, OJ 2010, L344/1 (hereafter 'Regulation No 1231/2010').

32 The personal scope of the former Regulations No 1408/71 and No 574/74 was also extended to these third-country nationals by Regulation (EC) No 895/2003, OJ 2003, L 124/1.

33 The CJEU recently specified that Regulation (EU) No 1231/2010 also covers third country nationals who temporarily reside and work in different Member States in the service of an employer established in a Member State provided that they are legally staying and working in the territory of the Member States. The duration of the presence of those nationals on the territory of a Member States and the fact that they retain their centre of interest in a third country are not relevant, as such, in order to establish whether they are 'legally resident in the territory of a Member State' within

find themselves in a cross-border situation between Member States.[34] Regulation No 1231/2010 has only one substantial provision which extends the provisions of Regulations No 883/2004 and 987/2009 to third-country nationals. The introduction of this extension by a separate legal instrument was needed because a different legal basis than the one used for the coordination regulations had to be used, more specifically the legal basis for the EU's immigration policy (Article 79(2)(b) TFEU).[35]

Persons are only covered by the social security coordination insofar as they are or have been subject to the legislation of one or more Member States. The question as to whether or not a person is covered by the legislation of a Member State depends on this legislation. Coverage may be based on mandatory or voluntary insurance (*Bismarckian* systems) or on residence in a Member State. In principle, it remains the prerogative of the Member States to decide which persons are covered by their systems, provided of course that they respect EU law. This definition of the personal scope is very broad, much broader than the initial coordination regulations of 1958 and 1971 which were limited to migrant workers. Now, the status under which a person is covered by the national legislation (workers, self-employed persons, or persons with another status) is irrelevant. As a result, almost all EU citizens and legally residing third-country nationals are nowadays covered by the EU social security regulations.

Besides being covered by a national social security scheme, the person involved must also be in a cross-border situation. This means that a person in a purely internal situation which has no relation with another Member State, does not fall under the personal scope of the EU social security regulations.[36] This can be the case if such a person is in a situation which only concerns a border between the regions of a Member State.[37] A cross-border situation can take different forms, such as the nationality of another Member State, residence outside a Member State, having worked in more than one Member State or the need for medical treatment during a stay in another Member State.

---

the meaning of this regulation: CJEU, 24 January 2019, Case C-477/17, *Balandin,* ECLI:EU:C:2019:60.

34 This extension does not apply to third-country nationals with regard to the United Kingdom and Denmark (Recitals 18 and 19 of Regulation No 1231/2010) nor with regard to the EEA States and Switzerland (for the latter see: CJEU, 18 November 2010, Case C-247/09, *Xhymshiti*, ECLI:EU:C:2010:698).

35 The CJEU has indeed decided that the scope of the legal basis for EU social security regulations (Article 48 TFEU, former Article 42 EC) is limited to the EU nationals in the context of their right to free movement, see: CJEU, 11 October 2001, Joined Cases C-95/99, C-98/99 and C-180/99, *Khalil et al.*, ECLI:EU:C:2011: 532.

36 CJEU, 22 September 1992, Case C-153/91, *Petit*, ECLI:EU:C:1992: 354.

37 CJEU, 1 April 2008, Case C-212/06, *Gouvernement de la Communauté française and others*, ECLI:EU:C:2008:178.

5.2.3.2 Material Scope

The material scope of Regulation No 883/2004 is defined in its Article 3. It refers to all legislation concerning benefits in case of sickness, maternity and paternity, invalidity, old age and survivors' benefits, benefits in respect of accidents at work and occupational diseases, unemployment and pre-retirement benefits as well as benefits concerning death grants and family benefits. This is an exclusive list, but it applies to general as well as to special schemes, whether contributory or not. However, social and medical assistance schemes are excluded.[38] Still, benefits which have characteristics of both social security and social assistance are covered. Such benefits are called "special non-contributory cash benefits", because they provide coverage against the risks listed in Article 3 while at the same time guaranteeing the persons concerned a minimum subsistence income in accordance with the economic and social situation in a Member State. They are subject to a special coordination regime laid down in Article 70 Regulation No 883/2004, based on the person's residence.

The term "legislation" is defined very broadly in Article 1(l) Regulation No 883/2004. It includes all types of legislative, regulatory and administrative measures adopted by the Member States that have a direct or sufficiently relevant link with these branches of social security. The categorisation of the measures under national law (for instance as taxes and not as social security contributions) does not matter in this respect.[39] However, contractual provisions, such as occupational pensions agreed between employers and employees, are excluded.[40]

The CJEU has given a very extensive interpretation of this material scope. It is settled case law that a benefit may be regarded as a social security benefit if it is granted to the recipients, without any individual and discretionary assessment of personal needs, on the basis of a legally defined position and relates to one of the risks expressly listed in Article 3(1) Regulation No 883/2004.[41] In addition, the precise nature of the benefit should not vary according to the particular features of each system of national law but rest upon objective criteria defined in a context specific to EU law. The risk covered by each benefit must be taken into consideration.[42]

38 Nevertheless, such schemes are considered as "social advantages" within the meaning of Article 7(2) Regulation No 492/2011 are also excluded: benefit schemes in relation to which a Member State assumes the liability for damages to persons (such as those for victims of war or terrorist attacks) and provisions in national legislation concerning a ship-owner's obligations.

39 CJEU, 15 February 2000, Case C-34/98, *Commission v. France*, ECLI:EU:C:2000:84; and CJEU, 25 February 2015, Case C-623/13, *de Ruyter*, ECLI:EU:C:2015:123.

40 Unless they serve to implement an insurance obligation arising from national legislation or unless a Member State has made a declaration to include such systems into the regulation.

41 CJEU, 30 June 2011, Case C-388/09, *da Silva Martins*, ECLI:EU:C:2011:439, para. 38.

42 CJEU, 21 July 2011, Case C-503/09, *Stewart*, ECLI:EU:C:2011:500, paras. 35-36.

The qualification of a benefit is not only relevant for assessing whether the benefit is subject to the provisions of the EU coordination regulations, but also for determining which provisions of these regulations are applicable. Indeed, the regulations contain a number of special provisions for each benefit (Title III). For instance, the CJEU qualified a number of long-term care benefits as sickness benefits within the meaning of the Regulation,[43] so that the relevant provisions regarding these benefits apply (Articles 17-35) and not the provisions on invalidity benefits (Articles 44-49). In a similar vein, the CJEU considered a parenting allowance, which is designed to enable one of the parents to devote himself or herself to the raising of a young child and which is intended as a kind of remuneration for bringing up that child and to mitigate the financial disadvantages entailed in giving up income from full-time employment, as a family benefit within the meaning of Regulation No 883/2004.[44] So, not only do such benefits fall within the scope of the regulation, but the provisions in the regulation on family benefits (Articles 67-69) apply to them as well.

5.2.4 General Principles

5.2.4.1 Equal Treatment

The principle of equal treatment, as confirmed in Article 4 Regulation No 883/2004, or the prohibition of discrimination on grounds of nationality, guarantees that in social security matters nationals of a Member State are treated by any other Member State as if they were nationals of the latter State. This principle is deeply rooted in EU law[45] and has always been interpreted broadly by the CJEU in social security matters. It is also the basic reason for the State-of-employment principle. This principle not only protects migrant workers against discrimination in the host State, but also seeks to prevent unfair competition between employers who employ migrant workers and those who employ domestic workers.[46] This would occur if the first category were allowed to pay lower social security contributions for migrant workers in the sending State compared to the contributions to be paid in the host State.

43 CJEU, 5 March 1998, Case C-160/96, *Molenaar*, ECLI:EU:C:1998:84; and CJEU, 1 April 2008, Case C-212/06, *Gouvernement de la Communauté française and others*, ECLI:EU:C:2008:178.

44 CJEU, 10 October 1996, Joined Cases C-245/94 and C-312/94, *Hoever and Zachow*, ECLI:EU:C:1996:379, paras. 23-25; and CJEU, 19 September 1013, Joined Cases C-216/12 and C-217/12, *Hliddal and Bornand*, ECLI:EU:C:2013:568, paras. 56-57.

45 See, *inter alia*, Articles 18 and 45 TFEU.

46 CJEU, 4 April 1974, Case C-167/73, *Commission v. France*, ECLI:EU:C:1974:35, para. 45.

This principle applies in the first place to direct and overt discrimination on grounds of nationality, which is nowadays rather rare in the field of social security.[47] But it also applies to all forms of discrimination which, through the application of other distinguishing criteria, lead in fact to the same result. For the CJEU a provision of national law must be regarded as indirectly discriminatory if it is intrinsically likely to affect migrant workers more than national workers and if there is a consequent risk that it will place the former at a particular disadvantage.[48] It is not necessary, in that respect, to establish that the provision in question does in practice affect a substantially higher proportion of migrant workers. It is sufficient that it is likely to have such an effect.[49]

A clear example of such provisions are residence clauses. The CJEU repeatedly confirmed that a distinction based on residence is likely to operate mainly to the detriment of nationals of other Member States, as in the majority of cases non-residents are foreign nationals.[50]

However, the Court accepts such provisions, provided that they are appropriate for securing the attainment of a legitimate objective and do not go beyond what is necessary to attain that objective.[51] As far as the justification for indirect discrimination on grounds of nationality is concerned, the Court has stated that administrative reasons or reasons of purely economic nature cannot constitute an overriding reason in the public interest which may justify such discrimination.[52] This means that additional costs caused by that equal treatment do not constitute an acceptable justification. Nevertheless, the Court was of the opinion that a

---

47 For recent examples see: CJEU, 9 November 2006, Case C-346/05, *Chateignier*, ECLI:EU:C:2006:711 (on Belgian unemployment benefits); and CJEU, 22 June 2011, Case C-399/09, *Landtová*, ECLI:EU:C:2011:415 (on old age pensions in Czechia).

48 CJEU, 27 November 1997, Case C-57/96, *Meints*, ECLI:EU:C:1997:564, para. 45; and CJEU, 18 January 2007, Case C-332/05, *Celozzi*, ECLI:EU:C:2007:35, para. 32.

49 See, e.g. CJEU, 23 May 1996, Case C-237/94, *O'Flynn*, ECLI:EU:C:1996:206, para. 21; CJEU, 18 January 2007, Case C-332/05, *Celozzi*, ECLI:EU:C:2007:35, para. 27; and CJEU, 18 December 2014, Case C-523/13, *Larcher*, ECLI:EU:C:2014:2458, paras. 30-33.

50 See *inter alia*: CJEU, 27 November 1997, Case C-57/96, *Meints*, ECLI:EU:C:1997:564; CJEU, 11 September 2008, Case C-228/07, *Petersen*, ECLI:EU:C:2008:494; and CJEU, 5 May 2011, Case C-206/11, *Commission v. Germany*, ECLI:EU:C:2011:283.

51 CJEU, 11 September 2008, Case C-228/07, *Petersen*, ECLI:EU:C:2008:494, para. 54; CJEU, 18 December 2014, Case C-523/13, *Larcher*, ECLI:EU:C:2014:2458, para. 38; and CJEU, 14 June 2016, Case C-308/14, *Commission v. United Kingdom*, ECLI:EU:C:2016:436, para. 79.

52 CJEU, 26 January 1999, Case C-18/95, *Terhoeve*, ECLI:EU:C:1999:22, para. 45; and recently CJEU, 21 January 2016, Case C-515/14, *Commission v. Cyprus*, ECLI:EU:C:2016:30, para. 53.

national arrangement could constitute such a justification if this is dictated by reasons of economic nature in the pursuit of an objective in the public interest, such as avoiding serious damage to the financial balance of the social security system of a Member State.[53] However, the Court added that it is for the competent national authorities, when adopting a measure derogating from a principle in Union law (such as the prohibition of discrimination on grounds of nationality and the right of free movement of persons), to demonstrate, with solid and consistent data, that there are genuine risks to the balance of the social security system.[54]

Recently it was also discussed whether Member States could subject the grant of social benefits falling under the scope of Regulation No 883/2004 to Union citizens who are not economically active to the condition that those citizens possess a right to reside lawfully in the host Member State. For the Court this condition is a form of indirect discrimination on grounds of nationality, since it is more easily satisfied by nationals of that Member State. But for the Court the need to protect the finances of the host Member State justifies, in principle, the possibility to check whether residence is lawful when a social benefit is granted to, in particular, and economically inactive persons from other Member States. For the Court such a grant could have consequences for the overall level of assistance accorded by that State.[55]

The principle of equal treatment is further developed in Article 5 Regulation No 883/2004 on the equal treatment of benefits, income, facts or events. It makes sure that aspects of a person's situation which might be relevant for his/her social security rights but which are linked to another Member State, should be taken into account. For instance, if under the legislation of a Member State entitlement to a benefit (such as a supplement to an old-age pension) depends on a person being already entitled to another social security benefit (in this case a basic old-age pension), the receipt of such a benefit acquired under the legislation of another Member State should be taken into account.

In addition, EU law not only prohibits discrimination on grounds of nationality regarding social security entitlement, but also all other measures capable of hindering or rendering less attractive the exercise by EU nationals of the right to free movement, even if they apply without regard to the nationality of the workers concerned. In particular measures which have the effect of causing persons to lose, as a consequence of the exercise of their right to freedom of movement, social security advantages guaranteed to them by the legislation of a Member State have been

53 See *inter alia:* CJEU, 28 April 1998, Case C-158/96, *Kohll*, ECLI:EU:C:1998:171, para. 41; and recently CJEU, 21 January 2016, Case C-515/14, *Commission v. Cyprus*, ECLI:EU:C:2016:30, para. 53.

54 CJEU, 21 January 2016, Case C-515/14, *Commission v. Cyprus*, ECLI:EU:C:2016:30, para. 54.

55 CJEU, 14 June 2016, Case C-308/14, *Commission v. United Kingdom*, ECLI:EU:C:2016:436, paras. 75-80.

classed as obstacles.[56] This was, for instance, the case with former legislation of the Flemish region in Belgium which made affiliation to a care insurance scheme dependent on the condition of residence in that part of Belgium, denying any entitlement to migrant workers coming from other Member States and working in that part of Belgium, but residing in another part.[57] The CJEU also condemned the legislation of a Member State which levied on a worker who had transferred his/her residence in the course of one year from one Member State to another in order to take up employment there, higher social security contributions than those which would be payable, in similar circumstances, by a worker who had continued to reside throughout the year in the Member State in question.[58]

Such non-discriminatory obstacles to the free movement can be justified only if they are based on objective considerations of public interest, independent of the nationality of the persons concerned and proportionate to the legitimate objective of the national provisions.[59]

5.2.4.2 Waiving Residence Clauses

Regulation No 833/2004 also contains a general rule on the waiving of residence clauses in the legislation of the Member States (Article 7). According to this rule, cash benefits payable under the legislation of a Member State shall also be paid when the beneficiary resides in an another Member State. This is the so-called principle of the export of benefits. This holds first and foremost for benefits like old-age pensions or invalidity and long-term care benefits. Moreover, the residence of a child in another Member State should not prevent a person from being entitled to child benefits for that child either.[60]

There are, however, a number of exceptions to the export principle. One such exception is the special coordination regime that applies to the so-called special non-contributory benefits that lie between social security and social assistance. For these kinds of benefits, a State-of-residence-based coordination system is in place.[61] Another exception are unemployment benefits, which only need to be exported for a maximum of three months if the benefit-entitled person moves to another Mem-

56 CJEU, 26 January 1999, Case C-18/95, *Terhoeve*, ECLI:EU:C:1999:22, para. 39; CJEU, 5 October 1994, Case C-165/91, *van Munster*, ECLI:EU:C:1994:359, para. 27; CJEU, 1 April 2008, Case C-212/06, *Gouvernement de la Communauté française and others*, ECLI:EU:C:2008:178, paras. 45-46; and CJEU, 5 November 2014, Case C-103/13, *Somova*, ECLI:EU:C:2014:2334, para. 38.

57 CJEU, 1 April 2008, Case C-212/06, *Gouvernement de la Communauté française and others*, ECLI:EU:C:2008:178.

58 CJEU, 26 January 1999, Case C-18/95, *Terhoeve*, ECLI:EU:C:1999:22.

59 CJEU, 18 July 2006, Case C-406/04, *De Cuyper*, ECLI:EU:C:2006:491, para. 40.

60 CJEU, 5 February 2002, Case C-255/99, *Humer*, ECLI:EU:C:2002:73, para. 39.

61 Article 70 Regulation No 883/2004.

ber State in order to seek employment.[62] In other words, there is in effect a residence requirement for unemployment benefits entitlement.

5.2.4.3 Aggregation of Periods

One of the essential measures to facilitate the free movement of persons within the EU is the aggregation of periods to which Article 48 TFEU explicitly refers. For entitlement to social security benefits the legislation of the Member States sometimes requires that the person concerned has completed certain periods. These periods can be periods of insurance, of residence or of employment. For instance, for the entitlement to unemployment benefits, the legislation of Member States often requires that the unemployed person has previously worked or been insured for unemployment during a certain period of time. For entitlement to old-age pensions, too, quite often the legislation of the Member States requires that the person involved has been insured for a certain period of time for this kind of benefits.

Such requirements become problematic for the exercise of the right to free movement if under the legislation of a Member State only periods fulfilled in that Member State are taken into consideration. Persons who recently moved from one Member State to another would run the risk of having their claim for a social security benefit denied by the latter Member State because they did not fulfil the necessary periods in that Member State. Let us take the example of the legislation of Member State A which submits entitlement to an unemployment benefit to a previous insurance period of 2 years in that Member State. A person who had first worked for some years in Member State B before he/she moved to work in Member State A, but became unemployed after only 1 year in Member State A, would not be entitled to unemployment benefits in that Member State because he/she did not fulfil the required 2 years of insurance there. Such a situation would clearly be to the detriment of migrant workers and would constitute an obstacle to free movement.

Therefore, the EU social security coordination contains a general principle, worded in Article 6 Regulation No 883/2004 according to which a Member State whose legislation makes the acquisition, retention, duration or recovery of the right to benefits or the coverage by its legislation conditional upon the completion of periods of insurance, employment, self-employment or residence shall, to the necessary extent, take into account such periods completed under the legislation of any other Member State. These rules are further detailed for each of the social security branches in the provisions of Title III of Regulation No 883/2004.

5.2.4.4 Determination of the Applicable Social Security Legislation

One of the most important tasks of the coordination system is to determine the legislation applicable in cross-border situations. The relevant rules are laid down in Title II of Regulation No 883/2004 (Articles 11 to 16). We will first give an overview of the general principles underlying these rules and of the specific provisions

62 Article 64 Regulation No 883/2004.

thereof. Next, an analysis in more detail on the specific rules applicable to posted workers and in cases of activities in two or more Member States will be conducted. These rules appear to be of the utmost importance for the position of cross-border transport workers.

From the outset it should be emphasised that these rules of conflict differ from the rules of conflict applicable in labour law and that, in principle, they do not influence the latter. Consequently, it is possible that an employment contract is subject to the legislation of another Member State than the State whose social security legislation is applicable to the employee and the employer involved.

General Principles

The rules of conflict of Regulation No 883/2004 are intended, in the first place, to prevent the simultaneous application of various national legislative systems and the complications that might ensue from this. This would for instance occur if a person works in a Member State where coverage for social security is based on employment, but resides in a Member State in which such coverage is based on residence. This would result in the obligation for the worker and the employer involved to contribute via contributions to the financing of social security benefits in both Member States. The rules of conflict also aim to ensure that a person in a cross-border situation between Member States is not left without social security coverage because there is no legislation applicable to him/her.[63] The latter would occur if a person resides in a Member State in which coverage for social security is based on employment, but works in a Member State in which such coverage is based on residence.

The provisions of Title II of Regulation No 883/2004 determine to which Member State's legislation a migrant person shall be subject. For the CJEU, Title II of the Regulation forms a complete system of conflict rules which has the effect of divesting the legislature of each Member State of the power to determine at its discretion the ambit and the conditions for the application of its national legislation.[64] These rules of conflict have a binding character, meaning that national affiliation conditions are overridden if their application is such as to deprive the conflict of law rule laid down in Regulation No 883/2004 of all practical effect. For instance, the condition in the legislation of a Member State that a person is only insured for

63 CJEU, 11 June 1998, Case C-275/96, *Kuusijärvi*, ECLI:EU:C:1998:279; CJEU, 10 February 2000, Case C-202/97 *Fitzwilliam*, ECLI:EU:C:2000:75, para. 20; CJEU, 18 April 2013, Case C-548/11, *Mulders*, ECLI:EU:C:2013:249, para. 39; and CJEU, 25 October 2018, Case C-451/17, *'Walltopia' AD*, ECLI:EU:C:2018:861, para. 41.

64 CJEU, 10 July 1986, Case C-60/85, *Luijten*, ECLI:EU:C:1986:307, para. 14; CJEU, 25 February 2015, Case C-623/13, *de Ruyter*, ECLI:EU:C:2015:123, para. 35; CJEU, 26 October 2016, Case C-269/15, *Hoogstad*, ECLI:EU:C:2016:802, para. 39; and CJEU, 25 October 2018, Case C-451/17, *'Walltopia' AD*, ECLI:EU:C:2018:861, para. 48.

social security if he/she resides in the territory of that Member State, will be overruled by the provision in Article 11(3)(a) Regulation No 883/2004 which, in principle, obliges a Member State to insure all persons economically active in its territory, even if they reside in another Member State.
Another starting point of the conflict rules of Regulation No 883/2004 is their exclusive effect or the single-State principle. It means that the persons to whom that Regulation applies are to be subject to the legislation of a single Member State only, which therefore excludes any possibility of an overlap of the national legislation of several Member States with regard to one and the same period. This principle is intended to avoid double insurance and double contributions. Indeed, the principle that the legislation of a single Member State applies in matters of social security aims at avoiding the complications which may ensue from the simultaneous application of a number of national legislative systems and at eliminating the unequal treatment which, for persons moving within the European Union, would be the consequence of a partial or total overlap of the applicable legislation.[65]

Rules on the Determination of the Applicable Legislation

The basis of these rules of conflict is the territorial application of the social security law of the Member State where the work is carried out (the State-of-employment principle: *lex loci laboris*). It means that a person employed in the territory of one Member State shall be subject to the social security legislation of that State, even if he/she resides in the territory of another Member State or if his employer is registered in another Member State.[66]
The choice of this principle is inspired by the legal context in which the European social security coordination is applied: to ensure the free movement of workers and to preclude discrimination based on nationality by the Member State where the migrating worker is employed (Article 45(2) TFEU). The main reason for this State-of-employment principle is, indeed, to ensure equal treatment of all people working on the territory of a Member State, in accordance with the right to equal treatment for migrant workers. This prohibition does not only hold for all conditions of employment and remuneration that apply in the State of employment, but also for social security provisions.[67] So, the State-of-employment principle is an expression of the premise that a migrating worker is entitled to the same rights in the State of employment as workers of that Member State.[68]

---

65 CJEU, 15 February 2000, Case C-34/98, *Commission v. France*, ECLI:EU:C:2000:84, para. 46; CJEU, 25 February 2015, Case C-623/13, *de Ruyter*, ECLI:EU:C:2015:123, paras. 36-37; CJEU, 26 October 2016, Case C-269/15, *Hoogstad*, ECLI:EU:C:2016:802, paras. 35-36; and CJEU, 6 February 2018, Case C-359/16, *Altun*, ECLI:EU:2018:63, para. 29.

66 Article 11 Regulation No 883/2004.

67 See, e.g. CJEU, 15 January 1986, Case C-41/84, *Pinna*, ECLI:EU:C:1986:1.

68 The relevance of the principle of equal treatment to the rules governing the determination of the applicable legislation was underlined by the CJEU in, among other judg-

Nonetheless, the application of the State-of-employment principle does not imply that a migrant worker is invariably entitled to social security benefits provided in the State of employment. If such a person resides in another Member State (e.g. frontier workers) then, for certain benefits (e.g. coverage of medical costs), he or she shall be entitled first and foremost in accordance with the legislation of the State of residence (albeit at the expense of the State of employment).[69]
However, the provisions of Regulation No 883/2004 contain a number of exceptions and special rules. Civil servants, for instance, are subject to the social security of the Member State for which they work, even when they are working on the territory of another Member State (Article 11(3)(b)). Article 11 Regulation No 883/2004 also contains specific rules for seamen (Article 11(4)) and for airline personnel (Article 11(5)). Particularly relevant for the transport sector are the special rules for posting and for the cases of simultaneous employment in two or more Member States. When a worker is posted by his/her employer to pursue temporarily on behalf of his/her employer activities in another Member State, or when a self-employed person goes to pursue temporarily his/her activities in another Member State, they remain, pursuant to Article 12 Regulation No 883/2004, subject to the social security legislation of the Member State in which they normally pursue their activities. For cases of simultaneous employment in two or more Member States the provisions of Article 13 Regulation No 883/2004 refer to the State of residence, provided that occupational activities are pursued in that country. In a number of other cases, it is the registered office or the place of business of the employing undertaking which determines to which country's social security legislation the person in question is subject.
The situations of posting and of simultaneous employment in two or more Member States will be discussed in more detail in the next section.
Persons to which Article 11 (3)(a) to (d) do not apply, such as those who are not (or no longer) economically active, the State-of-residence principle applies (Article 11(3)(e)).[70] The category of economically inactive persons is understood to include

ments: CJEU, 9 March 2006, Case C-493/04, *Piatkowski*, ECLI:EU:C:2006:167, para. 19; CJEU, 1 April 2008, Case C-212/06, *Gouvernement de la Communauté française and others*, ECLI:EU:C:2008:178, para. 48; and CJEU, 3 April 2008, Case C-103/06, *Derouin*, ECLI:EU:C:2008:185, para. 20. See also recital 17 of the preamble to Regulation No 883/2004, stating that: "With a view to guaranteeing the equality of treatment of all persons occupied in the territory of a Member State as effectively as possible, it is appropriate to determine as the legislation applicable, as a general rule, that of the Member State in which the person concerned pursues his/her activity as an employed or self-employed person." This was explicitly confirmed in CJEU, 6 September 2018, Case C-527/16, *Alpenrind*, ECLI:EU:C:2018:669, para. 98.

69 See Article 17 of Regulation No 883/2004.

70 For a recent application of this provision to a seaman working for an employer established in a Member State on a vessel flying the flag of a third State and travelling out-

pensioners (Article 11(2)). Unemployed frontier workers are likewise subject to the legislation of the State of residence (Article 11(3)(c)). However, this does not mean that inactive persons are exclusively entitled to social security benefits under the legislation of their State of residence. Retired persons who do not receive their pension from their State of residence, for example, are also subject to the legislation of the State which does pay their pension as far as sickness benefits in cash, such as long-term care benefits, are concerned. Consequently, these Member States must export those benefits.[71]

Finally, the implementation of the conflict rules in Articles 11 to 15 Regulation No 883/2004 does not always lead to appropriate results. Therefore, Article 16 offers the competent authorities of the Member States to provide, by common agreement, the possibility of exceptions to these rules. The only condition is that the exception is in the interest of the persons or categories of persons concerned.[72] The possibility offered by this provision is often used to extend the period of posting, sometimes up to 5 years. The agreement must have the consent of the institutions of both Member States involved.

5.2.5 Applicability and Enforcement of the Law in the Road Transport Sector

Particularly relevant for the road transport sector are the special rules applicable to posted employed and self-employed persons, as well as the special rules in cases of simultaneous employment in two or more Member States. Indeed, the inherent cross-border aspect of the international road transport very often leads to a situation in which these rules are applicable. In addition, it appears that in practice these rules are often used by the employers to make sure that they can pay social security contributions in a Member State with lower rates of contributions than the rates of the Member States in which the activities are carried out via so-called letterbox companies. Such companies can be defined as legal entities established on paper in a Member State without a substantial link to genuine economic activities carried out in that Member State, enabling "regime shopping" for lower taxes, wages, labour standards and social contributions.[73]

The applicable rules on posting and on simultaneous employment in two or more Member States and their implementation will now be discussed in more detail.

---

side of the territory of the EU: CJEU, 8 May 2019, Case C-631/17, *SF*, ECLI:EU:C:2019:381.

71 See Article 29 of Regulation No 883/2004.

72 In December 2013 the Administrative Commission published a 'Practical Guide on the applicable legislation', more specifically on the rules on posting and on the pursuit of an activity in two or more Member States. The guide can be found at: http://ec.europa.eu/social/main.jsp?catId=868. It is further referred to as 'Practical Guide'.

73 M. Houwerzijl, 'Letterbox strategies to avoid social security contributions', ETUC, *The hunters game: how policy can change to spot and sink letterbox-type practices* (December 2016), 49.

5.2.5.1 *Special Rules Applicable to Posted Employed and Self-Employed Persons*

Why Such a "Special Rule" for Posted Workers?

The derogation of the State-of-employment principle, which is currently the most disputed one, concerns the rules applicable to the posting of workers from one Member State to another. Article 12 provides for *"special rules"* applicable in the case of posting.[74] During 24 months at the most, a posted employee or a self-employed person seconding himself/herself remains subject to the social security legislation of the Member State to which he/she was subject before the posting. Contrary to the provisions of Posting Directive 96/71 this concerns the entire social security legislation of the Member State in question, and therefore the social security legislation of the host Member State does not apply for this period. As regards the employees, this provision specifies that the person concerned may not be sent to replace another posted worker. As far as the self-employed are concerned, this provision only applies if they go and carry out similar activities in the host State.

Principally, the intention is to avoid that, as a result of a strict application of the State-of-employment principle, a short and temporary employment situation in a certain Member State would lead to an equally short and temporary change of the applicable social security law. Not only could this lead to administrative complications, but also to insurance breaks that could work out badly for the person concerned. The application of the State-of-employment principle would then be an obstacle to the free movement of workers and service providers.[75] For short postings it is indeed in the interest of workers to remain affiliated to the social security system of the country where they normally work rather than to interrupt this in return for acquiring only small benefits rights under the system of the host State. During that short period, it is in the employer's interest to be able to continue paying social contributions in the State where he/she normally carries out his/her activities in order to avoid extra costs and administrative complications.[76] It is also in the interest of the social security institutions of the Member States, to avoid administrative complications caused by short periods of coverage by temporarily posted workers.

---

74 The provisions in Regulation No 883/2004 do not differ substantially from those in the former Regulation No 1408/71, more specifically Article 14. The case law of the Court of Justice on the posting provisions of this old Regulation continues to be relevant as well.

75 CJEU, 17 December 1970, Case C-35/70, *Manpower*, ECLI:EU:C:1970:120, paras. 10-12; CJEU, 10 February 2000, Case C-202/97, *Fitzwilliam*, ECLI:EU:C:2000:75, paras. 28-31; CJEU, 9 November 2000, Case C-404/98, *Plum*, ECLI:EU:C:2000:607, para. 19; and CJEU, 6 February 2018, Case C-359/16, *Altun*, ECLI:EU:2018:63, para. 32.

76 Houwerzijl (2016), 56.

Conditions to be Met in Order to Prevent Abuse of the Posting Provisions
Nonetheless, the Court explicitly regarded the posting provisions as an exception to the State-of-employment principle and held that they can only be applied if a number of conditions is met.[77] After all, this derogation means that the worker concerned will not be able to invoke the right to equal treatment with the workers of the Member State where he/she works. In addition, the application of the social security system of a Member State other than that where the activities are carried out could lead to competitive advantages for the sending company *vis-à-vis* the undertakings established in the host Member State. The special rules with regard to posting in Regulation No 883/2004 hover between the application of the State-of-employment principle as an expression of the principle of equal treatment and the removal of legal and administrative obstacles to the free movement of service providers. The balance between those two points of departure must be preserved by observance of a series of specific conditions to be met with a view to allowing exceptions to the State-of-employment principle as laid down by the Union legislator and interpreted by the Court of Justice. These conditions must prevent the posting provisions in Regulation No 883/2004 from being used in situations for which they were not meant and in which the employers or the posted self-employed persons try to avoid paying social security contributions in the Member State in which the work is carried out. The above-mentioned use of letterbox companies is the most widespread way to reach the latter goal.
Some of these conditions follow from the applicable provisions themselves, among which the provisions of Article 14 Regulation No 987/2009. These rules are further specified in Decision No A2 of the Administrative Commission for the coordination of social security systems.[78] Those could be summarised as follows.

Maximum Period of 24 Months
In the first place, there is the temporary character of the posting. The duration to be expected may not exceed 24 months.[79] This is quite a long period, the more so

77 CJEU, 17 December 1970, Case C-35/70, *Manpower*, ECLI:EU:C:1970:120, para. 10; CJEU, 10 February 2000, Case C-202/97, *Fitzwilliam*, ECLI:EU:C:2000:75, paras. 28 and 30; CJEU, 9 November 2000, Case C-404/98, *Plum*, ECLI:EU:C:2000:607, para. 14; and CJEU, 6 September 2018, Case C-527/16, *Alpenrind*, ECLI:EU:C:2018:669, para. 95.

78 Decision No A2 of 12 June 2009 concerning the interpretation of Article 12 of Regulation (EC) No 883/2004 of the European Parliament and of the Council on the legislation applicable to posted workers and self-employed workers temporarily working outside the competent State, OJ 2010, C 106/5. Decisions of the Administrative Commission are not directly binding but give an authoritative interpretation of the relevant provisions of the regulations and build on the case law of the CJEU.

79 The Administrative Commission decided that all periods of posting completed under the regulation shall be taken into consideration for the calculation of the uninterrupted posting period, so that the total period of the uninterrupted posting completed

because from the European Commission's "impact assessment" of the proposal for a change of the Posting Directive it is apparent that the average duration only amounts to 4 months.[80] The Practical Guide specifies that once a worker has ended a period of posting, no fresh period of posting for the same worker, the same undertaking and the same Member State can be authorised until at least two months have elapsed from the date of expiry of the previous posting period.

Prior Affiliation to the Legislation of the Sending State

Still, it is possible that the posted employee is recruited with a view to being posted to another Member State.[81] Thus, it is not required that the worker was employed in the posting undertaking immediately before his/her posting. But before being posted the worker concerned must have been subject to the legislation of the State in which his/her employer is established.[82] Regarding the requirement that the posted worker must have been subject to the legislation of the sending State immediately before the start of his/her employment, Decision A2 states that, as an indication, having been subject to the legislation of the Member State in which the employer is established for at least one month can be considered as meeting this requirement. Employment with any employer in the sending State meets this requirement. The condition is also fulfilled by students or pensioners or someone who is insured due to residence and subject to the social security system of the sending State.[83] Shorter periods would require a case-by-case evaluation taking account of all the other factors involved. If such previous period of insurance in the posting State is not fulfilled, the worker will be subject to the legislation of the receiving Member State.

The Continuation of a "Direct Relationship" Between the Employer and the Posted Worker

An additional condition is the continuation during the period of employment in another Member State of a "direct relationship" between the undertaking established in a Member State and the workers it has posted to the territory of another

under the application of both Regulations cannot exceed 24 months. See Decision No A3 of 17 December 2009 concerning the aggregation of uninterrupted posting periods completed under Council Regulation (EEC) No 1408/71 and Regulation (EC) No 883/2004 of the European Parliament and of the Council, OJ 2010, C149/3.

80 Document SWD(2016) 52 final of 8 March 2016.

81 This is, amongst other things, important for posting by temporary employment agencies. See: CJEU, 10 February 2000, Case C-202/97, *Fitzwilliam*, ECLI:EU:C:2000:75.

82 See expressly Article 14(1) Regulation No 987/2009. See also: CJEU, 25 October 2018, Case C-451/17, '*Walltopia*' *AD*, ECLI:EU:C:2018:861.

83 Practical Guide, 11.

Member State.[84] The CJEU stated that in order to ascertain the existence of such a direct relationship, the circumstances of the employment must show that during the posting period the employee works under the authority of that enterprise.[85] Decision A2 of the Administrative Commission further clarifies that, in order to establish whether a direct relationship between the worker and the employer continues to exist, assuming therefore that the worker continues to be under the authority of the employer who posted him/her, a number of elements have to be taken into account, including responsibility for recruitment, an employment contract, remuneration (without prejudice to possible agreements between the employer in the sending State and the undertaking in the State of employment on payment of the workers), dismissal, and the competence to determine the nature of the work or to impose disciplinary sanctions.

It also means that if the worker concludes an employment contract with the company in the Member State to which he is posted, the posting provisions are not applicable (any longer) and the social security legislation of the latter Member State will be applicable.

Habitual Activity in the Sending State

Furthermore, the sending undertaking must normally carry out activities and be habitually active on the territory of the State in which it is established.[86] In this respect Article 14(2) Regulation No 987/2009 specifies that its activities must be substantial and go beyond purely internal management. With the requirement of significant activities in the sending State by the sending company the Court of Justice clearly wanted to avoid that so-called letterbox companies would use the posting provisions to escape the application of the social security legislation of the Member State where they usually do carry out their activities. Indeed, by a fictitious construction they obviously would want to subject themselves to the (probably cheaper) social security legislation of another Member State.

For the posting of self-employed persons similar conditions apply. The Court of Justice stated that self-employed persons too must be able to prove that they usually pursue activities in the capacity as self-employed workers in the sending State. For the Court this obligation means that the person concerned usually carries out significant activities in his/her Member State of establishment.[87] Article 14(3) Regulation No 987/2009 further states that a self-employed person must have already

84 CJEU, 10 February 2000, Case C-202/97, *Fitzwilliam*, ECLI:EU:C:2000:75, para. 24; CJEU, 26 January 2006, Case C-2/05, *Herbosch Kiere*, ECLI:EU:C:2006:69, para. 19; and CJEU, 6 February 2018, Case C-359/16, *Altun,* ECLI:EU:2018:63, para. 34.

85 CJEU, 10 February 2000, Case C-202/97, *Fitzwilliam*, ECLI:EU:C:2000:75, para. 24.

86 CJEU, 10 February 2000, Case C-202/97, *Fitzwilliam*, ECLI:EU:C:2000:75, paras. 22, 23 and 43; and CJEU, 6 February 2018, Case C-359/16, *Altun,* ECLI:EU: 2018:63, para. 34.

87 CJEU, 30 March 2000, Case C-178/97, *Banks*, ECLI:EU:C:2000:169, paras. 25-27.

pursued his/her activity for some time before the date on which he/she wishes to take advantage of the posting provision. Such person also must continue to fulfil in the Member State in which he/she is established the requirements for the pursuit of his/her activities in order to be able to pursue these on his/her return.
In addition, Decision A2 of the Administrative Commission stipulates that in order to determine whether an employer ordinarily performs substantial activities in the territory of the Member State in which he/she is established, the competent institution in the latter is required to examine all the criteria characterising the activities carried out by that employer, including the place where the undertaking has its registered office and administration, the number of administrative staff working in the Member State in which it is established as well as in the other Member State, the place where posted workers are recruited and the place where the majority of contracts with clients are concluded, the law applicable to the contracts concluded by the undertaking with its workers, on the one hand, and with its clients, on the other, the turnover during an appropriately typical period in each Member State concerned and the number of contracts performed in the sending State. This is not an exhaustive list, as the criteria should be adapted to each specific case and take account of the nature of the activities carried out by the undertaking in the State in which it is established.
As for posted self-employed persons, Decision A2 further specifies that the fulfilment of the requirements in the Member State where the person is established is assessed on criteria such as having use of office space, paying taxes, having a professional card and a VAT number or being registered with chambers of commerce or professional bodies. It also says that, as an indication, the self-employed person must have pursued his/her activity in the sending State for at least two months before the posting to the receiving State. Shorter periods would require a case-by-case evaluation taking account of all the other factors involved.

Similar Activities for Self-Employed Posted Workers
Pursuant to Article 12(2) of Regulation No 883/2004 a posted self-employed person must pursue a "similar activity" in the receiving State. When determining whether a person is going to another Member State to pursue a "similar" activity to that pursued in the posting State, account must be taken of the actual nature of the activity. It does not matter how this type of activity is categorised in the State of employment, i.e. whether it is designated as employment or self-employment.[88]
The Practical Guide indicates that in order to determine if the work is "similar", the work which the person sets out to perform must be determined in advance, before departure from the posting State. The self-employed person should be able to prove this, for example by producing contracts regarding the work. In general, self-employed activity in the same sector would be regarded as pursuing a similar activity. However, it must be recognised that even within sectors, work can be very diverse and it may not always be possible to apply this general rule. For instance, a

88 CJEU, 30 March 2000, Case C-178/97, *Banks*, ECLI:EU:C:2000:169, paras. 20-23.

person who normally works as a self-employed carpenter in State X and moves to State Y where he/she works as a self-employed butcher, would not be regarded as pursuing a "similar activity" as the employment in State Y bears no similarity to his/her work in State X. However, a self-employed person who runs a construction company in State X and accepts commissions relating to the installation of piping and wiring systems, may benefit from the posting provisions since this activity can be regarded as similar.[89]

No Replacement for Another Posted Worker

In order to prevent permanent tasks in an enterprise from being carried out regularly by posted workers, replacement of posted workers performing the same tasks is not allowed. This prohibition mainly aims at preventing abuse of the posting provisions by undertakings which establish a kind of rotation system of successively posted workers coming from Member States where the social security contributions are lower than in the country of employment. The CJEU recently specified that if a worker, who is posted by his employer to carry out work in another Member State, is replaced by another worker posted by another employer, the latter employee must be regarded as being 'sent to replace another person', within the meaning of Article 12(1) of Regulation No 883/2004. As a consequence, she/he cannot benefit from the special rules laid down in that provision in order to remain subject to the legislation of the Member State in which his employer normally carries out its activities. The fact that the employers of the two workers concerned have their registered offices in the same Member State or that they may have personal or organisational links is irrelevant in that respect.[90]

Only in exceptional circumstances it would be possible to replace a person who has already been posted, provided the period allowed for the posting has not been completed. An example where this might arise would be a situation where a worker was posted for 20 months, became seriously ill after 10 months and needed to be replaced. In that situation it would be reasonable to allow another person to be posted for the remaining 10 months of the agreed period.

The posted worker cannot be replaced immediately in receiving Member State A by a posted worker from the same undertaking of posting Member State B, nor by a posted worker from a different undertaking based in Member State B or a posted worker from an undertaking based in Member State C. So, if an activity in the receiving undertaking of Member State A was previously pursued by a posted worker from posting Member State B, this worker cannot be replaced immediately by a newly posted worker from any Member State. It does not matter from which posting undertaking or Member State the newly posted worker comes.

When a posted worker is immediately replaced by another posted worker the newly posted worker shall be subject to the social security legislation of the State of work

89 Practical Guide, 15.

90 CJEU, 6 September 2018, Case C-527/16, *Alpenrind*, ECLI:EU:C:2018:669, para. 100.

from the beginning of his/her activity because the exception of Article 12 of Regulation No 883/2004 does no longer apply to him/her.[91]

Situations in Which the Application of the Provisions on Posting Are Ruled Out

The Practical Guide lists a number of situations which rule out *a priori* the application of the provisions on posting.[92] This is in particular the case when:

- the undertaking to which the worker has been posted places him/her at the disposal of another undertaking in the Member State in which it is situated;
- the undertaking to which the worker is posted places him/her at the disposal of an undertaking situated in another Member State;
- the worker is recruited in a Member State in order to be sent by an undertaking situated in a second Member State to an undertaking in a third Member State without the requirements of prior attachment to the social security system of the posting State being satisfied;
- the worker is recruited in one Member State by an undertaking situated in a second Member State in order to work in the first Member State;
- the worker is posted to replace another posted person;
- the worker has concluded a labour contract with the undertaking to which he/she is posted.

These exclusions are necessary to prevent wrongful use of the posting provisions.

5.2.5.2 Special Rules in Cases of Pursuit of Activities in Two or More Member States

Particularly relevant for the international road transport sector are the special rules applicable in cases where employed or self-employed persons pursue activities in two or more Member States. These rules are laid down in Article 13 of Regulation No 883/2004. Just like all the rules for determining the applicable legislation, these rules are designed to ensure that the social security legislation of only one Member State is applicable at the time.

Distinction Between Posting and Pursuit of Activities in Two or More Member States

According to Article 14(5) Regulation No 987/2009 a person who “normally pursues an activity as an employed person in two or more Member States” shall refer to a person who simultaneously, or in alteration, for the same undertaking or employer or for various undertakings or employers, exercises one or more separate activities in two or more Member States. The Practical Guide gives as an example of persons working simultaneously in two or more Member States, e.g. international road transport workers driving through different Member States to deliver

91 Practical Guide, 13-14.

92 Practical Guide, 12-13.

goods.[93] In general, it can be said that "normally pursuing activities in two or more Member States" refers to coinciding activities which are a normal aspect of the working pattern and the fact that there is no gap between the activities in one Member State or the other. Article 13 Regulation No 883/2004 also applies in case of activities that are performed in alternation, consisting in successive work assignments carried out in different Member States, one after another.

As for self-employed persons, these are persons who simultaneously or in alternation pursue one or more separate self-employed activities, irrespective of the nature of those activities, in two or more Member States (Article 14(6) Regulation No 987/2009).

For the purpose of distinguishing between the situation of posting and the situation of pursuing activities simultaneously in two or more Member States (so between the scope of application of Article 12 and Article 13 of Regulation No 883/2004), Article 14(7) Regulation No 987/2004 specifies that the duration of the activity in one or more other Member States (whether this is permanent or of an *ad hoc* or temporary nature) shall be decisive. For these purposes, an overall assessment shall be made of all the relevant facts including, in particular, in the case of an employed person, the place of work as defined in the employment contract.

Moreover, it is not always clear whether an employee who works under successive employment contracts in various Member States, must be considered as working during the term of each of those contracts only on the territory of one of those States at a time, or whether such person is concurrently working on the territory of more than one Member State. In the first case this person would be successively subject to the social security legislation of each of the Member States in which he/she is working (implementation of Article 11(3)(a)) Regulation No 883/2004). In the latter case, the applicable legislation would be determined by the provisions of Article 13 Regulation No 883/2004, which may lead to a different applicable legislation. With regard to this issue the CJEU decided in its judgment in *Format* that a person who, under successive employment contracts in which the place of employment is said to be situated on the territory of several Member States, but in fact works during the term of each of those contracts only on the territory of one of those States at a time, cannot fall within the concept of "a person normally employed in the territory of two or more Member States".[94]

Rules to Determine the Applicable Legislation in Cases of Pursuit of Activities in Two or More Member States

With regard to employed persons the starting point is that a person who normally pursues an activity as an employed person in two or more Member States shall be subject to the legislation of the Member State of residence if he/she pursues a substantial part of his/her activity in that Member State (Article 13(1)(a) Regulation No 883/2004).

93 Practical Guide, 24.

94 CJEU, 4 October 2012, Case C-115/11, *Format*, ECLI:EU:C:2012:606.

If he/she does not pursue a substantial part of his/her activity in the Member State of residence, then a number of specific rules apply (Article 13(1)(b) Regulation No 883/2004). This person will be subject to the legislation of the Member State in which the registered office or place of business of the undertaking or employer is situated if he/she is employed by one undertaking or employer. He/she shall be subject to the legislation of the Member State in which the registered office or place of business of the undertakings or employers is situated if he/she is employed by two or more undertakings or employers having their registered office or place of business in only one Member State. If he/she is employed by two or more undertakings or employers having their registered office or place of business in two Member States, one of which is the Member State of residence, then the employee involved will be subject to the legislation of the Member State in which the registered office or place of business of the undertaking or employer is situated other than the Member State of residence. And finally, if he/she is employed by two or more undertakings or employers, at least two of which have their registered office or place of business in different Member States other than the Member State of residence, he/she shall be subject to the legislation of the Member State of residence.

For instance: a lorry driver is employed by two transport companies whose registered offices are in the Netherlands and he/she has never worked in the Netherlands. The companies provide lorry drivers to various international transport companies. This driver does not work in the Netherlands, nor in Poland where he/she resides. As he/she does not pursue a substantial part of his activity in the Member State of residence, and receives all his/her income from the companies in the Netherlands, the legislation of the Member State where his/her employer has its registered office (outside the Member State of residence, i.e. the Netherlands), applies.

With regard to a person who normally pursues an activity as a self-employed person in two or more Member States the following rules apply (Article 13(2) Regulation No 883/2004). He/she shall be subject to the legislation of the Member State of residence if he/she pursues a substantial part of his/her activity in that Member State. If this person does not reside in one of the Member States in which he/she pursues a substantial part of his/her activity, he/she shall be subject to the legislation of the Member State in which the centre of interest of his/her activities is situated.

Article 13(3) Regulation No 883/2004 further specifies that a person who normally simultaneously pursues an activity as an employed person and an activity as a self-employed person in different Member States shall be subject to the legislation of the Member State in which he/she pursues an activity as an employed person or, if he/she pursues such an activity in two or more Member States, to the legislation determined in accordance with Article 13(1) Regulation No 883/2004. A person who is employed as a civil servant by one Member State and who pursues an activity as an employed person and/or as a self-employed person in one or more other Member States shall be subject to the legislation of the Member State to which the administration employing him/her is subject (Article 13(4) Regulation No 883/2004).

Finally, Article 13(5) Regulation No 883/2004 states that, for the purposes of the legislation determined in accordance with these provisions, the persons referred to in Article 13 Regulation No 883/2004 shall be treated as though they were pursuing all their activities as employed or self-employed persons and were receiving all their income in the Member State concerned. Pursuant to Article 14(5b) Regulation No 987/2009, marginal activities shall be disregarded when it comes to determining the applicable legislation under Article 13 Regulation No 883/2004.

Further Clarifications of the Concepts Used

Registered office or place of business

Article 14(5)(a) Regulation No 987/2009 further clarifies that "registered office or place of business" shall refer to the registered office or place of business where the essential decisions of the undertaking are taken and where the functions of its central administration are carried out.

As a general principle, letterbox operations, where the social insurance of the employees is linked to a purely administrative company without having actual decision-making powers, should not be accepted as satisfying the requirements in this area. As a specification of the definition in Article 14(5a) of Regulation No 987/2009, the Practical Guide gives the following criteria that could be taken into account:

- the place where the undertaking has its registered office and its administration;
- the length of time that the undertaking has been established in the Member State;
- the number of administrative staff working in the office in question;
- the place where the majority of contracts with clients are concluded;
- the office which dictates company policy and operational matters;
- the place where the principal financial functions, including banking, are located;
- the place designated under EU regulations as the place responsible for managing and maintaining records in relation to regulatory requirements of the particular industry in which the undertaking is engaged;
- the place where the workers are recruited.

The Practical Guide continues to say that if, having considered these criteria, it would still not be possible to eliminate the possibility that the registered office is a letterbox company, then the person concerned should be made subject to the legislation of the Member State in which the establishment is situated with which he or she has the closest connection in terms of the performance of employed activity. That establishment shall be considered to be the registered office or place of business employing the person concerned for the purposes of the social security coordination regulations. In this determination, it should not be forgotten that this establishment must actually employ the person concerned, and that a direct relationship must exist with the person.

Substantial part of employed or self-employed activity

As regards the issue of determining what is a "substantial part of employed or self-employed activity" pursued in a Member State, Article 14(8) Regulation No 987/2009 specifies that it means a quantitatively substantial part of all the activities of the employed or self-employed person pursued there, without this necessarily being the major part of those activities. To determine whether a substantial part of the activities is pursued in a Member State, the following indicative criteria shall be taken into account: in the case of an employed activity, the working time and/or the remuneration; and in the case of a self-employed activity, the turnover, working time, number of services rendered and/or income. In terms of an overall assessment, a share of less than 25% in respect of the criteria mentioned above shall be an indicator that a substantial part of the activities is not being pursued in the relevant Member State.

Centre of interest

For the purposes of the application of Article 13(2)(b) Regulation No 883/2004, the "centre of interest" of the activities of a self-employed person shall be determined by taking account of all the aspects of that person's occupational activities, notably the place where the person's fixed and permanent place of business is located, the habitual nature or the duration of the activities pursued, the number of services rendered, and the intention of the person concerned as apparent from all the circumstances (Article 14(9) Regulation No 987/2009).

Situation planned in the following 12 calendar months

Finally, Article 14(10) Regulation No 987/2009 says that for the determination of the applicable legislation under paragraphs 8 and 9, the institutions concerned shall take into account the situation planned for the following 12 calendar months.

5.2.5.3 Implementation of These Rules on International Transport Workers

The Practical Guide provides assistance in dealing with the particular working arrangements which apply in the international transport sector.[95] First it indicates that where it is clear from an initial assessment that a worker is substantially employed in his/her State of residence, the legislation of that Member State will apply to this worker. In assessing the "substantial part of the activity" for this group of workers it is considered that working time is the most appropriate criterion on which to base a decision. However, it is also recognised that dividing the activity between two or more Member States may not always be as straightforward for a transport worker as for those in "standard" cross-border employment. Accordingly, a closer examination of the working arrangements may be needed in order to deter-

95 Practical Guide, 29-30.

mine the applicable legislation in such cases when the working hours in the Member State of residence are difficult to estimate. Some transport workers have set work patterns, routes to be travelled and estimated journey times.

A person seeking a decision on applicable legislation should make a reasonable case (e.g. by providing duty rosters or travel calendars or other information) to apportion the activity between time spent working in the State of residence and time spent working in other Member States. Where the working hours spent in the Member State of residence are not available, or when it is not clear from the circumstances as a whole that a substantial part of the activity is spent in the Member State of residence, then another method other than working hours can be used for determining whether or not a substantial part of the activity is pursued in the Member State of residence. In this regard it is suggested that the activity is broken down into different elements or incidents and a judgment concerning the extent of activity in the State of residence is made on the basis of the number of elements occurring there as a percentage of the total number of incidents in a given period (the assessment should be based as far as possible on work patterns over a 12-months period).

In the case of road transport, the focus could be on the loading and unloading of cargo and the different countries in which this takes place, as illustrated in the following example. A truck driver lives in Germany and is employed by a Dutch transport company. The worker's activities are carried out mainly in the Netherlands, Belgium, Germany and Austria. In a given period, e.g. a week, he/she loads the lorry 5 times and offloads it 5 times. In total there are 10 elements (5 loadings, 5 off-loadings). During this week he/she loads and offloads once in Germany, his/her state of residence. This amounts to 2 elements which equals 20% of the total and is thus an indication that there is not a substantial part of activity pursued in the State of residence. Therefore, Dutch legislation will apply as the Netherlands is the Member State of the employer's registered office. Given the broad range of working arrangements that can apply in this sector, it would be impossible to suggest a system of assessment which would suit all circumstances. When assessing the substantial part of the activity, the regulations specifically provide for an assessment of working time and remuneration. However, the regulations provide for these to be used as indicators in the framework of an overall assessment of a person's situation. Accordingly, it is possible for the designated institutions responsible for determining the applicable legislation to use measures other than those outlined in the regulations and the Practical Guide which they consider to be more suited to the particular situations with which they are dealing.

The Practical Guide also recognises that working arrangements, e.g. for international transport workers, can be subject to frequent change. It would not be practical, nor in the interests of the persons concerned to review the applicable legislation every time their duty roster changed. Accordingly, once a decision is made on the applicable legislation this should, in principle and provided that the information given by the employer or person concerned was truthful to the best of their knowledge, not be subject to review for a period of at least the following 12 months. This is without prejudice to the right of an institution to review a decision it has made where it considers that such a review is warranted. The objective is to ensure legal stability and avoid the so-called "yo-yo" effect, especially for highly mobile workers, such as those in the international transport sector. Therefore, the applicable legislation under Article 13(1) of Regulation No 883/2004 shall be determined and in principle remain stable for the following 12 calendar months. In addition, the assumed future situation for the following 12 calendar months shall be taken into account. If there are no indications that the work patterns will change substantially in the following 12 months, the designated institution shall base the overall assessment on the contracts and working performance of the past 12 months and use this to project the situation for the following 12 months.

5.2.5.4 Abuses of the Rules on Posting and in Cases of Activities in Two or More Member States

The rules governing the determination of the applicable social security legislation in cases of posting or of activities pursued in two or more Member States are not always easy to implement, due in particular to a number of grey zones in defining the relevant criteria, such as "organic link", "habitual activity", "substantial activity", "replacement", "registered office", "place of business" and "centre of interest". Employers often make use of these difficulties to apply and interpret these rules or even to circumvent them in order to make their workers subject to the social security system of a Member State where the contributions are lower than in the Member State in which the workers concerned carry out their activities. These include posting through letterbox companies, letterbox companies employing workers who are pursuing activities in more than two Member States, the posting of workers followed by the simultaneous employment of these workers in two or more Member States, false declarations of posting, long-term postings, repeated replacements of posted workers, bogus self-employed persons, non-payment of social security contributions in the sending country, pyramids of sub-contractors that make controls difficult, lack of cooperation between the competent social security institutions of the Member States concerned, etc.

A notorious case of such abuse of the applicable rules in order to benefit from the payment of lower social security contributions is the *Bogdan* case. In this case an Irish temporary employment agency, but with its registered office in Cyprus, had sent a construction worker, who resided in Poland, successively to clients in several other Member States. This company did not pursue substantial activities in Cyprus. But it claimed that the social security legislation of Cyprus was applicable to this Polish worker and that consequently it had to pay (relatively low) social security contributions in Cyprus. The company based its claim on the provision of Article 13(1)(b)(i) of Regulation No 883/2004. The case was brought before the European Court of Justice (Case C-189/14), which eventually did not rule in this case because it was withdrawn by the referring Cypriot judge. It turned out that the company had taken the case to court without the consent of Mr Bogdan, only to have the confirmation of the CJEU that Cypriot social security was applicable.

5.2.5.5 Control Measures: The Role of the A1 Certificate

What Is an A1 Certificate?

Adequate control measures are crucial to guarantee a correct application of these rules. The Portable Document (PD) A1 (former E101 certificate) plays a key role in verifying whether or not the conditions for derogations of the State-of-employment principle are met. This is a document issued by the competent body of a Member State which proves that the persons concerned remain subject to the legislation of that Member State.[96] The body issuing the document is obliged to assess the relevant facts correctly and must guarantee the accuracy of the data that have been entered.[97] Thus, it could be an important instrument in combating fraud and abuse. However, it remains a unilateral document, the issuance of which only depends on the decision of the competent institution of the issuing Member State. But the implementation of the above rules on posting and of the pursuance of activities in two or more Member States, not only depends on factors and criteria that are to be verified in the issuing Member State, but also in other Member States such as the receiving Member States. Such criteria that come to mind are: the pursuance of substantial activities, the replacement of already posted workers, the place of business or the centre of interest.

In this context it is necessary to examine the legal significance of the A1 certificate issued by a competent body of a Member State. Is the delivery of such a declaration a sufficient condition to put into force a derogation of the State-of-employment principle? Can, if such a declaration has been issued by a Member State, the competent body of another Member State and, more specifically, of the Member State where the posted person temporarily carries out activities, still dispute that the above-mentioned fundamental conditions have been met?

The Validity of an A1 Certificate

In its case law the Court of Justice stated in this respect that the principle that a worker or self-employed person can only be subject to the social security legislation of one Member State at a time prevents that during the validity period of the A1 certificate this person would be subject to the regulations of a Member State other than the Member State that issued this certificate.[98] As long as the A1 certificate

96 See Article 19 Regulation No 987/2009.

97 This was expressly confirmed by the Court of Justice in: CJEU, 10 February 2000, Case C-202/97, *Fitzwilliam*, ECLI:EU:C:2000:75, para. 51; CJEU, 30 March 2000, Case C-178/97, *Banks*, ECLI:EU:C:2000:169, para. 38; and CJEU, 4 October 2012, Case C-115/11, *Format*, ECLI:EU:C:2012:606, para. 46.

98 CJEU, 26 January 2006, Case C-2/05, *Herbosch Kiere*, ECLI:EU:C:2006:69, para. 21; and very recently confirmed in: CJEU, 27 April 2017, Case C-620/15, *A-Rosa Flussschiff*, ECLI:EU:C:2017:309, para. 38; and CJEU, 6 February 2018, Case C-359/16, *Altun*, ECLI:EU:2018:63, para. 36.

has not been withdrawn or declared invalid, the competent body of the receiving Member State must take into account that the workers concerned are already subject to the legislation of another State, meaning that it may not subject them to its own social security legislation.[99] For the Court of Justice, the opposite result would undermine the principle that employees are to be covered by only one social security system, would make it difficult to know which system is applicable and would consequently undermine legal certainty. In cases in which it was difficult to determine the applicable system, each of the competent institutions of the two Member States concerned would be inclined to take the view, to the detriment of the workers concerned, that its own social security system was applicable to those workers.[100] It could mean that the person and employers concerned must pay social security contributions in two Member States at the same time which would amount to an obstacle to the free movement of services.

What in Case of a Dispute between the Institutions of the Member States on the Validity of a Certificate?

The Court of Justice stated that in the case of a dispute between the competent bodies of the Member States on the question whether or not the certificate had been issued correctly, first of all, they have to contact each other. At the request of the body of the receiving State the body of the sending State must re-examine whether or not the issued A1 certificate was correct and, if necessary, withdraw it. If they cannot reach an agreement, the Member States concerned can submit their dispute to the Administrative Commission.[101] If the Administrative Commission fails to reconcile the positions of the competent bodies, the receiving State has the right, whilst retaining the possibility to give notice of appeal in the Member State of the issuing body, to bring a non-compliance case within the meaning of Article 227 EC Treaty (now Article 259 TFEU) before the Court of Justice. That way the

99 CJEU, 30 March 2000, Case C-178/97, *Banks*, ECLI:EU:C:2000:169, para. 42; CJEU, 27 April 2017, Case C-620/15, *A-Rosa Flussschiff*, ECLI:EU:C:2017:309, paras. 41-43; CJEU, 6 February 2018, Case C-359/16, *Altun,* ECLI:EU:2018:63, paras. 38-41; and CJEU, 6 September 2018, Case C-527/16, *Alpenrind*, ECLI:EU:C:2018:669, para. 64.

100 CJEU, 26 January 2006, Case C-2/05, *Herbosch Kiere*, ECLI:EU:C:2006:69, para. 25; and CJEU, 27 April 2017, Case C-620/15, *A-Rosa Flussschiff*, ECLI:EU:C:2017:309, para. 42.

101 This Administrative Commission was established by Article 71 Regulation No 883/2004 and consists of a government representative from each of the Member States. The duties of this Administrative Commission are listed in Article 72 Regulation No 883/2004. See in this respect also: Article 5 Regulation No 987/2009 and Decision No A1 of 12 June 2009 concerning the establishment of a dialogue and conciliation procedure concerning the validity of documents, the determination of the applicable legislation and the provision of benefits under Regulation (EC) No 883/2004, OJ 2010, C106/1.

Court would have the possibility to examine the question regarding the applicable legislation and the accuracy of the data in the A1 certificate.[102]
The Court also noted that it follows from the principle of sincere cooperation that any institution of a Member State must carry out a diligent examination of the application of its own social security system. It also follows from that principle that the institutions of the other Member States are entitled to expect the institution of the Member State concerned to fulfil that obligation.[103]
But as long as it has not been withdrawn or declared invalid, the A1 certificate takes effect in the internal legal order of the Member State to which the employee goes in order to work and, therefore, binds the institutions of that Member State. The above-mentioned procedure must be followed, even if it was established that the conditions under which the workers concerned carry out their activities clearly do not fall within the material scope of the provision on the basis of which the A1 certificate was issued.[104] This case law was meanwhile codified in Article 5 of Regulation No 987/2009.
Moreover, the Court also decided that the national courts of the receiving Member State cannot disregard an A1 certificate. It expressly stated that a judicial body of the receiving Member State is not authorised to verify the validity of an A1 certificate as regards the substantiation of the facts on the basis of which such a certificate has been issued, notably the existence of an organic link between the undertaking posting the employee and the posted worker.[105]

What with Cases of Abuse and Fraud?
However, the effectiveness of these procedures largely depends on the *goodwill* of the bodies concerned. Meanwhile, this has led to much discontent on the part of a number of Member States, especially with regard to situations in which an A1 certificate validly issued was used to escape the application of the national security legislation in circumstances in which the conditions for a derogation of the State-of-employment principle were not complied with, especially in cases of posting or of simultaneous employment in two or more Member States. As a reaction to this, Belgium unilaterally took a number of measures such as the provisions of Articles

102 See for the procedures to be followed: CJEU, 10 February 2000, Case C-202/97, *Fitzwilliam*, ECLI:EU:C:2000:75, paras. 57-59; CJEU, 30 March 2000, Case C-178/97, *Banks*, ECLI:EU:C:2000:169, paras. 44-45; CJEU, 4 October 2012, Case C-115/11, *Format*, ECLI:EU:C:2012:606, para. 47; CJEU, 27 April 2017, Case C-620/15, *A-Rosa Flussschiff*, ECLI:EU:C:2017:309, paras. 44-47; and CJEU, 11 July 2018, Case C-356/15, *Commission v. Belgium*, ECLI:EU:C:2018:555, paras. 89-92.

103 CJEU, 6 February 2018, Case C-359/16, *Altun*, ECLI:EU:2018:63, para. 42.

104 CJEU, 27 April 2017, Case C-620/15, *A-Rosa Flussschiff*, ECLI:EU:C:2017:309, para. 53.

105 CJEU, 26 January 2006, Case C-2/05, *Herbosch Kiere*, ECLI:EU:C:2006:69, para. 32; and CJEU, 27 April 2017, C-620/15, *A-Rosa Flussschiff*, ECLI:EU:C:2017: 309, para. 49.

22 to 25 of the Law of 27 December 2012. These provisions are intended to fight abuse of law. According to Article 23 of this law, abuse of law occurs when, with regard to a worker or self-employed person, the provisions of the coordination regulations are applied to a situation in which the conditions laid down in the regulations are not observed, with the aim to shirk the Belgian social security legislation that should have been applied in that situation. This especially concerns the use of letterbox companies. As for social security, Articles 24 says that when a national court, a public social security institution or a social inspector finds such abuse to have occurred, the worker or self-employed person concerned will be subjected to the Belgian social security legislation. The Belgian social security scheme will apply from the first day on which the conditions for its application are satisfied. This measure does run counter to the above explained provisions of Regulation No 883/2004 and Regulation No 987/2009 as well as the case law of the Court of Justice, which do not permit unilateral actions by the Member States if an A1 certificate has been issued by the competent body of a Member State. The European Commission too held the view that this legislation constitutes a violation of the applicable Union law, commenced an infringement procedure against Belgium and brought the case before the Court of Justice. In its judgment of 11 July 2018, the Court confirmed the Commission's position and declared the Belgian law contrary to EU law.[106]

In the meantime, national courts from Belgium, Austria and France asked for a preliminary ruling from the Court of Justice about the question whether in case of fraud the courts of the Member States may ignore an A1 certificate and therefore also the provisions in Regulation No 883/2004 regarding posting. In that case they would be able to apply the social security of the State of employment.[107]

On 6 February 2018, the Court of Justice delivered its judgment in Case C-359/16 (*Altun*). The Court confirmed its previous case law on the validity of an E101 certificate (now A1 certificate), but added that this must not result in individuals being able to rely on EU law for abusive or fraudulent ends. The Court confirmed that the principle of prohibition of fraud and abuse of rights, is a general principle of EU law which individuals must comply with. The Court further added that findings of fraud are to be based on a consistent body of evidence that satisfies both an objective and a subjective factor. The objective factor consists in the fact that the conditions for obtaining and relying on an E101 certificate are not met. The subjective factor corresponds to the intention of the parties concerned to evade or circumvent the conditions for the issue of that certificate, with a view to obtaining the advantage attached to it. The Court recognised that the fraudulent procurement of an E101 certificate may thus result from a deliberate action, such as the misrepresentation of the real situation of the posted worker or of the undertaking posting that worker, or from a deliberate omission, such as the concealment of rele-

106 CJEU, 11 July 2018, Case C-356/15, *Commission v. Belgium*, ECLI:EU:C:2018:555.

107 See the following cases: Case C-359/16, *Altun*; C-527/16, *Alpenrind* and Case C-370/17, *Vueling Airlines* (case in progress).

vant information, with the intention of evading the conditions governing the posting provisions. If the institution of the Member State to which the workers have been posted puts before the institution that issued the E101 certificates concrete evidence that suggests that those certificates were obtained fraudulently, it is the duty of the latter institution, by virtue of the principle of sincere cooperation, to review, in the light of that evidence, the grounds for the issue of those certificates and, where appropriate, to withdraw them. However, if the latter institution fails to carry out such a review within a reasonable period of time, it must be possible for that evidence to be relied on in judicial proceedings, in order to satisfy the court of the Member State to which the workers have been posted that the certificates should be disregarded. The persons, who are alleged in such proceedings to have used posted workers ostensibly covered by fraudulently obtained certificates, must, however, be given the opportunity to rebut the evidence on which those proceedings are based before the national court decides, if appropriate, that the certificates should be disregarded and gives a ruling on the liability of those persons under the applicable national law.[108]

This new development in the case law of the Court of Justice offers the Member State to which the workers have been posted the possibility, in cases of fraud and under certain conditions, to ask its judiciary to disregard an A1 certificate and to apply its own social security legislation, including the recovery of contributions.

Recent Proposals of the European Commission

It is in this context as well that on 13 December 2016, the European Commission put a number of proposals to make the receiving States' verification of the postings more efficient.[109] For instance, the Commission suggests to include in Article 5 Regulation No 987/2009 that the documents (such as an A1 certificate) issued by the institution of a Member State are only valid if all sections indicated as compulsory are filled in on the form. Moreover, the Commission proposes that, if the institution of a Member State which has some doubts about the validity of a document or the accuracy of the facts on the basis of which it has been issued asks the issuing body for clarification or withdrawal of this document, the latter has to respond to this within 25 workdays. If the inquiring body indicates that the matter is urgent, the other body has to respond within two workdays. If, furthermore, it is clear that fraud is involved, the document must be corrected or withdrawn immediately and retroactively. In addition, the Commission proposes to include, explicitly, in Article 19 Regulation No 987/2009 the obligation for the institutions of the Member States to make a proper assessment of the relevant facts and to guarantee that the information on the basis of which the certificates are issued is correct.

These changes are meant to offer the Member States the opportunity to obtain clarity, without delay, about the question to which Member State's legislation the

108 CJEU, 6 February 2018, Case C-359/16, *Altun,* ECLI:EU:2018:63, paras. 48-56.

109 Proposal of 13 December 2016 to amend Regulation No 883/2004 and Regulation No 987/2009, COM(2016) 815 final.

posted worker or self-employed person concerned is subject in the case of disputes about, *inter alia*, the A1 certificate. Moreover, these adaptations will increase the pressure on the Member States that want to issue or have issued an A1 certificate to actively examine whether all the conditions for posting have really been met. Whether or not this new text will effectively lead to fighting fraud in the case of posting will naturally depend on the willingness of all Member States to take this seriously.

5.3 Case Law

List of the most relevant case law of the Court of Justice of the European Union:

CJEU, 17 December 1970, Case C-35/70, *Manpower*, ECLI:EU:C:1970:120.
CJEU, 5 March 1998, Case C-160/96, *Molenaar*, ECLI:EU:C:1998:84.
CJEU, 10 February 2000, Case C-202/97, *Fitzwilliam*, ECLI:EU:C:2000:75.
CJEU, 30 March 2000, Case C-178/97, *Banks*, ECLI:EU:C:2000:169.
CJEU, 9 November 2000, Case C-404/98, *Plum*, ECLI:EU:C:2000:607.
CJEU, 26 January 2006, Case C-2/05, *Herbosch Kiere*, ECLI:EU:C:2006:69.
CJEU, 9 March 2006, Case C-493/04, *Piatkowski*, ECLI:EU:C:2006:167.
CJEU, 1 April 2008, Case C-212/06, *Gouvernement de la Communauté française and others*, ECLI:EU:C:2008:178.
CJEU, 11 September 2008, Case C-228/07, *Petersen*, ECLI:EU:C:2008:494.
CJEU, 5 May 2011, Case C-206/11, *Commission v. Germany*, ECLI:EU:C:2011:283.
CJEU, 4 October 2012, Case C-115/11, *Format*, ECLI:EU:C:2012:606.
CJEU, 18 April 2013, Case C-548/11, *Mulders*, ECLI:EU:C:2013:249.
CJEU, 5 November 2014, Case C-103/13, *Somova*, ECLI:EU:C:2014:2334.
CJEU, 18 December 2014, Case C-523/13, *Larcher*, ECLI:EU:C:2014:2458.
CJEU, 12 February 2015, Case C-114/13, *Bouman*, ECLI:EU:C:2015:81.
CJEU, 25 February 2015, Case C-623/13, *de Ruyter*, ECLI:EU:C:2015:123.
CJEU, 21 January 2016, Case C-515/14, *Commission v. Cyprus*, ECLI:EU:C:2016:30.
CJEU, 26 October 2016, Case C-269/15, *Hoogstad*, ECLI:EU:C:2016:802.
CJEU, 27 April 2017, Case C-620/15, A-*Rosa Flussschiff*, ECLI:EU:C:2017:309.
CJEU, 6 February 2018, Case C-359/16, *Altun*, ECLI:EU:2018:63.
CJEU, 11 July 2018, Case C-356/15, *Commission v. Belgium*, ECLI:EU:C:2018:555.
CJEU, 6 September 2018, Case C-527/16, *Alpenrind*, ECLI:EU:C:2018:669.

5.4 Further Reading

5.4.1 Academic Literature

R. Cornelissen, 'Conflicting Rules of Conflict: Social Security and Labour Law', in: H. Verschueren (ed.), *Residence, Employment and Social Rights of Mobile Persons.*

On How EU Law Defines Where They Belong (Cambridge-Antwerp-Portland: Intersentia, 2016), 255-284.

M. Fuchs and R. Cornelissen (eds.), *EU Social Security Law. A Commentary on EU Regulations 883/2004 and 987/2009* (Munich-Baden-Baden-Oxford: Beck-Hart-Nomos, 2015).

M. Houwerzijl, 'Letterbox strategies to avoid social security contributions', ETUC, *The hunters game: how policy can change to spot and sink letterbox-type practices* (December 2016), 45-85.

J. Paju, *European Union and Social Security Law* (Oxford: Hart, 2017).

F. Pennings, *European Social Security Law*, 6th ed. (Cambridge-Antwerp-Portland: Intersentia, 2015).

5.4.2 Other Documents

'Practical Guide on the applicable legislation', to be found at: http://ec.europa.eu/social/main.jsp?catId=868.

Websites with additional information:
Website of the European Commission: http://ec.europa.eu/social/main.jsp?catId=849.

Website of the network of legal exports in the field of free movement of workers and social security coordination (FreSsco) (including reports of this network, a regulations database and an e-learning tool): http://ec.europa.eu/social/main.jsp?catId=1098&langId=en.

Website of the network of experts on statistics (including annual reports on labour mobility and reports on the portable A1 document): http://ec.europa.eu/social/main.jsp?catId=1154&langId=en.

6 The European Social Dialogue in the Road Transport Sector

*Monika Tomaszewska & Michał Szypniewski**

6.1 Introduction

6.1.1 Curriculum Outline

The social dialogue attempts to facilitate the cooperation between a vast array of stakeholders representing different positions, also in forms of collective bargaining, which in essence contributes to an overall improvement of strategic legal instruments by taking into account a wider perspective negotiations and consultations among stakeholders. At the European level, social dialogue plays an important role between the associations of employers, trade unions and essentially the EU institutions that are obliged to take into account the stakeholders' opinions on the legislative proposals. Therefore, as described, social dialogue cannot be omitted, nor disregarded, quite the contrary, it needs to be strengthened to achieve a fair level playing field for all involved in the cross-border road transport.

An alternative form of the General Social Dialogue is a Sectoral social dialogue on selected industries (sectors) and representing these ones (e.g. road transport) of active partners. Dialogue at European level differs from the traditional sectoral-level collective bargaining in operation within the Member States and are of a different nature: that is, multi-level, with close cooperation with the European authorities, numerous coordination processes, and subtle forms of mutual learning and dissemination of ideas.[1] Moreover in practice, European (sectoral) dialogue including road transport sector is quite challenging. Sectoral social partners have to

* Monika Tomaszewska is Professor of Labour Law, Michał Szypniewski is a PhD Researcher, University of Gdańsk. The authors would like to express their gratitude to Mijke Houwerzijl (Tilburg University) for contributing to this chapter.

1 P. Pochet, E. Léonard and E. Perin, *Dynamics of European sectoral social dialogue*, (European Foundation for the Improvement of Living and Working Conditions: Luxemburg, 2009), 3.

represent national member organisations that operate in different countries but, what is worth mentioning, they are subject to different socioeconomic realities, objectives, type of structures and their roles in their domestic system of industrial relations could be different.[2] Taking into account the above perspective, it is important to understand the entire consultation process that leads to the agreement of a common position between social partners.

The general academic aim is to provide readers with an understanding of the meaning, the tools and the actors involved in the European social dialogue within the context of the road freight sector.

6.1.2 Specific Learning Outcomes

Readers will gain a general understanding of the European social dialogue with a specific focus on the road freight transport sector. More specifically they will know:

1. What the European Social Dialogue consists of, including the representative (sectoral) social partner organisations, specifically in the road freight transport sector.
2. What differences exist between national collective representation and the European (sectoral) social dialogue.
3. What issues are discussed in the European (sectoral) social dialogue regarding intra-EU mobility of truck drivers in the road freight transport sector.

6.2 Demarcation of the Road Freight Transport Sector

6.2.1 What Are We Talking About?

The Sectoral Social Dialogue Committee in Road Transport dates back from the advisory and joint committees created as part of the European Coal and Steel Community Treaty. An informal dialogue was set up in 1965 the road transport sectoral social dialogue was formally established in 1999 with internal rules of procedures adopted in 2000. That means informal joint committee functioned since the Treaties of Rome was signed. However, only in 1999 when came into force as a first Maastricht Social Agreement and then it was included into general provisions by the Amsterdam Treaty governing the social dialogue as such – Articles 138 and 139 of the EC Treaty[3], they triggered off the dialogue at European level. At those Treaty bases, the older joint committees and informal work parties were transformed into homogenous 'sectoral social dialogue committees' by European Commission Decision 98/500/EC of 20 May 1998. The number of committees was extended to 36 at that time by added some newly created committees.

2 Ibid., 5.

3 Treaty of Amsterdam amending the Treaty on European Union, the Treaties establishing the European Communities and certain related acts, was signed on 2 October 1997, and entered into force on 1 May 1999. Full text of the Amsterdam Treaty: https://europa.eu/european-union/sites/europaeu/files/docs/body/treaty_of_amsterdam_en.pdf.

The ESSD Committee in Road Transport meets 3-4 times a year in plenary and in dedicated working groups.

Social Partner Organisations are considered 'sector related' if they are active in the fields described in Statistical Classification of Economic Activities in the European Community (NACE). These requirements are set in order to ensure the real capacity to negotiate and representation. For the purpose of this chapter, it is therefore necessary to demarcate the specific sector we are focusing on. Data for employee and employer organisations in the road transport and logistics sector on domain coverage, membership, sectorial density, collective bargaining, consultation arrangements, and national, European and international affiliations are provided in a Eurofound study of 2015.[4]

In the Eurofound study, the road transport and logistics sector is defined according to the NACE system to ensure the cross-national comparability of the findings. The domains of the trade unions and employer organisations and the scope of the relevant collective agreements vary from this precise NACE definition, therefore also organisations with a broader domain are included, as long as they are (also) active in the road transport and logistics sector.[5]

From the Eurofound study, information on representative social partners at EU level and national level is selected below only as far as relevant for the focus of the textbook which is on the position of international truck drivers. This means that we narrow our focus to international freight transport by road only. Hence, professional passenger transport (including public transport) is excluded from our analysis as far as possible.

The European and national social partner organisations mentioned below in sections 2 and 3 are active in the subsector freight transport by road and cover at least the occupation of international truck drivers. Organisations that only represent white-collar workers are therefore excluded from the scope. It is assumed (but not checked) that organisations representing international truck drivers include those with other than standard employment contracts in freight transport by road (self-employed, temporary agency workers, fixed-term contracts...).

4 P. Sanz de Miguel, 'Representativeness of the European social partner organisations: Road transport and logistics sector', *Eurofound* 10 April 2015 (Observatory: EurWORK, Topic: Social dialogue, Social partners, Representativeness, Industrial relations); https://www.eurofound.europa.eu/observatories/eurwork/comparative-information/representativeness-of-the-european-social-partner-organisations-road-transport-and-logistics-sector.

5 More specifically, the road transport and logistics is defined as embracing the following sectors of NACE (Rev. 2): 49.31 Urban and suburban passenger land transport; 49.32 Taxi operation; 49.39 Other passenger land transport, not elsewhere classified; *49.41 Freight transport by road*; 49.42 Removal services; 52.10 Warehousing and storage; 52.29 Other transportation support activities; 53.2 Other postal and courier activities.

6.2.2 Haulage Companies and Courier Companies – What Is the Difference?[6]

As we shall see below in sections 6.3 and 6.4, in most instances it is impossible to clearly pinpoint employee and employer organisations active in the different areas of freight logistics and transport by road, simply because they organise more than just international truck drivers and employers in freight (haulage) transport by road alone. This means e.g. that both (drivers employed or deployed by) haulage companies and courier companies are represented by the social partner organisations below.

6.2.2.1 What Is the Difference Between the Two?

Although both types of companies are involved with "Carriage of Goods" they have quite a few differences between them. For example haulage contractors often have specific contracts to whom they distribute to on a regular basis. They often have pre-booked appointments and they know exactly what they are carrying before the goods are loaded and transported.

Couriers generally don't have specific contracts however they may be contracted by certain businesses to carry out their parcel delivery needs. They tend to advertise and get customers for transporting one-off items. The size and type of goods a haulier carries would also be on a larger scale than a courier. Haulage companies carry palletized goods and containers, whereas couriers transport goods on a smaller scale such as parcels and letters. Due to the size of products distributed, the size of vehicles used to transport these goods would also be much larger for a road haulage company than a courier.

In general, the key difference between couriers and hauliers other than size of goods and vehicle type is that anyone could contact a courier or courier company at any time on any given day, and they aren't always aware of the packages they are transporting. Generally, couriers provide parcel delivery services nationwide and many of these companies offer parcel delivery worldwide as well. In general, every haulage trip comes from point of origin to the address where the package is scheduled to deliver – instead of having multiple stops and starts carried out by couriers. On average, hauliers focus in hauling freight in large heavy vehicles, and sometimes, warehousing. They also handle container shipping. Simply put, couriers transport hand-carry packages while hauliers transport freight.

The maximum authorized dimensions that are allowed for national and international traffic and the maximum weights and dimensions in haulage transport that are allowed for certain vehicles in international traffic were prescribed in the EU Council Directive 96/53/EC of May 25th 1996[7] and amended by Directive (EU)

6 https://www.dmg-freight.com/haulage-companies-and-courier-companies-what-is-the-difference/ (1 July 2015).

7 Council Directive 96/53/EC of 25 July 1996 laying down for certain road vehicles circulating within the Community the maximum authorized dimensions in national and

2015/719/EU of 29 April 2015.[8] Based on dates reported by *Improved Performance of European Long Haulage Transport*[9] in international long haulage transport within the EU articulated vehicles, usually called semitrailer combinations, are dominant. Their regular loading capacity, of about 85 m3 and 26 tonnes is provided by a 13.6-metre long semi-trailer (the maximum total weight being 40 tonnes or 44 tonnes if the cargo consists of a 40-foot ISO container). Also road trains, consisting of a lorry and a centre-axle trailer, are used. The maximum loading capacity is approximately 96 m3 and 26 tonnes.

6.2.3 Statistics on the National and European Road Freight Transport Sector[10]

Relative to population size, road freight transport was highest among the EU Member States in *Luxembourg,* where, on average, 15.5 thousand tonne-kilometres (tkm) of freight were transported by road for each inhabitant in 2015; this was 70 % higher than the next highest level of road freight transport per inhabitant, recorded in Lithuania (9.1 thousand tkm). In both cases, the vast majority — more than 85 % — of the freight transported by road was international movements performed by vehicles registered in these two EU Member States. These road freight statistics are based on worldwide movements of vehicles registered in the reporting country ('nationality principle').

The split between national and international road freight varied considerably across the EU Member States: the highest proportions of national road freight transport

international traffic and the maximum authorized weights in international traffic, OJ L 235, 17 September 1996, 59–75.

8 Directive (EU) 2015/719 of the European Parliament and of the Council of 29 April 2015 amending Council Directive 96/53/EC laying down for certain road vehicles circulating within the Community the maximum authorised dimensions in national and international traffic and the maximum authorised weights in international traffic (Text with EEA relevance), OJ L 115, 6 May 2015, 1–10.

9 Improved Performance of European Long Haulage Transport, http://modularsystem.eu/download/facts_and_figures/final_report_extra.pdf.

10 http://ec.europa.eu/eurostat/statistics-explained/index.php/Freight_transport_statistics#Road_freight (data extracted on 1 April 2017). Road freight transport statistics are collected under the framework provided by Regulation No 1172/98 on statistical returns in respect of the carriage of goods by road, substantially amended several times, and recast as Regulation No 70/2012. The data are based on sample surveys carried out in the reporting countries and record the transport of goods by road, as undertaken by vehicles registered in each of the EU Member States. It is important to note that almost all of the Member States apply a cut-off point for carrying capacity under which vehicles are not surveyed; this should not be greater than 3.5 tonnes carrying capacity, or 6 tonnes in terms of gross vehicle weight; some of the Member States also apply a limit on the age of the vehicles surveyed.

in 2015 were recorded in Cyprus (97.3 %) and the United Kingdom (95.5 %), while shares in France and Sweden were also above 90 %. By contrast, in 2015, half of the Member States reported that foreign road networks accounted for the majority of the goods transported by vehicles registered in their Member State. The share of international road freight transport in total road freight was particularly high in Latvia (81.3 %), Slovakia (84.4 %), *Luxembourg* (87.5 %), Slovenia (88.4 %), and Lithuania (89.0 %).

Road transport has the highest share of freight transport in the European Union. In 2015 the volume of goods transport, measured by transport performance in EU countries, amounted to 1767.8 billion tkm and was by 2.4% higher than in 2014. Germany was the leader in terms of transport performance (314.7 million tkm), Poland ranked second (260.7 million tkm), followed by Spain (209.4 million tkm).

Structure of transport performance in EU countries by modes of transport

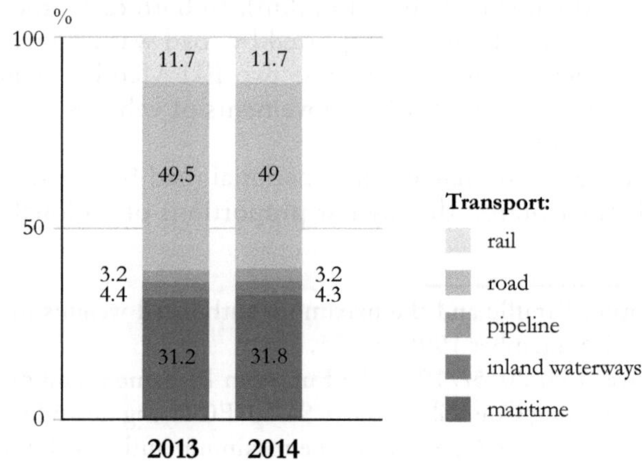

Source: own compile on the basis of EUROSTAT data.

Road transport has become the important economic activity in such countries as Poland or Lithuania. In Poland, for example, revenues from overall activities in all road transport entities accounts nearly 6% of the gross national product.[11] Most of transport companies in Poland are small companies – almost 80% comprising not more ten transport vehicles. Such companies are particularly sensitive to economic and the legal uncertainty or changing business environment.

The increasing importance of transport sector is presented by Eurostat statistics. The rate of change in inland freight transport was around one third higher than the overall growth in economic activity during the period 2004-2014 in Poland and

11 https://trans.info/pl/polski-transport-ze-swietnym-wynikiem-80368.

Lithuania.[12] More detailed data is presented by the Polish Central Statistical Office (GUS). According to GUS statistics, companies employing more than 9 people growed in the transport service by 12.3 % in 2017 in comparison with 2016. In 2017, 245.3 million tons of cargo was transported in road transport in Poland. This result is better by 11.9 % in comparison with 2016. In December 2017, 19.7 million tons of cargo were transported which gave increasing of 6.6 % on a yearly basis.

Income growth is connected with the increase in employment in the road transport sector in Poland. The average paid employment on the basis of an employment contract in entities employing more than 9 persons in 2015 amounted to 251.1 thousand persons and was by 5.9% higher in comparison with 2014; employment in the public sector growth by 0.4%, and in the private sector by 7.6%.[13]

Accusations of social duping caused by the low earnings of truck drivers from Poland seem to be exaggerated. Rely on GUS data, the average monthly gross wages and salaries of workers employed on the basis of an employment contract in entities employing more than 9 persons in 2015 amounted to 3098.4 PLN (about 737 EUR). In comparison with 2014 they were higher by 3.9%; an increase of wages and salaries was higher in the private sector (by 4.6%) than in the public sector (by 4.2%). The amount 3098.4 was an average income in Poland in comparison with minimum income 1600 (381 EUR) in 2014.[14]

6.3 Social Partner Representation at European Level

6.3.1 Brief Introduction into the European Social Dialogue

At the European level, social dialogue plays an important role between the associations of employers, trade unions ("management and labour"), and essentially the EU institutions that are obliged to take into account the stakeholders' opinions on the legislative proposals. Therefore, (sectoral) social dialogue cannot be omitted, nor disregarded, quite the contrary, it needs to be strengthened to achieve a fair level playing field for all involved in the cross-border road transport.

6.3.1.1 What Is the European Social Dialogue About?

There is no uniform pattern of social dialogue. Each country has its own rules, customs and practices which define social dialogue. The International Labour Organisation (ILO) tries to capture the universal elements of all varying traditions, in its definition of social dialogue as "all types of negotiation, consultation or simply exchange of information between, or among, representatives of governments,

12 http://ec.europa.eu/eurostat/statistics-explained/index.php/Freight_transport_statistics#Road_freight.

13 Road transport in Poland in the years 2014, 2015,. 67. The Statistical Office presents statistical data every two years. Therefore, there are no current reports on employment situation.

14 Road transport in Poland in the years 2014, 2015, 67.

employers and workers, on issues of common interest relating to economic and social policy."[15]
According to the website of the European Commission, DG Employment, Social Affairs & Inclusion, the European social dialogue refers to discussions, consultations, negotiations and joint actions involving organisations representing the two sides of industry (employers and workers). It takes two main forms:
- a tripartite dialogue involving the public authorities,
- a bipartite dialogue between the European employers and trade union organisations. This takes please at cross-industry level and within sectoral social dialogue committees.[16]

The European social dialogue is enshrined in Articles 152, 154-155 TFEU.[17] **Article 152**, which was newly introduced by the Lisbon Treaty, further strengthened the role of social dialogue by providing that the Union as a whole – not only the Commission – is committed to promoting the role of the social partners. It also highlights the role of the so-called Tripartite Social Summit.
Article 154 is the basis of EU social dialogue. Pursuant to Article 154(2) TFEU, the European Commission shall first consult the social partners before submitting proposals in the field of social policy. As Even notices: 'Judging from the words used in this provision (the Commission *shall* consult as opposed to *can* consult), this is not a discretionary power of the Commission, but an obligation'.[18] Actually, such an obligation laid down in law, is rather at odds with national traditions of 'bargaining in the shadow of the law'.

6.3.1.2 In Line with National Traditions?

However, while the 'European Social Dialogue' at least builds upon strong collective labour traditions in the Nordic, Western-European and Mediterranean European Member States, this is not true for the former Communist countries, who joined the EU in 2004, 2007 and 2013. In its 2002 Communication 'the Euro-

15 International Labour Organisation, 'Social dialogue sector'. Available at: www.ilo.org/public/english/dialogue/.

16 http://ec.europa.eu/social/main.jsp?catId=329&langId=en. Financial support is given to transnational projects carried out by social partners and others active in the field of industrial relations through the social dialogue budget lines. It is also provided through the European Social Fund (ESF) for capacity-building of social partner organisations at national level.

17 See: E. Franssen, *Legal aspects of the European Social Dialogue* (Cambridge-Antwerp-Portland; Intersentia, 2002, 3). Also, Z.H. Even, *Transnational Collective Bargaining in Europe*, (PhD Thesis) (Den Haag: BJu, 2008). Retrieved from http://hdl.handle.net/1765/13755, Chapter 5 and 6, and for the history of the social dialogue, Chapter 3 and Franssen (2002), Chapter 3.

18 Z.H. Even, 'Transnational collective bargaining in the European Union', *ArA* No 2, 2008, 18. This subsection draws on parts of Even's contribution to *ArA* 2008.

pean Social Dialogue, a force for innovation and change', the European Commission addressed this issue. The Commission envisaged an important role for the European social dialogue with regard to the enlargement of the European Union with the then candidate-countries from Central and Eastern Europe.[19] The Commission pointed out that the social dialogue 'is enshrined in the Treaty and forms an integral part of the *acquis communautaire*'. Therefore, the social partner structure in the candidate countries needed to be strengthened. The social partners in the old Member States (the EU-15) were called upon to assist in this strengthening process. According to the Commission the social partners of the candidate countries had an important role to play in the context of the pre-accession strategy.[20]
In a response, the large cross-industry social partners, the European Trade Union Confederation ('ETUC'), the Union of Industrial and Employers' Confederation ('UNICE'; renamed into BUSINESS-EUROPE), the European Association of Craft, Small and Medium Sized Enterprises ('UAPME') and the European Centre for Public Enterprises ('CEEP') expressed in their joint contribution to the Laeken European Council of 7 December 2001, their intent to reposition their role. Basically, they planned not to be fully dependent on the Community institutions anymore. Instead of solely acting after having been consulted by the Commission and to have their subsequent agreements exclusively implemented by a Council decision on the basis of the European social dialogue as they did before, the European social partners would now rather take the initiative themselves and implement their agreements autonomously, with the instruments of industrial relations available to them at the national level.[21]

6.3.1.3 'Top-Down' Transposition of the Social Dialogue in the 'New' Member States

Social dialogue and industrial relations in the Central and Eastern European countries have indeed been experiencing radical changes since joined to the European Union. A range of institutions and mechanisms for consultation and social dialogue have been put in place at different levels in order to be compliant to the social dialogue in so-call old European countries.[22] However, still some important differences remain.

19 COM(2002)341, final.

20 See: C. Welz and T. Kauppinen, 'The Role of Social Dialogue in the Acceding Countries during the Preparatory Phase for Economic and Monetary Union (EMU)', *The International Journal of Comparative Law and Industrial Relations*, Winter 2004, 583 ff.

21 For a critical review see S. Smismans, 'The European Social Dialogue in the Shadow of Hierarchy', *Journal of Public Policy*, No. 1, 2008, 171.

22 Y. Ghellab, *Sectoral Social Dialogue in Future EU Member States: The Weakest Link* (Budapest, 2003), https://books.google.pl/books?hl=pl&lr=&id=-JzvlAmSLgsoi=fnd&pg=PR10&dq=social+dialogue+eu&ots=mHRZaRSXKy&sig=8YoOYv6&lGrAPxS3BtrCTytOmYvI&redir_esc=y#v=onepage&q=social%20dialogue%20eu&f=false.

The problem of the newly acceded EU countries (EU 10) from the former communist Eastern Bloc is that the original "socialist" labour codes in these countries were of an anti-liberal and imperative nature. Against the idea of liberation from that background, the EU 'acquis' on labour law were seen as likewise restricting freedom of contract of the parties in an employment relationship.
In the "old member states" of the EU, a mature system of labour law balancing between freedom and constraints was already in place when the European Union started to gradually interfere with its directives. The character of national labour law was only slightly modified by the transposition of EU directives, also due to the fact that they were mainly requesting 'minimum-harmonisation', leaving much room for the Member States to stick to their own national preferences and peculiarities. In Poland, on the other hand, the Communist legacy of anti-liberal legislation was strengthened by the transposition of the EU directives. Therefore, the predominant perception in Poland is that the implementation of Union directives in the field of labour law has not contributed to the flexibility of Polish labour law, on the contrary. Notwithstanding, the important role of social dialogue in resolving industrial relations conflicts is acknowledged also in the new Member States, for instance by giving social dialogue a constitutional basis, such as in Poland (Article 12 Polish Constitution).[23] But the question remains how the acknowledgement of solidarity, dialogue and cooperation between the social partners as crucial elements of a Social Market Economy, enshrined in Article 3 Treaty on the European Union (TEU)[24] and in national constitutions (e.g. Poland - Article 12 Polish Constitution), can be turned into tangible results for Union citizens all across the EU.

6.3.1.4 Levels of the European Social Dialogue

Social dialogue between representative organisations of workers and employers at all levels – company, local, regional, sectoral, national, and European is recognised as **a pillar of the European social model.**

Three European levels of social dialogue are distinguished:

1. Cross-industry level: a dialogue between the social partners whose scope covers the whole EU economy and labour market in general. This form of social dialogue is opened to those of the social partners that are representative for all economic sectors. General cross-industry organisations represent workers and employers in the private sector, the public sector and small and medium-sized enterprises, and professional and managerial staff. The most important three are:

23 I. Palinkaš, *The legal and institutional framing of collective bargaining in CEE countries: Between Europeanisation and decentralization*, (PhD Thesis) (Tilburg: Tilburg University, 2016).

24 M. Tomaszewska and, M. Szypniewski, 'The social market economy - balance between fundamental freedom to provide cross-border services and social protection of workers' rights', *Gdańskie: Studia Prawnicze t. XXXVII*, 2017, 63.

- **BUSINESSEUROPE** - with 41 national employers' and industrial confederations from 35 European countries as its members. It represents 20 million companies of all sizes, mainly in the private sector.
- **European Centre of Employers and Enterprises Providing Public Services** (CEEP) - representing individual enterprises and employers' associations in public services. It has 19 national sections and 4 affiliated European-level sectoral organisations. CEEP's members employ 30 % of the EU workforce.
- **European Trade Union Confederation** (ETUC) - The main cross-industry trade union organisation is made up of 83 national union confederations from 36 countries and 12 European trade union federations, which bring together national unions operating in particular sectors. In total, the ETUC represents 60 million union members across Europe.

Some legislative initiatives affect small and medium-sized businesses (SMEs) causing necessity to consult the following representative organization:
- **The European Association of Craft, Small and Medium-sized Enterprises** (UEAPME) - bringing together 40 national cross industry federations for SMEs and craft businesses from 26 EU Member States, plus associate members including national SME organisations from outside the EU and 29 European level sectoral SME organisations. UEAPME represents over 12 million enterprises with 55 million employees.[25]

2. Sectoral level: European Sectoral Social Dialogue Committees are the place for consultations on sector-specific issues. For this reason, the sectoral committees are attended by representatives of employers and employees representing the field or a particular industry. Each Sectoral Social Dialogue Committee consists of a maximum of **66 representatives** of the social partners with an equal number of employers 'and workers' representatives pursuant to the Commission's decision of 20 May 1998 – 98/500/EC.[26] Currently, in the EU sectoral social dialogue committees **62 European-level employers' organisations** participate. By contrast, only **17 trade union organisations** participate in the EU-level sectoral dialogue.[27] Each Committee adopts its own rules of procedure, and holds at least one plenary meeting per year.

Such committees play the double function: on the one hand, they are consultative bodies able to influence European public policies – such as transport; on the other hand, they should be capable of developing bilateral relations and reaching an

25 It participates with BusinessEurope and CEEP in the employers' group for dialogue and negotiations with the ETUC.

26 Commission Decision of 20 May 1998 on the establishment of Sectoral Dialogue Committees promoting the Dialogue between the social partners at European level, available as modified by Commission Regulation No 1792/2006.

27 VADEMECUM – A Practical Guide for European Social Partner Organisations and their National Affiliates (Brussels: European Commission, 2017), 10.

agreement, if possible. A special **sectoral committee** is focused on **road transport** issue. Program and recent achievements is presented on European Commission website.[28]

3. Company level: The main forums for European-level social dialogue within companies are European Works Councils (EWCs). Based on an EU Directive adopted in 1994 (and revised in 2009),[29] EWCs can be set up – following negotiations initiated by employees or by management – in multinational companies with at least 1,000 employees within the 30 European Economic Area member states and at least 150 employees in each of at least two member states. Up till now, more than 60 EWCs transnational company agreements have been signed on topics such as restructuring, corporate social responsibility (CSR), equality and health and safety.

6.3.1.5 Implementation of EU-Level Agreements

Article 155 TFEU sets out that dialogue between management and labour at EU level may, if they so wish, lead to 'contractual relations' including agreements. If the social partners decide to negotiate after a consultation by the Commission on a proposal for EU action in the social policy field, prior they must inform the Commission about their initiative. After that, Commission temporarily suspends its work on the proposal. The partners in such a case have nine months to reach an agreement, unless they agree jointly with the Commission to extend this period. There is no such deadline for negotiations among the contractual parties if the negotiations arise solely on the social partners' will.

Two options for implementing an EU-level agreement reached by the social partners:

1. The first option is applicable in all cases, the agreement can be implemented autonomously, that means 'in accordance with the procedures and practices specific to management and labour and the Member States' — in other words, the agreement will be implemented by the signatories' national member organisations, in ways compliance with legal systems in each Member State. Such agreements are called **autonomous agreements**, e.g.:
   - The autonomous agreement on telework (2002),
   - The autonomous agreement on work-related stress (2004),
   - The autonomous agreement on harassment and violence at work (2005),
   - The autonomous agreement on inclusive labour markets (2010).

28 http://ec.europa.eu/social/main.jsp?catId=480&langId=en&intPageId=1850.

29 Directive 2009/38/EC of the European Parliament and of the Council of 6 May 2009 on the establishment of a European Works Council or a procedure in Community-scale groups of undertakings for the purposes of informing and consulting employees.

2. The second option where the agreement deals with employment/social matters which fall within the EU's competence.[30] In such a case the social partners have the option of asking the Commission to propose a decision (in practice only a directive) to be adopted by the Council, giving the agreement legal force across the EU. Such agreements are called **framework agreements.** The most important intersectoral ones are:
   - The agreement on parental leave (1995) - Council Directive 2010/18/EU of 8 March 2010 implementing the revised Framework Agreement on parental leave concluded by BUSINESSEUROPE, UEAPME, CEEP and the ETUC and repealing Directive 96/34/EC, OJ L68, 18 March 2010,
   - The agreement on part-time work (1997) - Council Directive 97/81/EC of 15 December 1997 concerning the Framework Agreement on part-time work concluded by UNICE, CEEP and the ETUC - Annex: Framework agreement on part-time work,
   - The agreement on fixed-term work (1999) - Council Directive 1999/70/EC of 28 June 1999 concerning the framework agreement on fixed-term work concluded by ETUC, UNICE and CEEP

The European Commission recognises also slightly different categories of documents important for social dialogue as well as being an effect of social dialogue:[31]

1. 'Process-oriented texts' contain clear provisions and processes pertain to monitor implementation. This category covers all texts making explicit reference to a monitoring process. In this category, the Commission distinguishes between the framework for action, code of conduct, guidelines and policy orientation.
2. 'Joint opinions and tools' are divided into three subcategories:
   a. Joint opinions – These are generally intended to provide input to the European institutions and/or national public authorities. They include texts that: respond to a Community consultation, such as Green and White papers, consultation documents or Communications; adopt a joint position with regard to a given Community policy; explicitly ask the Commission to adopt a particular stance, or ask the Commission to undertake studies or other actions. Joint opinions often relate to sectoral policies and aim to influence Community policymaking. Employers sometimes use social dialogue as a mechanism for reinforcing requests made directly to the relevant Directorate General (DG) of the Commission. As an instrument, joint opinions can prove useful for trade unions too, since they do not always have access to the DGs responsible for sectoral policy. Thus, joint opinions may be considered as '**joint lobbying**'

30 As laid down in Article 153 TFEU, which clarifies the (shared) competences of the EU legislator in the field of social policy.

31 Pochet et al. (2009), 18. See also: Z.H. Even, *Transnational Collective Bargaining in Europe*, (PhD Thesis) (Den Haag: BJu, 2008), pp. 151-154.

b. 'Declarations' – These are addressed to the social partners but are vague and do not contain monitoring procedures;
c. 'Tools' – These mainly comprise studies, training packages or dissemination media such as websites. The criterion for inclusion in this group is that they are adopted by the social partners; for example, this definition excludes studies carried out by consultants.

3. 'Procedural text' concerns the rules of the procedure for social dialogue.

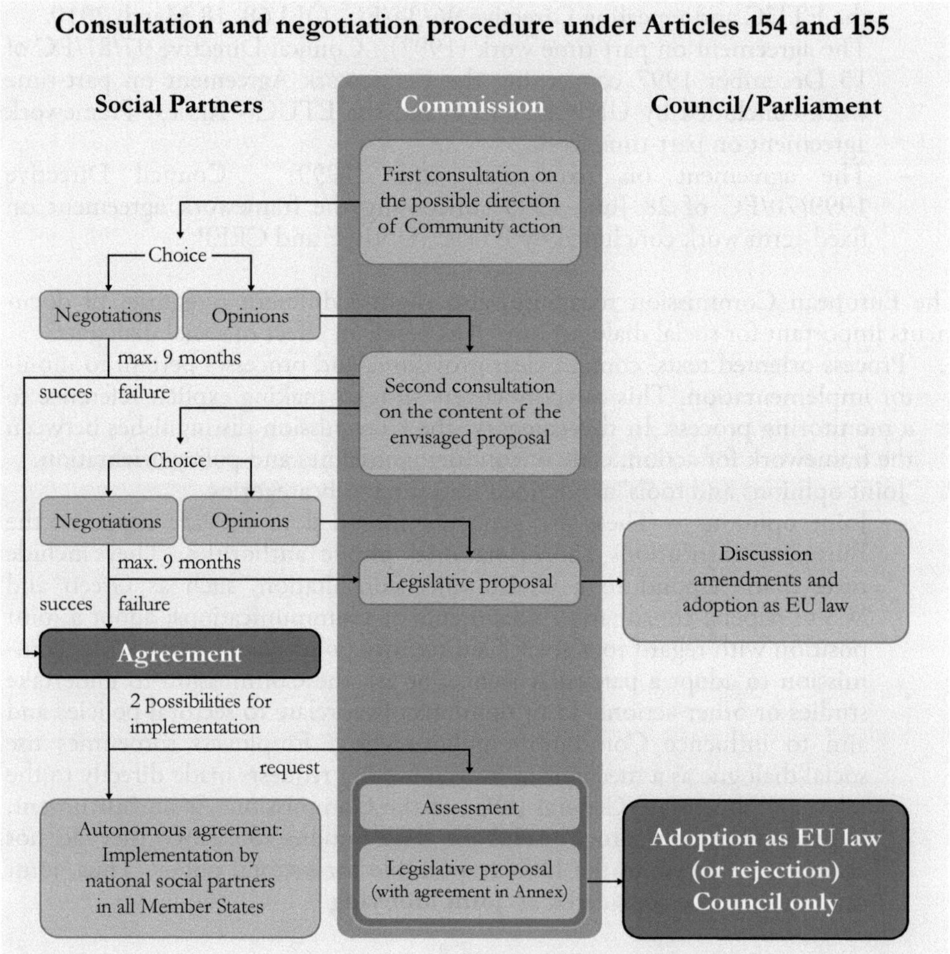

Source: Commentary in Consulting European social partners: Understanding how it works (Brussels: European Commission, 2011), 8.

6.3.1.6 Comparison with National Collective Bargaining Systems

The European social dialogue has led to both intersectoral and sectoral European collective agreements. Nevertheless, its outcomes are modest if compared to (most) national systems of collective bargaining and social dialogue. Yet, the European social dialogue is a process that stipulates a relationship between collective bargaining and law specific to the EU that cannot simply be equated with such systems at the national level. First, it implies a flexible relationship between social dialogue at all levels and is contingent upon national traditions of social dialogue within the Member States. Second, collective bargaining and social dialogue within Member States is regarded as reflecting a balance of power between labour and capital, exercised traditionally through industrial conflict. The Treaty does not address even the possibility of industrial conflict at EU level. Indeed, Article 153(5) TFEU seems explicitly to exclude regulatory competences on the right to strike, which would be most relevant. Also, unlike in many national industrial relations systems and despite longstanding calls by the ETUC (as well as, from time to time, certain EU institutions), the European level has not yet seen the establishment of a European system of mediation and conciliation for solving (collective) labour conflicts, which could also be useful for solving questions of interpretation and/or application of the framework agreements. Crucial elements are lacking, such as the possibility of intervention by the European social partners in proceedings before the European Court of Justice (CJEU), in particular in cases concerning their framework agreements. This justifies reviving the longstanding ETUC demand for a European Labour Chamber at the CJEU or at least a clear right of intervention in such cases.

6.3.2 Representativeness Criteria

The TFEU does not set out whom the social partners are that need to be consulted. In order to fill this lacunae, the Commission defined the criteria that organisations must meet. In its Communication concerning the application of the Agreement on Social Policy (COM (93) 600 final, Brussels, 14 December 1993), the Commission indicated that 'management and labour' are to be understood as the European social partner organisations, organised cross-industry or by sector. It defined criteria of representativeness and drew up a list (subject to regular revision) of organisations to be consulted under Article 154 TFEU, which currently consists of 57 organisations.

6.3.2.1 The UEAPME Judgment

Nevertheless, representativeness was the key issue of a dispute between *UEAPME v. Council of the European Union* (Case T-135/96).[32] On 17 June 1998, the European Court of Justice rejected a case brought by UEAPME, the European organisation which seeks to represent SMEs. UEAPME had claimed that the EU Directive on parental leave should be annulled or ruled inapplicable to its members, as it had

32 CJEU, 17 June 1998, Case T-135/96, *UEAPME v. Council of the European Union*, ECLI:EU:T:1998:128.

been excluded from the negotiating process for the agreement on which the Directive was based.
The European Association of Craft and Small and Medium-sized Enterprises (UEAPME) had brought the case, seeking principally the annulment of the June 1996 EU Directive on parental leave (96/34/EC), or secondarily the annulment of the Directive's applicability to small and medium-sized enterprises (SMEs). The CJEU dismissed the case as inadmissible, finding that UEAPME did not meet the legal requirements for being "concerned" by the Directive, and could thus not bring a case relating to it. At the same time, the Court affirmed the legitimacy of the process of decision-making and arriving at European legislation laid down by the social policy Protocol and Agreement. Nevertheless, it did not rule out future challenges against EU Directives based on framework agreements between the social partners by organisations which can successfully prove to be insufficiently represented by the organisations sitting around the negotiating table.
The Court ruled that "The Commission and the Council are obliged to verify the representativeness [...] [t]hat means that they must verify whether, having regard to the content of the agreement in question, the collective representativeness of the signatories representing management and labour was sufficient". In other words, the Commission should regularly assess if the criteria for representativeness of social partners' which were set out in a Communication of 1993 are fulfilled by the social partners at the European level.

6.3.2.2 Current Rules for Assessing Representativeness of European Social Partners

Currently, the representativeness of the social partners is assessed in two phases. First, prior to the creation of any new committee, the second phase takes place after the committee has been established.
Eligibility for consultation and participation in social dialogue is linked to three criteria defined under Article 1 of Commission Communication COM(1998) 322 final. A social partner organisation must have the following attributes:

a. (...) relate to specific sectors or categories and be organized at European level;
b. (...) consist of organizations which are themselves an integral and recognised part of Member States' social partner structures and have the capacity to negotiate agreements, and which are representative of several Member States;
c. (...) have adequate structures to ensure their effective participation in the work of the Committees.

In terms of social dialogue, the constituent feature is the ability of such organisations to negotiate on behalf of their members and to conclude binding agreements.
The European sectoral social partners should be able to prove their capacity to negotiate on behalf of their members and to enter into 'contractual relations, including agreements' (Article 155 TFEU), that is, the capacity to commit themselves and their national affiliates.

Criterion (b) refers to the negotiation of agreements as provided for in Article 155 TFEU; negotiating other types of joint texts such as joint opinions, frameworks of action and guidelines is not considered to be sufficient in this context.
This capacity to negotiate entails the existence of a mandating procedure of the member associations to the EU-level organisation. The mandate/mandating procedure can be either 'statutory' (that is, laid down in the statutes (constitution) of the organisation or annexed to them) or 'non-statutory' (that is, laid down in secondary (formal) documents, such as rules of procedures, memoranda of understanding or decisions by the governing bodies of the organisation). If no such formal mandating procedure can be identified, the condition concerned is not fulfilled.
Where a mandate exists, it can be further described or qualified in terms of the conditions and procedure for the European social partner organisation to be given the authorisation to enter into a specific negotiation, as well as for the ratification of a possible agreement. In this respect, specific attention is paid to the type of applicable decision procedures (unanimity, different types of majority voting). The frequency of making use of this mandating procedure and/or the number of concluded agreements are expressions of the real capacity to negotiate of social partner organisations.

6.3.2.3 Criteria Used in the Eurofound Study 2015

Starting point of the Eurofound Study on which the rest of this contribution draws, is affiliation to a European social-partner organisation and/or involvement in national collective bargaining. These two criteria are of utmost importance to the European sectoral social dialogue, since they are the two constituent mechanisms that can systematically connect the national and European levels. In the Eurofound study, the following criteria are used to define relevant sector-related interest associations.[33]
A European association is considered a relevant sector-related social partner if:
- it is on the Commission's list of interest organisations to be consulted on behalf of the sector under Article 154 TFEU;
- and/or it participates in the sector-related European Social Dialogue;
- and/or it has requested to be consulted under Article 154 TFEU.

6.3.2.4 Challenges Concerning the Representativeness of Sectoral Social Partners

In an analysis on the functioning and potential of in particular the European sectoral social dialogue in 2010, the Commission underlined the challenges, faced in particular in the European sectoral social dialogue.
In its 1998 Communication on European social dialogue, the Commission encouraged the development of joint actions and negotiations at both cross-industry and sectoral level. It particularly highlighted the potential of European sectoral social dialogue. As a result, the capacity to negotiate agreements at European level was included among the conditions for participating in a committee. However, accord-

33 Eurofound study (2015), 40.

ing to the Commission, sectoral social partners may not yet have fully exploited the potential that this framework offers for sectoral negotiation. For instance, major sectors where large transnational companies are prevalent (steel, telecommunications, chemical industry, civil aviation) tend to pay less attention to the European sectoral level because the social partners prefer to negotiate directly at company level, including also within European Works Councils).

Most European sectoral social partners' organisations are characterised by a low degree of centralisation. They have limited capacity to influence their national affiliates. Follow-up at the national level of dialogue held at the European level depends on involving national sectoral social partners effectively in EU dialogue, and on the interaction between the EU social dialogue mechanisms and various national industrial relations systems. Effective follow-up at national level is also clearly linked to the representativeness of social partners, and this is why it is important that committees are as inclusive as possible, and able to involve new players when relevant: national organisations which are not involved in the work of the committees at European level may not want to implement provisions that they did not contribute to.

> "The European social partners are increasingly involved in the European policy-making process. Under Article 154 of the Treaty, European social partners are consulted by the Commission on the principle and content of any European social policy initiative. In recent years, the pace and number of these formal consultations have increased. Moreover, the European social partners are consulted by Commission services dealing with sectoral policies (such as trade, internal market, education, industrial or transport policies). The Commission has developed a methodology and procedure for Impact Assessment of all its initiatives. Assessment guidelines include a specific reference to consulting European sectoral social dialogue committees, offering them a new opportunity to contribute towards shaping European policies.
> If the partners are to be effective in this new role, they have to have the capacity to deliver timely reactions to such consultations. (...) However, their capacity depends on that of their national affiliates whose strengths and resources may be limited, or whose structures may still be evolving in particular, in the new Member States and in sectors experiencing structural change, including the entry of new actors. It is crucial that national sectoral social partners and authorities develop and assess their own capacity, partly by making full use of European funding from the social dialogue budget headings and the European Social Fund. Given the key role that the European sectoral social partners can play in the policy-making process, this issue of capacity is of utmost importance."[34]

34 See section 3.1 of SEC(2010)964 staff working document on the functioning and potential of European sectoral social dialogue.

6.3.2.5 A New Start?

According to the Commission Juncker: "The social market economy can only work if there is social dialogue. Social dialogue suffered during the crisis years. Now it must be resumed at national and especially at European level. I would like to be a President of social dialogue."[35]

6.3.3 The EU Sectoral Social Dialogue in the Road Transport Sector

The Sectoral Social Dialogue Committee in Road Transport dates back from the advisory and joint committees created as part of the European Coal and Steel Community Treaty. An informal dialogue was set up in 1965, the road transport sectoral social dialogue was formally established in 1999, with internal rules of procedures adopted in 2000. The ESSD Committee in Road Transport meets 3-4 times a year in plenary and in dedicated working groups.

Organisations listed by the European Commission as a (sectoral) social partner organisation consulted under Article 154 of the TFEU are, on the employees' side, the **European Transport Workers' Federation (ETF)**. On the employers' side, the **International Road Transport Union (IRU)**.[36] Both ETF and IRU clearly fulfil the criteria mentioned above under b. ETF has 74 direct affiliations (59% of the unions identified in the study) in 26 Member States, of which 66 participate in sectoral collective bargaining. IRU has 50 direct affiliations in 27 Member States (33% of all the employers' organisations included in the study and 29% when also taking companies into consideration) of which 20 of the affiliated employer organisations (42%) are involved in sectoral collective bargaining.

6.3.3.1 Membership Domain ETF and IRU[37]

According to its website, **the European Transport Workers' Federation (ETF)** represents more than 2.5 million transport workers from 231 transport unions and 41 European countries in the transport sector and in the tourism and fishery sector.

According to its website, **the International Road Transport Union (IRU)** represents 170 associations in 73 countries across all five continents in the road trans-

---

35 Jean-Claude Juncker, president of the European Commission in his opening speech at the European Parliament, 22 October 2014.

36 IRU participates together with the International Association of Public Transport (UITP) in the European road transport Sectoral Social Dialogue Committee (SSDC), on the basis of a cooperation agreement. UITP leads the employers' delegation, which apart from IRU, also includes the European Centre of Employers and Enterprises providing Public Services (CEEP) and the Community of European Railway and Infrastructure Companies (CER) in the SSDC's Urban Public Transport Working Group (CEEP is a cross-industry employers' organisation that represents public services including urban public transport and railways).

37 Eurofound study (2015), 25.

port and logistics sector and sectors linked to the transport such as manufacturers of vehicles, fuels, tyres and information systems.

6.3.3.2 *Mandate ETF and IRU*[38]

ETF

ETF has a general mandate to negotiate as part of its constitution.

The Executive Committee, which is the governing body of the ETF between congresses, decides the guidelines governing the procedure for negotiations and agreements between social partners in the EU. These guidelines are subject to ratification by the affiliated organisations from EU countries represented at Congress. The ETF Section concerned (that is, the ETF institution each affiliated union has the right to participate in, to the extent that it represents workers from the sector concerned) adopts a negotiation mandate and strategy. The Section president, who is a member of the Executive Committee, keeps the Executive Committee informed about the progress of the negotiations and the final results. In practice, it is the Section concerned that ratifies possible agreements.

So far, ETF has used the mandate to conclude an agreement on certain aspects of the working conditions of mobile workers engaged in interoperable cross-border services in the railway sector. This agreement was transformed into Council Directive 2005/47/EC. Also an Agreement on driving licence was concluded by ETF and CER.[39]

IRU

IRU has one common mandating procedure for all kinds of initiatives. Article 2 of its statues states that IRU 'will build increasingly productive relations with European trade unions via the European sector social dialogue, after full discussion and adoption of a common position by the IRU member associations'. Regarding the voting procedure, Article 18 of the IRU constitution* stipulates: 'in the IRU Transport Councils, each active member has, at its disposal, the number of votes attributed to it according to Article 15, whatever the number delegates present.

Decision by the IRU Transport Councils shall be taken by a show of hands and by a majority of active members present, irrespective of the number of votes attributed to them. However, at the prior request of at least five active members, voting on the decisions submitted to the Transport Council shall take place by secret ballot. In the event of a secret ballot, the decision shall be taken by a majority of votes of the active members taking part in the vote. In the framework of the functions defined in Article 16 a) and b), voting by correspondence is permitted in respect of written proposals transmitted to it by their respective President or the IRU Secre-

38 Ibid., 34-35.

39 See www.cer.be/publications/charters-and-agreements/charters-and-agreements-details/agreement-on-driving-licence/.

tary General. For the functions in Article 16 c), neither voting by correspondence, nor voting by proxy is permitted. Any decision taken by the IRU Transport Councils shall be immediately transmitted to the IRU Presidential Executive'.

Regarding sectoral social dialogue, IRU positions are negotiated and agreed internally in the IRU Committee on Social Affairs (CAS), the statutory committee for social issues at both global and EU level. Should the EU social partners decide to enter into official negotiations to conclude an agreement as per Article 155 TFEU, a mandate for these negotiations would be submitted to CAS and voted on by the members following the procedure outlined above.

The annual CAS work programme refers to this procedure and general cooperation with the trade unions: '(a) Develop, at global level, a pro-active and structured social dialogue, seeking common areas of understanding with trade union organisations. This should be initiated after adoption of a common position by the IRU Member Associations.

(b) In particular, at EU level: monitor the evolution of the EU social and employment area and the intention of the EU Commission in these areas and coordinate the political action of the IRU in relation to the EU in relation to the EU institutions; build increasingly productive relations with European trade unions via the European sectoral social dialogue, after full discussion and adoption of a common position by the IRU Member Associations'.

Mandate applied in the past IRU has not signed to date an agreement as per Article 155 TFEU.

6.3.3.3 Overview of Recent Achievements in the ESSD on Road Transport[40]

- 2016 - Joint Statement: 'Towards sustainable urban mobility'
- 2014 - 'Taxi – for a level playing field'
- **2014 - Joint terms of reference of the EU Road Transport Agency**
- 2014 - Joint recommendations: Strengthening women employment in urban public transport
- 2014 - Joint statement: The implication, application and further development of Directive 2003/59/EC on initial qualification and continuous training for professional bus drivers in urban public transport
- **2013 - Joint proposal for a policy package for the next revision of EU Regulations 1071/2009 on access to the profession & 1072/2009 on access to the road haulage market**
- **2012 - Joint statement on the further opening of the EU road haulage market**
- **2010-12 - Joint project on skills, training & the road transport sector (STARTS)**
- 2010-12 - Joint project on women employment in urban public transport sector

40 Information from EC website Sectoral social dialogue – Road transport: http://ec.europa.eu/social/main.jsp?catId=480&langId=en&intPageId=1850.

Key areas where the sectoral dialogue Committee is currently focusing on:

- **social conditions in the sector**
- **better enforcement of EU driving & rest time rules**
- **improving rest facilities**
- logistics qualifications
- **training requirements & their impact on employment in road transport**
- **driver shortages, image & recruitment in road transport**
- promoting urban public transport

6.3.3.4 Other Employer Organisations: UETR and CLECAT

In the Eurofound study, two other organisations have been identified at the employer's side that could be potentially deemed representative for subsections of the sector. However, the two European associations mentioned below do not cover all Member States:

- European Road Haulers Association (UETR);
- European Association for Forwarding, Transport, Logistics and Customs Services (CLECAT).

Both organisations are sector-related and, according to information on their websites, have affiliations in approx. 10 countries (UETR) and 15 countries (CLECAT). UETR has a high proportion of members (nine out of 11 in eight countries) that meet the criteria necessary to be included in the Eurofound study (that is, they are sector-related and involved in collective bargaining). However, from the countries involved in SENSE, UETR has members in Belgium only, namely:

- Transport en logistiek Vlaanderen;
- Union Professionelle du Transport et de la Logistique (UPTR).

CLECAT has only six members (out of 16 in 15 countries) that meet these criteria. Both UETR and CLECAT are not on the European Commission's list of interest organisations to be consulted on behalf of the sector under Article 154 TFEU. Neither do they participate in the sector-related European social dialogue nor have they requested to be consulted under Article 154 TFEU. For this reason, their capacity to negotiate was not explored in the Eurofound study of 2015.

UETR

Still, it is interesting to look a bit more in detail to UETR, since the domain of this entrepreneurs/employer association matches fully with the main focus of SENSE, which is on the position of international truck drivers in the subsector of European Road Haulers.

According to information on the website[41] on its mission and organisation, UETR was founded in 1998 and represents today more than 200,000 road transport

41 www.uetr.eu/en/ (last accessed: 13 November 2017).

undertakings in Europe (Micro, Small and Medium Enterprises; MSME's) with a total capacity of 430,000 commercial vehicles.

UETR's mission:
To have a regular dialogue with EU institutions as well as other stakeholders, networks and sectoral organisations; to give members an effective chance to give their input into EU policy-making; to gather intelligence on current and future policies and legislation; to represent an effective hub for national associations to cooperate and engage in joint projects and activities.
UETR is associate member (sectorial organization) of UEAPME, the European Association of Craft, Small and Medium-sized Enterprises incorporating 83 member organisations consisting of national cross-sectorial SME federations, European branch federations and other associate members and representing over 12 million enterprises with nearly 55 million employees.
UETR takes the lead and chairs the **UEAPME Transport Forum**, a co-operation platform bringing together small and medium-sized enterprises from manufacturing and repair of road vehicles as well as road transport. The Forum aims to develop joint positions on all transport-related issues. On its website[42] recent position papers include e.g.:
- July 2017: UEAPME response on a possible revision of the Road Transport Working Time Directive.
- 22/03/2017: UEAPME Transport Forum response to inquiry on social legislation revision on road transport.
- March 2017: UEAPME Transport Forum position on Social Legislation.
- February 2017: UEAPME Transport Forum Position on access to the occupation of road transport operator and to the international road haulage market.

6.4 Social Partner Representation at National Level

6.4.1 Criteria Used in the Eurofound Study 2015

As already set out above under 6.3.2, two criteria are of utmost importance to the European sectoral social dialogue:
- affiliation to a European social-partner organisation
  - and/or
  - involvement in national collective bargaining.

These two criteria are of utmost importance to the European sectoral social dialogue, since they are the two constituent mechanisms that can systematically connect the national and European levels. In the Eurofound study, the following criteria are used to define relevant sector-related interest associations. National associations must meet both criteria **A** and **B**:
a. The association's domain relates to the sector.

42 www.ueapme.com/spip.php?rubrique23 (last accessed: 13 November 2017).

b. The association is:
   a. either regularly involved in sector-related collective bargaining,
   b. and/or affiliated to a 'sector-related' European association of business or labour on the Commission's list of European social partner organisations consulted under Article 154 of the TFEU and/or that participates in the sector-related European social dialogue.

In the Eurofound study[43] it has also been considered whether statutory extension schemes for collective agreements have been applied to the sector. This analysis is confined to extension schemes that widen the scope of a collective agreement to employers not affiliated to the signatory employers' organisation. Extension regulations targeting the employees are therefore not included in the research.[44]
Representativeness obliges that each European sectoral social partner covers organisations in all Member States, with a variety of sizes, roles and structure. However, there are various methods of recognition sectoral domain that could give effect include not necessarily the same sectoral domain. Differentiates four types of situation:[45]

1. 'congruence' – where the domain of the organisations in a given country corresponds to the particular demarcation in the General industrial classification of economic activities within the
2. European Communities (Nomenclature générale des activités économiques dans les Communautés européennes, NACE);
3. 'sectionalism' – where the organisations' domain is narrower than the NACE demarcation;
4. 'overlap' – where the organisations cover not only the NACE domain but also parts of other sectors;
   – 'sectional overlap' – where the organisations cover parts of the NACE demarcation and parts of other sectors.

6.4.2 Trade Unions[46]

In the Eurofound study all sector-related employee organisations are listed that are either involved in collective bargaining and/or are affiliated to the European Trans-

43 Ibid., 42-43.

44 Regulations concerning the employees were not seen as significant for two reasons. 1) Extending a collective agreement to employees who are not unionised in a company covered by the collective agreement is a standard rule of the International Labour Organization, aside from any national legislation. 2) If employers did not extend a collective agreement concluded by them, even when not formally obliged to do so, they would set an incentive for their workforce to unionise.

45 Source: Philippe Pochet, Evelyne Léonard, Emmanuelle Perin, *Dynamics of European sectoral social dialogue*, European Foundation for the Improvement of Living and Working Conditions, Luxemburg 2009, p. 34.

46 Eurofound study (2015), 34-35.

port Workers' Federation (ETF). All countries have at least one sector-related trade union. A total of 126 sector-related trade unions were identified that fulfilled the criteria to be included in this representativeness study. According to the Eurofound study a pluralistic union landscape prevails in the road transport and logistics sector: only three countries have one sector-related union; five countries have two sector-related unions; five countries have three sector-related unions. A fragmented landscape is seen in the other 15 Member States, with four or more sector-related unions.

Only three unions (around 2% of all the unions) demarcate their domain in a way that is congruent with the sector definition. This implies that statistical definitions of business activities in the road transport and logistics sector differ from the lines along which employees identify their interests. Sectional overlap is the dominant sector-related domain pattern in the sector, occurring in 58% of cases. This circumstance usually derives from domain demarcations that focus on certain categories of employees that are then organised across several sectors, including activities outside the road transport and logistics sector. A frequent mode in the sector relates to various forms of multi-sector domains, covering other sectors apart from road transport and logistics, generally other transport activities such as aviation, railways, maritime transport and so on.

6.4.2.1 Membership Figures and Organisational Strength[47]

Membership of a sector-related trade union is, in principle, voluntary in the 28 Member States. However, the numbers of active trade union members differ widely from around 1,600,000 (CSC Services publics/ ACV Openbare diensten in *Belgium*) to less than 1,000 (such as TSSA in Ireland). The density figures used by Eurofound refer to net ratios: they are calculated only on the basis of active members (those who are employees) rather than by taking all union members (that is, those in a job and those who are not) into account. In *Luxembourg*, the unions active in the transport sector compete to represent workers' interests and to participate in professional elections.

Sectoral density rates were available only for 38 of the sector-related organisations covered out of 126 cases (or 30%). The Statistics show that:

- sectoral density exceeds 20% in four (*10%*) of the trade unions that document figures on density. In Denmark, the sole trade union in the sector records a sectoral density close to 55%;
- six (*16%*) of the trade unions claim they gather 10%–20% of the sector's employees;
- 12 (or *32%*) of the trade unions, for which data are available, claim to organise 5%–10% of the active employees in the sector;
- 16 (or *42%*) of the trade unions record a sector density rate of less than 5% of the employees in the sector.

47 Ibid., 1-14.

- Most of the unions record low and very low sectoral densities – less than 10%. This is generally explained by the existence of a fragmented union landscape, where the domains of the unions overlap with each other. In a few countries, such as *Belgium*, Cyprus or Finland – where there are several trade unions whose domains overlap – some unions record relatively high sectoral densities while others record low sectoral densities.

A total of 81 (or 64%) of the unions included in the study reported having members in the largest companies in the sector (no information was available on this for 19 unions)

6.4.3 Employer Associations[48]

A total of 153 sector-related employers' organisations were identified, indicating a fragmented landscape also on the employers' side:

- six countries have only one employers' organisation;
- five countries have two employers' organisations;
- two countries have three employers' organisations;
- 15 countries have four or more employers' organisations.

In six countries (Greece, Ireland, Latvia, Lithuania, *Poland*, the UK), none of the sectoral employer associations included in the Eurofound study are party to collective bargaining. In some countries (Austria, Czech Republic, Croatia, Estonia, Finland, France, Germany, Italy, *Luxembourg*, *the Netherlands*, Sweden and Slovenia), at least one of the employers' organisations is not involved in collective bargaining.
Generally, business organisations may also deal with interests other than those related to industrial relations. Those organisations that specialise in matters other than industrial relations are commonly defined as 'trade associations'. All the 36 organisations of 153 sector-related employers' organisations not involved in collective bargaining in the road transport and logistics sector, either primarily or exclusively act as trade organisations in their country. Such sector-related trade associations thus account for a significant share (23%) of the employers' organisations recorded in the study. Information on involvement in collective bargaining is not available for 24 employer organisations. All these organisations are members of one of the sectoral European-level employer organisations. According to the selection criteria, all national organisations affiliated to a European level employers' association are included in the study irrespective of whether or not they are involved in collective bargaining.
Although the domain of employer organisations tends to be narrower than that of the trade unions in the road transport and logistics sector, domain overlap arises with organisations that cover other transport activities such as port, aviation, railways and maritime transport. In addition, there are find cases or cross-sectoral domains (such as *Pracodawcy RP in Poland*). Only 5% of the associations show a

48 Ibid., 14-17.

membership domain that is more or less congruent with the sector definition. This means that the domain of these organisations focuses largely on the road transport and logistics sector. Only in Austria do sector-related employer organisations rely on obligatory membership: membership of the seven organisations that are sub-groups of the Federal Economic Chamber (WKÖ) is mandatory.

6.4.3.1 Domain Overlaps and Intercompetition

In countries with a pluralist structure in relation to employer organisations, these organisations have usually managed to achieve non-competing relationships (Bulgaria, Croatia, Czech Republic, Denmark, Finland, Germany, Italy, *Luxembourg, Netherlands*, Slovenia, Spain, Sweden, the UK). In the case of *Poland*, there is no competition because one of the two organisations (ZMPD) is not interested in concluding collective agreements. Other employer organization in Poland in this sector is TLP (Transport and Logistic Poland) which is a member of Leviatan Confederation and The Global Compact. This active association represents mostly commercial, economic and legal interests for its members rather than involving in the process concluding collective agreements.

Rivalries and competition are reported in France and Hungary. In the case of France, rivalries and competition concern the right to conclude collective agreements. In Hungary, competition is over member's recruitment. In other countries, the activities of the different organisation are complementary to each other as a result of inter-associational differentiation by their membership demarcation (as is the case in Austria, *Belgium*, Estonia and Portugal). Other countries such as Romania and Slovakia did not report information on this matter.

6.4.3.2 Membership Figures and Organisational Strength

According to the Eurofound study, data on the sectoral density of the employer organisations were available for 85 organisations in terms of companies and 44 in terms of employees. Generally, sectoral densities are low, with only four employers' organisations having a sectoral domain density in terms of companies greater than 50%. This may be explained by the fragmented landscape that prevails in most of the countries. When information is available for both kind of densities (38 cases), the sectoral domain densities of companies tend to be lower than the densities in terms of employees. This happens in 33 out of the 38 cases, possibly indicating a slightly higher propensity of larger companies to associate than smaller ones. A total of 82 organisations (or 54%) reported having members in the largest road transport and logistics companies. No information is available on this for 40 organisations.

6.4.4 Collective Bargaining Coverage

Information on collective bargaining coverage in 2013 in the countries involved in the project SENSE:[49]

CBC	(%)	Share of MEB (%)	Extension practices
BE	100	100	2
LU	100	MEB prevailing	2
NL	100	90	1
PL	1	0	0

CBC = collective bargaining coverage: employees covered as a percentage of the total number of employees in the sector.
Eurofound study 2015 author's own elaboration from national contributions (2013). Please note that MEB is short for multi-employer bargaining relative to single-employer bargaining and SEB is short for single-employer bargaining.
0 = no practice.

The situation regarding collective bargaining coverage differs widely between countries. Of the 24 countries with available data:

- nine have high rates of collective bargaining coverage, exceeding 80%. These countries are Austria, *Belgium*, Finland, France, Italy, *Luxembourg, the Netherlands*, Sweden and Slovenia.
- The Czech Republic, Denmark, Estonia, Hungary and Romania have medium coverage rates that oscillate between 50% and 70%.
- The remaining countries with available information (Bulgaria, Cyprus, Croatia, Ireland, Lithuania, Portugal, Slovakia, UK) have a rate of collective bargaining coverage that oscillates between 5% and 40%.
- In Malta, collective bargaining is practically non-existent. In *Poland*, collective bargaining is very low (close to 1%) and it is only conducted at company level.

Several factors that sometimes interact with each other, such as the predominance of multi- employer bargaining or the existence of pervasive extension practices, generally explain the highest coverage rates. Similarly, the predominance of single-employer bargaining and lack of extension practices explain the lowest coverage rates (Cyprus, Ireland, Lithuania, Malta, *Poland*).

49 Ibid., Table 4, 19-20.

6.4.4.1 *Tripartite Participation*[50]

Genuine sector-specific bodies have been established in 17 of the 28 Member States. Tripartite bodies have been established in *Belgium*, Bulgaria, the Czech Republic, Germany, Denmark, Spain, Finland, France, Croatia, Hungary, Italy, Latvia, *the Netherlands*, Romania, Slovenia, Slovakia and the UK. In some of the countries there are several bodies dealing with different issues (Italy or France) or *focused on specific subsectors (Belgium)*. The scope of activity of the tripartite and bipartite bodies is focused on *education and training* (France, Italy, *the Netherlands*, Denmark, UK), environmental issues (Denmark), welfare funds and *social security issues (Netherlands*, France or Italy), undocumented work (Germany), payroll system (Finland) or health and safety (Italy, Finland, France, UK). Other bodies have wide ranging scope of activities (Spain, Bulgaria, Hungary, Croatia, Romania or Slovakia).

6.4.5 Overview of National Trade Unions Active in Road Freight Transport, Limited To 'SENSE Countries'[51]

In 2013, the following national trade unions were affiliated to ETF:

Belgium:
CSC/ACV Transcom, Christian trade union
ABVV-BTB/ FGTB-UBOT,
ACLVB-CGSLB, liberal trade union
All three trade unions are active in collective bargaining, both multi-employer and single bargaining in the whole country

Luxembourg:
LCGB Transports,
ÖGB-L Syndicat Transport sur Route/ACAL (www.ogbl.lu/syndicat-transport/)
Both trade unions are active in multi-employer collective bargaining only in the whole country

The Netherlands:
FNV (sector transport&logistics), https://www.fnv.nl/sector-en-cao/alle-sectoren/transport-en-logistiek/ (FNV is the largest trade union federation in the Netherlands. It exists since 1975 and is a merger of social-democratic trade union federation NVV and Catholic trade union federation NKV. End 2014 most of the member trade unions of the FNV merged in one big organisation)
CNV Vakmensen (sector transport), https://www.cnvvakmensen.nl/wie-we-zijn/raden CNV Vakmensen is a Christian trade union and member of the umbrella trade union federation CNV.

50 Eurofound study (2015), 21.
51 Ibid., 26, 28.

Both FNV Transport sector and CNV vakmensen are active in multi-employer and single collective bargaining in the transport sector in the whole country.

Poland:
KSTD NSZZ 'Solidarność', https://www.solidarnosc.org.pl/kstd/ is active in single-employer collective bargaining only in transport sector in the whole country. The sections of Road Transport have been separated within NSZZ 'Solidarność' and represents drivers.

6.4.6 Overview of National Employers' Organisations Active in Road Freight Transport, Limited to 'SENSE Countries'[52]

In 2013, the following national employer associations were affiliated to IRU:

Belgium:
Febetra https://febetra.be/, active in multi-employer collective bargaining only in the whole country

Luxembourg:
CLC (confédération luxembourgeoise du commerce) www.clc.lu/fr Not active in collective bargaining. Represents the interests of entrepreneurs in three sectors: commerce, transport, services in the whole country and at supra-national level

The Netherlands:
Evofenedex https://www.evofenedex.nl/ Not active in collective bargaining. Represents the interests of trade- and production companies in national and international logistics in the whole country
TLN https://www.tln.nl/, represents 5.500 members in road transport and logistic services sector
KNV https://www.knv.nl/ (Koninklijk Nederlands Vervoer (KNV)) is an umbrella employer organisation with (subsectoral side) activities in the road transport sector. Both TLN and KNV are active in multi-employer collective bargaining only in the whole country.

Poland:
ZMPD www.zmpd.pl/ Not involved in collective bargaining. Represents interests of Polish transport companies in the whole country and at EU level.
TLP (Transport and Logistic Poland) which is a member of Leviatan Confederation and The Global Compact http://tlp.org.pl/aktualnosci/ Represents interests of Polish transport companies in the whole country and at EU level (as a member of Leviatan Confederation)

52 Ibid., 29.

6.5 Social Partner Positions on the Social Conditions for Intra-EU Mobility of Truck Drivers

Here information on the position of the respective (sectoral) social partners regarding the initiatives of the Commission on social conditions for intra-EU truck drivers will be provided (including the discussion about excluding "posted" truck drivers from the PWD)

So the standpoints from:
- ETF(ETUC),
- IRU(BusinessEurope),
- UEAPME(UETR)

and
- joint positions, if any, in the ESSD for road transport

and (if this would have any added value)
- national social partner organisations from the 'SENSE countries'

6.6 Further Reading

6.6.1 Academic Literature

K.W. Baran, *Labour law in dispute in Polish legal system* (Warsaw: www.Ksiegarnie.beck.pl, 2017) (The book presents a comprehensive analysis of the issue of labour disputes under the Polish labour law system. It presents both disputes that arise under individual labour law and those arising under collective labour law.)

A. Branch, 'The Evolution of the European Social Dialogue Towards Greater Autonomy: Challenges and Potential Benefits', *IJCLLIR,* Vol. 21, 2005, 321, 322.

S. Clauwaert, '2011: 20 years of European interprofessional social dialogue: achievements and prospects', *Transfer: European Review of Labour and Research*, 2011, Volume 17, No 2, 169-179.

Dynamics of European sectoral social dialogue (European Foundation for the Improvement of Living and Working Conditions, 2009).

Z.H. Even, *Transnational Collective Bargaining in Europe*, (PhD Thesis) (Den Haag: Bju, 2008). Retrieved from http://hdl.handle.net/1765/13755.

Z.H. Even, 'Transnational collective bargaining in the European Union', *ArA*, No. 2, 2008

E. Franssen, *Legal aspects of the European Social Dialogue* (Cambridge- Antwerp-Portland: Intersentia: Intersentia, 2002).

Y. Ghellab, *Sectoral Social Dialogue in Future EU Member States: The Weakest Link* (Budapest 2003).

M. Keune, 'Shaping the future of industrial relations in the EU: Ideas, paradoxes and drivers of change', *International Labour Review,* 2015, 154, 47–56.

A. Lo Faro, *Regulating Social Europe: Reality and Myth of Collective Bargaining in the EC Legal Order* (Oxford-Portland: Hart Publishing, 2000).

P. Marginson and M. Keune, 'European social dialogue as multi-level governance: Towards more autonomy and new dependencies', *EIoP*, Vol. 16, 2012.

I. Palinkaš, *The legal and institutional framing of collective bargaining in CEE countries: Between Europeanisation and decentralization* (PhD Thesis), Tilburg: Tilburg University, 2016.

P. Sanz de Miguel, 'Representativeness of the European social partner organisations: Road transport and logistics sector', *Eurofound,* 10 April 2015.

S. Smismans, 'The European Social Dialogue in the Shadow of Hierarchy', *Journal of Public Policy,* No. 1, 2008, 171.

M. Tomaszewska and M. Szypniewski, 'The social market economy - balance between fundamental freedom to provide cross-border services and social protection of workers' rights', *Gdańskie Studia Prawnicze t. XXXVII,* 2017.

C. Welz and T. Kauppinen, 'The Role of Social Dialogue in the Acceding Countries during the Preparatory Phase for Economic and Monetary Union (EMU)', *The International Journal of Comparative Law and Industrial Relations*, Winter 2004, 583 ff.

6.6.2 Other Sources

Webpage European Commission DG Employment, Social Affairs & Inclusion on the social dialogue: http://ec.europa.eu/social/main.jsp?catId=329&langId=en.

Printed by Libri Plureos GmbH in Hamburg,
Germany

9 789462 369641